Heart of the Community
The Libraries We Love

Treasured Libraries of the United States and Canada

Edited by Karen Christensen and David Levinson
Berkshire Publishing Group
with
Leslie Burger, Nancy Kranich, Kathleen de la Peña McCook,
Tom Phelps, Sally Reed, and others

BERKSHIRE
PUBLISHING GROUP
Great Barrington, Massachusetts

Copyright © 2007 by Berkshire Publishing Group

Published by:
Berkshire Publishing Group LLC
314 Main Street
Great Barrington, Massachusetts 01230
www.berkshirepublishing.com

Berkshire books are available at special quantity discounts to use as premiums and sales promotions. Custom editions are also available. For more information, please write to Special Sales, Berkshire Publishing Group, 314 Main Street, Great Barrington, Massachusetts 01230, cservice@berkshirepublishing.com.

Printed in China

Library of Congress Cataloging-in-Publication Data
Heart of the community : the libraries we love : treasured libraries of the United States and Canada / edited by Karen Christensen and David Levinson.
    p. cm.
Includes index.
ISBN 0-9770159-2-0 (alk. paper)
  1. Public libraries—United States.   2. Public libraries—Canada.   3. Libraries and community.
4. Libraries—United States—Pictorial works.   5. Libraries—Canada—Pictorial works.   6. Library buildings—United States—Pictorial works.   7. Library buildings—Canada—Pictorial works.
8. Library architecture—United States—Pictorial works.   9. Library architecture—Canada—Pictorial works.   I. Christensen, Karen, 1957–   II. Levinson, David, 1947–
  Z731.H38 2007
  027.473—dc22   2006033460

Contents

Advisory Board   iv

Editorial and Production Staff   v

Mary Pope Osborne on the Magic of Libraries   vi

Henry Winkler: Library Memory   vii

Library Locator   viii

Introduction: The Libraries We Love   xi

Treasured Libraries   2

Libraries of Distinction   163

Index   168

Advisory Board

Editorial and Production Staff

Editors
Karen Christensen and David Levinson

Project Coordinators
Carrie Owens and Marcy Ross

Writer
Pauline Clarke

Cover and Interior Designer
Joseph DiStefano

Compositor
Brad Walrod/High Text Graphics, Inc.

Editorial and Production Staff
Scott Eldridge II, Rachel Christensen, Tom Christensen, Jake Makler

Copyeditor
Mike Nichols

Proofreader and Indexer
Mary Bagg

Printer
Kings Time Printing Press, Ltd.

Mary Pope Osborne on the Magic of Libraries

Mary Pope Osborne, the author of the popular Magic Tree House books for children, happens to spend part of her time in Great Barrington, Massachusetts (where Berkshire Publishing Group is based) and agreed to be on the advisory board for Heart of the Community: The Libraries We Love. *Readers of her books know that librarians are important participants in the Magic Tree House stories. Her characters Jack and Annie go back in time, through magical books laid out by the librarian of Camelot, Morgan Le Fay, and many of their adventures are part of a quest to become "Master Librarians." Mary eloquently expresses her own love of libraries in the extract below:*

When I was young in New York City and wanted to be a writer, I started spending all my free time reading and writing in libraries. I sat for many hours at the Jefferson Market Library and the Hudson Park Library in my neighborhood in Greenwich Village. I discovered the Mechanic's Library in midtown. I was a regular visitor at the libraries of the Carl Jung Institute and the Museum of Natural History. I loved the reading room at the New York Public Library on 42nd Street and the austere stacks of the New York University Bobst Library where a village resident could apply for a community card.

I spent a great deal of time searching for old books about mythology, folklore, and fairy tales. For a collection of mermaid legends, I found a Japanese Sea Queen at the Jung Library and an Algonquin waterfall maid at the library of the Museum of Natural History. When I decided to write a book called *American Tall Tales,* I went to the 42nd Street Library and found the first article written about Johnny Appleseed in a nineteenth-century *Harper's Magazine,* and I read an 1848 play featuring New York tall tale hero, Mose the Fireboy.

For my book, *My Brother's Keeper,* I studied old newspapers at the New York Historical Society; and for another book, *My Secret War,* I studied articles published the day after the attack on Pearl Harbor. When I began the Magic Tree House series, I spent years visiting all my favorite libraries to research dinosaurs, knights, mummies, pirates, ninjas, the rainforest, and dozens of other subjects and places. The imaginary worlds I've discovered in libraries over the years are as real to me as if I'd truly visited them. That's why libraries seem magical to me. And that's why the mysterious heroine in the Magic Tree House books—the woman who sends Jack and Annie on all their missions through time and space—is (you guessed it) a librarian.

Henry Winkler

LIBRARY MEMORY
Heart of the Community: The Libraries We Love
BERKSHIRE PUBLISHING

My library is on Amsterdam Avenue and 81st Street in New York City. It has four or five narrow stone steps leading up to the front door. They are much more narrow than the massive steps of the main library on 42nd Street in New York. I first got my library card in the 1950's. And, even though it was so difficult for me to read, it was always exciting to take out a book using my card.

There was a whole wall filled with long slender drawers. They, in turn, were filled with 3x4 index cards that contained the name of every book in the building. Oh my, was that confusing for me! You had to know the author's name, and how to spell it, and the title of the book, and how to spell it. And, at the bottom of the card was this long number with a decimal point contained in it. Oh my, was that confusing!

Actually, none of that mattered when I finally found the books I was looking for, and brought them to the front desk to check them out. Every book was covered in plastic to keep them fresh and in good condition for the next reader. On the inside flap, there was a little envelope that held the check-out card. The librarian used a rubber stamp to mark the date that the books had to be returned by. She took a record of my library card, and home I went, which was only 4 blocks away, with *Huckleberry Finn* and *The History of the Howitzer* neatly tucked under my arm.

Even if you didn't see the sign, somehow you just knew to be very, very quiet, that you were in a really important place.

The library is a living place – you have to visit it, use it, enjoy it to keep it healthy.

Read your heart out!

Henry Winkler

Library

Zip Code	Library	Page
01247	North Adams Public Library	2
02116	Boston Public Library–Central Library	4
02445	Brookline Public Library	6
02630	Sturgis Library	8
02806	Barrington Public Library	10
03246	Laconia Public Library	12
04843	Camden Public Library	14
05091	Norman Williams Public Library	16
06058	Norfolk Library	18
06770	Howard Whittemore Memorial Library	20
08542	Princeton Public Library	22
08753	Toms River Branch–Ocean County Library	24
10928	Highland Falls Public Library	26
11355	Flushing Library–Queens Borough Library System	28
11720	Middle Country Public Library	30
13501	Utica Public Library	32
15213	Carnegie Library of Pittsburgh–Main	34
16365	Warren Public Library	36
19023	Darby Free Library	38
21009	Abingdon Branch–Harford County Public Library	40
23607	West Avenue Library–Newport News Library System	42

Zip Code	Library	Page
25443	Shepherdstown Public Library	44
25701	Cabell County Public Library	46
30606	Athens-Clarke County Library	48
33138	Brockway Memorial Library	50
33607	West Tampa Library–Tampa-Hillsborough County Library	52
35203	Birmingham Central Public Library	54
37733	Thomas Hughes Public Library	56
38111	Benjamin L. Hooks Central Library–Memphis Public Library and Information Center	58
40504	Village Branch–Lexington Public Library	60
44514	Poland Branch–Public Library of Youngstown and Mahoning County	62
45219	Corryville Branch–Public Library of Cincinnati and Hamilton County	64
47630	Ohio Township Public Library System–Central Library	66
47711	Oaklyn Branch–Evansville Vanderburgh Public Library	68
48038	Clinton-Macomb Public Library	70
48076	Southfield Public Library	72
48323	West Bloomfield Township Public Library	74
48843	Howell Carnegie District Library	76
52001	Carnegie-Stout Public Library	78

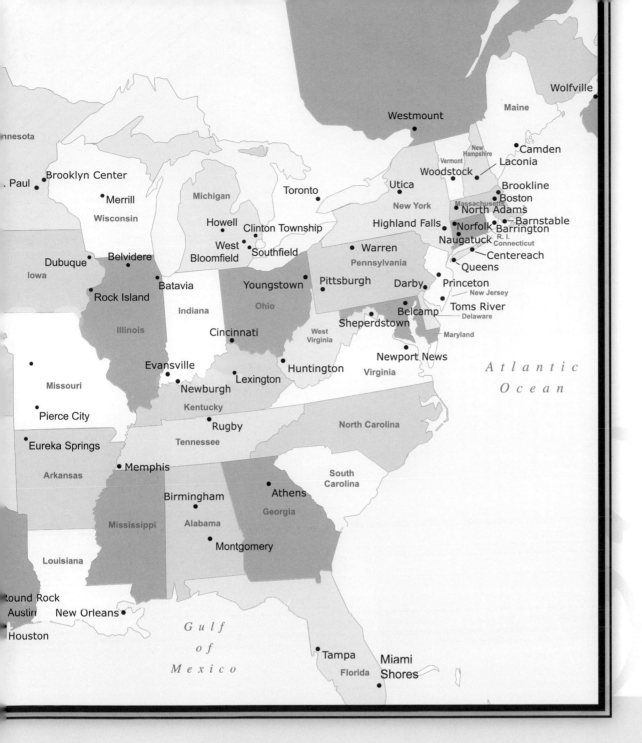

Zip Code	Library	Page
54452	T. B. Scott Free Library	80
55108	Saint Anthony Park Branch Library–Saint Paul Library	82
55430	Brookdale Library	84
58501	Bismarck Veterans Memorial Public Library	86
59829	Darby Community Public Library	88
60510	Batavia Public Library	90
61008	Ida Public Library	92
61201	Rock Island Public Library	94
65301	Sedalia Public Library	96
65723	Pierce City Branch–Barry-Lawrence Regional Library	98
66212	Johnson County Library–Central Resource Library	100
70118	Milton H. Latter Memorial Branch–New Orleans Library	102
72632	Eureka Springs Carnegie Public Library	104
74848	Grace M. Pickens Public Library	106
76443	Cross Plains Public Library	108
77002	Houston Public Library–Julia Ideson Building	110
78664	Round Rock Public Library	112
78746	Westbank Community Library	114
80204	Denver Public Library–Central Library	116
80302	Boulder Public Library	118
84057	Orem Public Library	120

Zip Code	Library	Page
84111	City Library–Salt Lake City Public Library System	122
85331	Desert Broom Branch Library–Phoenix Public Library	124
87106	Ernie Pyle Branch Library–Albuquerque-Bernalillo County Library System	126
87410	Aztec Public Library	128
89523	Northwest Reno Library	130
90022	East Los Angeles Library–County of Los Angeles Library	132
90071	Los Angeles Public Library–Central Library	134
91201	Brand Library and Art Center–Glendale Public Library	136
93023	Ojai Library–Ventura County Library	138
95112	Dr. Martin Luther King, Jr. Library	140
95969	Bayliss Library–Willows Public Library	142
97205	Multnomah County Central Library	144
98107	Ballard Branch–Seattle Public Library	146
98110	Bainbridge Public Library and Gardens	148
98201	Everett Public Library	150
99503	Z. J. Loussac Library	152
B4P 2A1	Wolfville Memorial Library	154
H3Z 1G1	Westmount Public Library	156
M6S 1M8	Runnymeade Branch–Toronto Public Library	158
S4P 3Z5	Regina Public Library	160

Introduction
The Libraries We Love

Karen Christensen, Berkshire Publishing Group

This celebration of libraries began one bright spring morning in Stone Ridge, New York. My husband David Levinson and I were driving to his father's summer home in the Catskills, along our usual path on Route 209 along the Roundout Creek in the Hudson River Valley. As we passed through Stone Ridge, a village noted for its old, stone houses and strictly enforced speed limit, David (who is also my business partner and president of Berkshire Publishing) pointed out that one of those houses was the village library. He then mused about how libraries were often among the grandest buildings in town, architecturally striking, and valued by their communities. As publishers, our thoughts quickly turned to books, and David said that he didn't think he'd ever seen a book that celebrated the unique qualities and contributions of America's public libraries. I couldn't think of one either, and as soon as we could get to a computer, we went looking for such a book—and found none. Queries to librarian friends also turned up a blank.

We realized that this was a book we had to do. Within a week, we had a plan, and not long thereafter an advisory board to help us decide exactly how to tackle our project. We came up with a list of criteria to consider in selecting libraries for inclusion in the book, decided that illustrations would play a major role and that the book would have to be in full color. Soon after, we took a field trip to Chatham, New York. The stunning Tiffany stained-glass window of Chatham's library provided a beautiful illustration, along with those from our own town's Mason Library (seen on the book's cover), for our preliminary designs.

When we talked to our local library about the project, word quickly spread. An architect from the southwest wandered into our office one day asking if he could buy a copy, saying he'd heard about the book at the library (sadly, we didn't get his card, so we hope he will come across the book on his own). And when I mentioned the project to a cab driver in Chicago, he extolled the virtues of his hometown library, in Ghana, and talked about how the librarians were, first and foremost, storytellers.

Through the counsel of Sally Reed of Friends of Libraries U.S.A., we came to see that the book would also be a celebration of America, as libraries are one of America's foremost contributions to the world.

The Tiffany window at Chatham Public Library, New York

At the June 2005 American Library Association (ALA) Annual Meeting in Chicago, we introduced the project to the library community. We spoke with four ALA presidents (past, present, and incoming), who were all enthusiastic and encouraging. Our old friend Nancy Kranich (a past president) and incoming president Leslie Burger joined our advisory board. Nancy suggested other key people in the library community for the board.

"The Fonz" Loves Libraries, Too

We also garnered support from actor/director/producer/children's author Henry Winkler, whose testimonial letter about his childhood library is reproduced in the front of the volume. Winkler wrote to us about the excitement he felt every time he took out a book as a child, closing his letter with the admonition: "The library is a living place—you have to visit it, use it, enjoy it to keep it healthy. Read your heart out!"

Henry Winkler himself is beloved by librarians. When his *Happy Days* character, the Fonz, said, "'Hey Ritchie, you can get a library card, and they're free," library cards issued in the United States reportedly went up 500 percent. More recently, Winkler has moved from promoting library use to writing books for their shelves. His children's novels feature Hank Zipzer, "the world's best underachiever," who has to cope with learning challenges, just as Winkler himself did in his own childhood.

Everywhere we went, in the United States and abroad, people were enthusiastic about our project. Brad Walrod, our compositor (also the compositor on the U.S. editions of books 4, 5, and 6 in the Harry Potter series) got into the game and sent photos of his hometown library in Arcade, New York. Francesca Forrest, Berkshire's senior copy editor, shared photos of her local library, the stately Clapp Memorial Library in Belchertown, Massachusetts.

Our Love of Libraries

Berkshire Publishing—as a creator of major multivolume encyclopedias—has always focused, first and foremost, on libraries. We know the stacks, the reference room, and the databases; we and our expert authors depend on them, and when we developed the *Encyclopedia of Community* in 2003 we came to understand just how important libraries are as public places, as well.

But our interest in libraries isn't merely professional; it's personal, too. One of David's first jobs was counting all the books in the Newark Public Library his junior year of high school. And during his army service, the post library at Ft. Bragg offered a break from the daily routine at the hospital where he worked. At Yale, he was spoiled by the Sterling Library, and on moving to Great Barrington, his local research has been greatly aided by the local-history collection at Mason Library.

I myself feel my life was transformed by libraries, starting with my school library in Bloomington, Minnesota, where I discovered Beatrix Potter and later started reading about Japan and China. I have belonged to public libraries on three continents: I fondly recall walking home with grocery bags full of books from the Cupertino Public Library, being introduced to England through the books at the Frimley Green Library in Surrey (highlights included Beverley Nichols's gardening books from the 1930s and Elizabeth Gaskell's *Cranford*), discovering M. F .K. Fisher in the stacks at the Santa Barbara Public Library, and reading all the novels of Anthony Trollope during the summer after college, because the Sydney Public Library in Australia had them all.

We also asked the Berkshire Publishing staff involved with the project to tell us how libraries had an impact on their lives. Carrie Owens, the editor who took on the challenging task of organizing the nomination and selection process, told us of the regular trips she took with her two young daughters to their local Stockbridge, Massachusetts, library, returning home with dozens of books.

Clapp Memorial Library in Belchertown, Massachusetts.

Marcy Ross, the Berkshire staff editor who coordinated the later stages of the project, recalls:

I didn't realize until we'd finished all the text how much this book mirrors my own hometown library in New Jersey, the Bayonne Public Library. Located smack-dab in the center of town, the Carnegie-funded Bayonne Library opened in 1903—a grand building in Beaux Arts and Classical Revival styles with Ionic and Doric columns. I felt I was the luckiest kid in the world to have the library located right next to my elementary school, within walking distance of our home. The expensive hardcover children's picture books I craved were just not in our family's budget. But our library had any Dr. Seuss I wanted—along with everything else I could imagine.

Marcy, who is also a former president of her local Friends group at the Roeliff Jansen Community Library in Hillsdale, New York, has watched the charming rural library move swiftly into the computer age—offering not only an incredible array of books via interlibrary loan, but also an amazing selection of audio books and quality DVDs, all of which she can order from home by accessing the library's website. The library's electronic resources even dazzle our high-tech book designer, Joe DiStefano, who found he could download his favorite science fiction titles onto his MP3 player.

Pauline Clarke, the writer who penned many of the entries in the book, recalls her first visit to her hometown library, Bushnell-Sage Library, in Sheffield, Massachusetts:

> My first trip to my hometown library came in second grade, when we lined up and walked down the school drive, crossed Main Street, and were welcomed through the heavy front doors to a room filled with books and silence. I remember being awestruck by the sheer number of books available to me now that I could read. Think of all those people to meet, places to learn about, adventures to share! I still feel that way. Opening the door to a library opens doors to whole worlds, especially now that libraries have become full-fledged learning centers. What's not to love about a library?

Mike Nichols, copyeditor on the project—and the author of *Balaam Gimble's Gumption*, an award-winning novel about life in a small Texas town—offered this witty remembrance:

> The way I saw it, if not for Andrew Carnegie, I might have been the boy who never returned. The year was 1959. I was ten years old. The Kingston Trio had captured the popular imagination with the song "Charlie on the MTA," which told about the Massachusetts Transit Authority subway rider who was doomed to "ride forever 'neath the streets of Boston" as "the man who never returned."
>
> My hometown, Fort Worth, Texas, had only one public library at the time—the big Carnegie cathedral downtown. But that was miles from my home. Too far to walk, too far to bicycle. My father worked long hours; my mother did not drive.
>
> "Why don't you just take the bus downtown to the library?" my mother said.
>
> But the thought of traveling alone on a city bus frightened me. I did not understand bus routes and tokens and transfers and the clanging, churning change machine that was mounted next to the driver. Even the pull cord intimidated me. I just knew that if I got on a city bus alone I'd never return, like Charlie on the MTA.
>
> Ah, but then all of a sudden a bookmobile from the downtown library began to visit my neighborhood every Saturday morning. It parked just two blocks from my home!
>
> It was as if the ghost of ol' Andrew Carnegie himself—the richest man in the world—had thundered, "What's that you say? A little boy in Fort Worth wants to read books, but he's afraid to ride the city bus to my downtown library? Then by all means we must take the library to *him*!"
>
> Suddenly, instead of being condemned to ride forever on the city bus system, each Saturday I just walked two blocks to that bookmobile. There I checked out books about everything a boy is interested in: snakes and turtles and frogs, jet fighters of the Cold War, biographies of sports heroes, juvenile mysteries, classics such as *Treasure Island* and *Don Quixote*. That's also where I met and fell in love with Mark Twain. When I get to Heaven, Twain will be the first angel I want to meet. After my parents, of course.
>
> Oh, and ol' Andrew.

❦ ❦
A Celebration—Not a Contest

We have made this book a celebration of libraries and their contribution to American and Canadian life. Public libraries are a foundation of democracy. Without them, we would not have informed citizens who can make the best choices for their nation. In selecting libraries for inclusion in the book, our guiding principle was that we wanted about eighty libraries that as a group display the full range of the diversity, potential, style, history, and contributions of libraries in the United States and Canada. We looked for regional diversity from east to west and north to south, and temporal coverage, from the earliest libraries to the very newest. And we also wanted libraries that have successfully undergone change, whether it is relocation, renovation, expansion, new missions, or new clientele.

We guessed that the best people to select the libraries were people who, like us, love libraries—librarians and avid users and supporters of libraries. So, we decided to turn the selection process into a contest of sorts. We say "of sorts" because we weren't looking for winners but for those libraries that, as a group, met our goals for the book. We announced the Libraries We Love nomination contest to the library world through mailings to various lists, at our ALA exhibit, and through announcements on our website and in the library media. The Friends of Libraries U.S.A. circulated the announcement to its members. We asked people to nominate their library by writing an essay highlighting its unique and significant features (past and present) and by submitting photos and other material. The key features nominators were asked to speak to were (1) the historical significance of the library, (2) association with an important event, (3) association with an important person, (4) architectural design, features, or innovations, and (5) significance to community life.

❦ ❦
Myriad Entries

We received nearly three hundred nominations ranging from single-page essays to bulging binders filed with newspaper clip-

The final nomination packages arriving on Valentine's Day.

The reading room of Mason Library in Great Barrington, Massachusetts. When the library was built in 1913, *Architecture* magazine described it as "the most exquisitely complete piece of architectural design which has appeared in a long time."

pings, annual reports, and color photos. Most nominations came from the libraries themselves or members of local Friends of Libraries chapters. A few came from architects who had designed libraries, and a few others from more unusual sources. For example, at a dinner shortly after Hurricane Katrina, I met Martin Covert, a staff writer with the New Orleans *Times-Picayune* who was interested in our project and recommended we include the Milton H. Latter Memorial Library. And a scholar in Canada who has worked with us on our sports encyclopedias suggested the Thomas Hughes Public Library in Tennessee. You'll see that both made this book!

The deadline for nominations was Valentine's Day 2006, and we received one packet in a red bag decorated with shiny paper hearts. Some packets contained page after page of testimonials from the community. We were overwhelmed not just by the quantity of materials we received, but also by the level of support and affection we were seeing for libraries. We were also overjoyed by the diversity of libraries represented by the deluge of nomination packets—large urban ones that had been brought back from the dead, those that had recovered from tornadoes and fires, old ones made totally modern without losing their past, new ones that blend into the environment, and a few associated with famous people such as Mark Twain, Garrison Keillor, and Kurt Vonnegut.

Narrowing the list to 80 was a difficult task. We involved several members of the advisory board in the process and managed to cut the list of nominees to 140, then to 90, then to 86. Six of the 86 did not respond to numerous queries for more information and photos, so are not included in the volume. Especially difficult

was selecting only a few libraries from states such as New York, Ohio, Pennsylvania, Massachusetts, and California, from which we had many nominations.

Mason Library

While we realized that it wouldn't be fair to feature our own Mason Library in the book, it's been featured in our advertising, on our website, and on our popular "Libraries Make the World a Better Place" buttons. We also used it as a test run for the book to see just what would be involved in gathering the needed information and photos for the articles. As frequent users, we already knew a good bit about the library; David, as a member of the Historic District Commission, had also been involved in reviewing and approving plans for the library's expansion and renovation.

David walked over to the library one afternoon and told Peggy Sullivan, the assistant librarian, of our plans for the book and our need for information about Mason. She very much liked the idea and told him to wait while she fetched a box of historical materials from downstairs. Downstairs houses the children's room, a display case of local archaeological artifacts, and storage rooms. She returned with a cardboard box and told him to go through it and take whatever he wanted.

The box was a treasure chest—original architect's renderings from 1913, invitations to the cornerstone laying and dedication, the original dedication bookplate, photographs of the completed but unoccupied library, copies of the 1913 issue of *Architecture* magazine that featured the new library, postcards of the library over the years, and a collection of postcards of other libraries. David took what seemed most useful for our immediate needs. A few days later he was in the local history room and saw a covered file box labeled "Library History"; it contained additional historical material.

We were to learn that many libraries had their information about themselves better organized and more accessible than Mason. Many libraries had full or part-time public relations staff, almost all had websites with historical and current information, several had a book written about them, and Friends of Libraries chapters had collections they were willing to share, including photographs of the library, its important and unique features, and its staff and patrons. And, if they didn't, they were happy to accommodate us with new photographs.

Organization of the Book

This book is organized very simply for maximum reader satisfaction. Each of the libraries is featured in a two-page spread of text, photographs, and other illustrations. Basic information for each library is at the top of the first page in each spread. Here and there, the text is supplemented by quotes from famous and influential people about books and libraries. The libraries are listed in zip code/postal code order, beginning with 01247 for North Adams, Massachusetts, and ending with S4P 3Z5 for Regina, Saskatchewan. A map in the front shows where each library is located, and an index in the back lets readers see which libraries are related to one another by topic. Libraries that were nominated and merited serious consideration but were not among the final eighty are listed in the appendix: Libraries of Distinction.

Acknowledgments

In addition to the wise counsel we received from the aforementioned members of our advisory board—Sally Reed, Nancy Kranich, and Leslie Burger—we want to acknowledge all the help and support we received from the other members of our advisory board: Clara Bohrer, Barbara Chubb, Dana Cummings, Rebecca Hamilton, Kathleen R. T. Imhoff, Deborah Jacobs, Kathleen de la Peña McCook; Mary Pope Osborne, Tom Phelps, Sally Reed, Loriene Roy, Jervey Tervalon, Nancy Tessman, Bernard Vavrek, and Peter R. Young.

Among Berkshire's staff, there was an incredible team effort from start to finish. Carrie Owens brought her considerable talents to the complex process of coordinating the nomination and selection process. Marcy Ross worked on the later stages of overseeing the text editing and photo collection, making sure each library got the care and attention it deserved. David Levinson and Pauline Clarke skillfully wrote most of the entries, and Mike Nichols added his sharp writing and copyediting talents to polish the prose until it shone. Mary Bagg lovingly and meticulously proofed each page and prepared the entries for the index.

Joseph DiStefano, our gifted designer, said from the beginning that "we had to hit this one out of the park"—and proceeded to design and refine the pages until they were truly home runs. Our newest staff member, Scott Eldridge II, dove right in and took on the mighty task of preparing all the photos for publication with skill and good cheer. And Brad Walrod, our compositor, brought it all together—with great talent and professionalism.

Our thanks go as well to our IT wizard, the magical Trevor Young, who devised the electronic map for our website that allowed us to show the geographic scope of the entries, and to Rachel Christensen who worked on the data entry and web work required for the project. Thanks also to Tom Christensen and Jake Makler, our interns, who labored much of their summer vacation to help us on many of the editorial and photo tasks that needed to be done.

This book would not have been possible without the help of all the dedicated librarians and other library staff, along with Friends groups, who worked so hard to get us the information and photos we needed. Special thanks to the photographers and architects who graciously let us use their images. And, of course, we appreciate the efforts of everyone who nominated their beloved libraries.

Heart of the Community: The Libraries We Love is only the beginning of our effort to publicize the vital role of public libraries and to sing the praises of the host of librarians, civic leaders, citizens, and readers who devote so much energy—and love—to maintaining and improving them. We at Berkshire Publishing join with you in celebrating the magnificent contribution they make to our public and private lives. Public libraries truly are the heart of our communities.

As Henry Winkler says, "Read your hearts out!"

And for more about our publishing plans, please see page 170. Do send us your ideas and suggestions, and share your dreams. You can do this at our website, or by writing to me:

Karen Christensen

Karen Christensen/CEO
karen@berkshirepublishing.com

Berkshire Publishing Group
314 Main Street
Great Barrington, MA 01230
www.berkshirepublishing.com

www.librarieswelove.org

North Adams
Public Library
◆

North Adams, Massachusetts

Address: 74 Church Street
North Adams, MA 01247
Date Founded: 1898
Date Built: 1866; 2005 (renovation)
Architect: Best Joslin and Bartels Architecture
(2005)
Director: Marcia Gross
Special Collections: Local History; Image Collections

The North Adams Public Library finds that it *is* easy being green—contrary to the opinion of Kermit the Frog. And "green" buildings (like green frogs) are good for the Earth.

When the library underwent a major renovation and expansion in 2003–2005, the goal was to preserve the historic features of the building while making it an energy-efficient "green" building that includes all the elements of a modern library. "Preserving a legacy, building for tomorrow" was the motto. During the design phase, the building committee and architects used the rating system of United States Green Building Council (USGBC)—a system known as Leadership in Environment and Energy Design (LEED). The result is an energy-efficient library that is also beautiful. The renovated library opened to the public on 31 May 2005 and is a community treasure, listed in the State and National Registers of Historic Places.

The "Sol" in "Solution"

A geothermal system heats and cools the building using the 58 degree water from two 150 foot wells. Arrays of 10 kilowatts of photovoltaic panels on the flat roof of the new addition generate approximately 5 percent of the total electricity needs of the building. Electrical output of the photovoltaic panels can be monitored at the library's website (www.naplibrary.com). For example, on 16 June 2006, the panels had produced 7,340 kilowatt-hours of electricity—enough to power more than 444 million minutes of cell phone chat and to offset 7,202 pounds of CO_2 emissions.

Other "green" features include:

- A sustainable site reusing a historic building located in an Economic Target Area and reachable by public transportation.
- Water-efficient landscaping using native and adaptive vegetation requiring no permanent irrigating system.
- An energy-efficient building with 20 percent of energy needs met by photovoltaic panels, structural insulated panels, geo-

> ## Some books are to be tasted, others to be swallowed, and some few to be chewed and digested.
>
> —Francis Bacon

thermal heat exchanger, and energy-efficient lights with time-clock lighting controls.

- Reuse of materials and resources, including antique bookcases, fireplaces, gilt mirrors, chandelier, portraits, tables, and chairs.
- 100-percent rehabilitation of the original building; 55 percent of materials were manufactured or harvested, extracted, or recovered within five hundred miles.
- Indoor environmental quality includes CO_2 monitoring, low-emitting materials, and operable windows.

History

Sanford Blackinton built this Victorian mansion in 1866, and at that time it was the most extravagant dwelling in North Adams, costing $85,000. The mansion was purchased by the city's first Mayor, A. C. Houghton, in 1896 and donated to the city. The mansion was converted into the North Adams Public Library and opened to the public in 1898.

During the $4.3 million renovation and expansion, the 17,800-square-foot building was enlarged by 10,876 square feet at the rear using a building lot purchased for expansion. Architect Ken Best, of the Best Joslin architectural firm, met the challenges of preserving this Victorian mansion and making it a state-of-the-art, "green" building. The building itself has many unique features, including service desks designed by the staff and built

Heart of the Community: **The Libraries We Love**

The reading room preserves elements of the building's original function as an opulent private residence. Courtesy of Marcia Gross.

locally, antique furniture, and a skylight. Located in the vestibule of the new addition, a stained glass window—designed and created by Deborah Coombs—recognizes the major donors to the building project.

❦ ❧

The Community's Living Room

The library is known as the community's living room, and the rooms of the library are used by patrons reading newspapers or magazines, attending a program, or enjoying the library's monthly teas. As a member of C/WMARS, a resource-sharing collaborative, the North Adams library benefits from a daily delivery of materials to serve its patrons. Toddler and preschool story times are held year around. The library also participates in the statewide Summer Reading Program, which draws local children every summer. The children's Activity Center is a hub for children and parents.

Meeting rooms are available free of charge to non-profit groups and are in demand by groups ranging from chess players to scholars. The library has a state-of-the-art computer lab, and offers instruction on computers and the Internet.

Back issues of the local newspapers to 1844 are available on microfilm as well as vital statistics, city directories, and city reports. Local history resources include materials on the Hoosac Tunnel, the Randy Trabold Photograph Collection from the *North Adams Transcript,* the Ruth Brown Collection, and the

papers of Jane Swift—a native of North Adams—from her time as acting governor of Massachusetts.

The library website has a page devoted to PEARL (People Embracing Aging, Retirement, and Life). It offers resources to older community members facing transitions such as retirement, loss of a partner, or a change in financial or medical status.

Long-time Mayor John Barrett III believes a public library is a reflection of the community and important to its economic revival. During the capital campaign the community raised $1 million—despite the fact that North Adams has struggled economically since the 1980s, when its major employer, Sprague Electric Co., closed. That, in itself, is a lot of green.

The children's activity center. Courtesy of Katherine Westwood.

Heart of the Community: **The Libraries We Love**

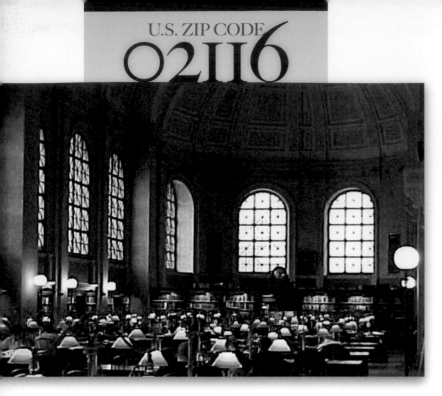

Boston Public Library

◆

Central Library
Boston, Massachusetts

Address: 700 Boylston Street
Boston, MA 02116
Date Founded: 1848
Date Built: 1895 (McKim Building.);
1972 (Johnson Building)
Architect: McKim, Mead, and White; Philip Johnson
Director: Bernard Margolis, President
Special Collections: Art; Art History; American History; Rare Books and Manuscripts; President John Adams Library

Boston is a city of firsts—the first school (Boston Latin School, 1635), the first American college (Harvard, 1636), the first medical school for women, the first vaudeville theater, and the first underground streetcar. According to William James Sidis in his book, *The Tribes and the States,* Boston was also the site of America's first public library, although that distinction may be disputed. The Boston Public Library has its own list of firsts. Established in 1848, it was the first publicly supported municipal library in the United States and the first to allow patrons to borrow books and other materials without a subscription fee. It was also the first U.S. library to build a branch library and the first to designate a separate children's room.

❦ ❦

More Firsts

According to Bernard Margolis, president of the Boston Public Library, the first subscription library in Boston was established in 1657, a gift from sea captain Robert Keene. The library and gallery burned to the ground in 1711, with only one book surviving the fire. The American Antiquarian Society returned the book to the library in 1956. Alexandre Vattemare, a French ventriloquist who visited Boston in 1848, introduced the idea of an "exchange of books." He convinced a group of influential Bostonians to create an institution that would expand on this idea. Shortly thereafter the first public library in Boston was founded. A collection of books donated to the people of Boston by Parisians echoes a collection in the Municipal Library of Paris donated by Bostonians.

The first library building was a former schoolhouse located on Mason Street. Opened in 1854, the library contained sixteen thousand volumes. In 1870 the first branch library was opened in east Boston. Between 1872 and 1900 twenty-one additional branches were opened throughout Boston's neighborhoods. Today the library has twenty-seven branches.

An exterior view of the Johnson Building.

❦ ❦

Still More Firsts

The Boston Public Library was the first library to introduce a formal story hour in the Children's Room. European storyteller Marie Shedlock first read there in 1902. The library was the first to issue an annual report by library trustees, the first public reference library to be established by a gift from a private citizen, and the first to have an audio-visual department. The library was also one of the original twenty-two public libraries designated as patent depository libraries by the U.S. Department of Commerce, is the only public library in the country that serves as a presidential library, and is the largest public

An exterior view of the McKim Building, which resembles a sixteenth-century Italian palazzo.

research library in New England. It is also a depository for United Nations documents.

McKim and Johnson Buildings

The exterior of the McKim Building, completed in 1895 on Copley Square, resembles a sixteenth-century Italian palazzo with a central courtyard and a sculpture garden. It has been referred to as a "palace for the people." Noncirculating research and reference materials, including those of the Fine Arts Department, general reference services, government documents, microtext, music, newspapers, maps, prints and photographs, rare books and manuscripts, and special collections, are housed here. Bates Hall, located on the second floor, is named for Joshua Bates, a London merchant banker born in Weymouth, Massachusetts, who donated fifty thousand dollars to the library in 1852. The hall's barrel-arched ceiling soars over English oak bookcases and a carved limestone balcony. Long wooden research tables hide Internet connections beneath their polished tops. The walls surrounding the grand staircase leading to the second-floor gallery feature murals painted by French artist Pierre Puvis de Chavannes, including eight depicting the main disciplines of poetry, philosophy, and science. The Abbey Room, also on the second floor and named for American artist Edwin Austin Abbey, holds his murals *Quest for the Holy Grail*. John Singer Sargent's Italian Renaissance frescos decorate the Sargent Room on the third floor. The library offers tours of its architecture and art.

The Johnson Building, a 1972 addition to the McKim Building, is named for its designing architect, Philip Johnson. It contains the circulating collections as well as public access computers equipped with adaptive technology for the handicapped. Materials pertaining to education, literacy, and citizenship as well as information services are located here. The Visual Services Department circulates DVDs, VHS tapes, books on tape, and audio cassettes. Children's Services is located in the Margaret and H. A. Rey Children's Room, whereas older children can check out materials in the Young Adult Room.

Highlights

The Boston Public Library is a researcher's paradise. In addition to more than 6.1 million books, 1.2 million of which are rare, it houses a wealth of maps, original music scores, folios of first edition Shakespearean works, the personal library of President John Adams, books on art history, and prints. More than five thousand programs a year are offered at varying locations, including talks by famous authors and public figures, concert series, films, lectures, seminars, and classes. There are reading programs, book clubs, a homework assistance program, outreach services, and the statewide MassAnswers reference project, which is available around the clock.

Boston has been called "the hub of the universe." President Margolis has called the Boston Public Library "the hub of the hub of the universe."

With all the library's firsts, its 2.2 million patrons each year might second that.

U.S. ZIP CODE
02445

Brookline Public Library

Brookline, Massachusetts

Address: 361 Washington Street
                        Brookline, MA 02445
Date Founded: 1857
Date Built: 1910
Architect: R. Clipston Sturgis
Director: James C. Flaherty
Special Collections: Local History; Chinese and Russian
                        Materials

For more than a century Brookline Public Library has put children first. One of the library's most important innovations was the establishment of one of the country's first separate reading rooms for children in 1890. The Brookline model was influential in sparking the expansion of library services to children across the country.

By 1898 the Brookline Library was sufficiently impressive to elicit this evaluation by Melvil Dewey of decimal system fame: "There are few institutions of the country concerning which I should be willing to speak more frankly to one of their officials. The Brookline Public Library is commonly looked on by those familiar with library work of its type through the country, as among the foremost in efficiency and influence. It has won a place where it is often quoted and referred to as the type of the best American public library."

Architectural Elegance

Although not the first public library in Massachusetts, Brookline was the first to be organized under 1851 state legislation allowing communities to tax themselves for such purposes. In a vote at the 30 March 1857 town meeting, the residents of Brookline Village established a free library.

The present library, dedicated on 17 November 1910, is the second on the site, replacing the 1869 mansard-roofed building. The Georgian Revival building was designed by Boston architect R. Clipston Sturgis. Built with red brick and Indiana limestone trim, it sits atop a knoll with a circular drive. One of its most impressive features is the oak-paneled reference room with ceiling-high windows and sterling silver chandeliers. The interior of the building was altered and an addition erected in 1970. A further renovation, completed in 2003, added more than 18,000 square feet of public space by eliminating the closed stacks and moving staff offices to newly created third-floor locations, all within the original footprint of the building. The renovation restored

the original double entrances, uncovered the grand-columned entrance hall, opened up access to the wings, which had been restricted in 1970, and doubled the floor space of the children's room. It also allowed the library to display a large portion of its art collection. Handicapped accessibility was enhanced by adding ramps that continue the design of the original balustraded terrace. This restoration renewed the facility for the twenty-first century while restoring and preserving almost all of the original architectural elegance.

The Children's Room

Again putting children first, in 1899 the library added a reading room for children with its own librarian. Until 1969 the public school libraries were under the auspices of the public library. With the 2003 renovation, a child-sized door was added at the entrance to the new children's room, the space doubled in size, and a large multipurpose room created for story hours and other activities. Programs include a Friday morning film series for children and story hours for toddlers and three- to four-year-olds. The staff prepares ongoing exhibits and book displays and leads book discussion groups for children (sixes and sevens; fourth and fifth graders), and young adults.

Cultural and Social Center

In addition to the services provided in the library, staff established school and social welfare libraries, outreach programs in the public schools, deposit branches, book delivery to servicemen during the wars, and services to the homebound. The library has been the home to many Brookline organizations: the Brookline Library Music Association, the Brookline Bird Club, the Brookline Art Association, the Brookline Education Society, and the

An exterior view of Brookline Public Library, a Georgian Revival building designed by R. Clipston Sturgis. Courtesy of Anne Clark.

Brookline Civic Association. The Brookline Historical Collection, with photographs and archival material, was established in 1894. Friends of the Brookline Public Library, established in 1981, conducts book sales and sponsor programs for the community and staff enrichment. Incorporated in 1999, the Brookline Library Foundation raises funds to support Brookline libraries.

The Brookline Library Music Association sponsors a concert series. An all-town reading program, *Brookline Reads,* has been established to inspire Brookline residents to read the same book and engage in community-wide discussions about the work. In celebration of the town's tercentenary, the library sponsored a town-wide photography contest, *Picturing Brookline,* that was open to all residents, from fourth-grade students to professional photographers. All the submissions have been placed in albums that will be kept in the library's archive and made available for future generations. The library also houses the recently established Brookline 300 display case, which will be an ever-changing window on Brookline's past.

The reference room. Courtesy of Anne Clark.

Famous Clientele

Over its 148 years the Brookline Public Library has encouraged many icons of local, regional, and national culture. They include landscape architects Charles Sprague Sargent and Frederick Law Olmsted (Sr. and Jr.); art-world patron Isabella Stewart Gardner and sculptor Theo Ruggles Kitson; abolitionists William I. Bowditch and Edward Atkinson; filmmakers William A. Wellman and the Maysles brothers; musicians Arthur Fiedler and Roland Hayes; social activists Minna Hall and Harriet Lawrence Hemenway (founders of the Massachusetts Audubon Society); politicians John F., Robert F., and Edward M. Kennedy; scientist Percival Lowell; Nobel Prize winners George Minot, William Murphy, and Norman F. Ramsay; personalities Mike Wallace and Conan O'Brian; writers Olive Prouty, Amy Lowell, Jane Holtz Kay, Ellen Goodman, and Arthur Golden; actress Jane Alexander, vaudevillian B. F. Keith; and sports executives Theo Epstein and Bob Kraft.

Heart of the Community: **The Libraries We Love**

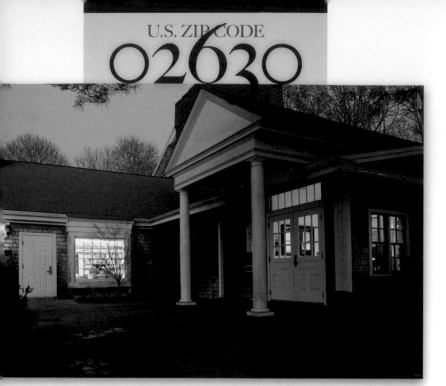

Sturgis Library
◆
Barnstable, Massachusetts

Address: 3090 Main Street
                      Barnstable, MA 02630
Date Founded: 1867
Date Built: 1644
Architect: Unknown
Director: Lucy Loomis
Special Collections: Local History; Genealogy; Maritime
                      Collection

The building that houses the Sturgis Library was standing before there was a United States. The library itself was lending books before Melvil Dewey invented his decimal classification system.

The Sturgis Library is located in Barnstable Village, a classic Cape Cod hamlet founded by European settlers in 1639. Barnstable Village is one of the seven villages in the Town of Barnstable, which is located on the bicep of the Cape Cod arm, bordered by Cape Cod Bay on the north and Nantucket Sound on the south.

Referred to by locals as "the gem of Barnstable Village," the Sturgis Library is often a meeting place for local organizations such as the Civic Association, the Barnstable Historical Society, and the Barnstable Fire District Committee. The Academy for Lifelong Learning holds a number of its courses at the library. In a village of fewer than three thousand people, the library staff members know their patrons by name and favored genre.

Oldest U.S. Library Building

Barnstable Village's reputation lies in its past—its deep-water sailors and captains, who brought great wealth to the village. By the 1700s trading was established with the Northwest for furs and then with the Far East for silks, spices, tea, and porcelain.

Constructed in 1644 for Reverend John Lothrop, founder of Barnstable, the house that forms the original part of the library is the oldest library building in the United States. The building is also one of the oldest houses on Cape Cod. Because Reverend Lothrop used the front room of the house for public worship, the Sturgis Library is also the oldest structure still standing in the United States where religious services were regularly held. The room, now called "the Lothrop Room," with its beamed ceiling and pumpkin-colored wide-board floors, retains the character of authentic Cape Cod houses.

On 25 February 1782, William Sturgis, a descendant of Reverend Lothrop, was born in the house. To help support his fam-

ily after the death of his father, William went to sea at the age of fifteen. In 1810 he founded Bryant and Sturgis, clipper ship owners engaged in the Northwest and China trades. In 1863, after a successful career, Captain Sturgis willed his former home, plus $15,000 in bonds, to establish a library in Barnstable. The library opened in 1867 with 1,300 volumes, many of which came from Sturgis's private library.

The Sturgis Library is listed on the National Register of Historic Places and is situated on the Old King's Highway, recently named as "one of the ten most scenic byways in America."

Cape Cod History and Genealogy

People come from across the country to the Sturgis Library to explore their Cape Cod roots and pay homage to their Cape Cod ancestors. Hundreds of members of the Lothrop and Sturgis families visit each year.

The library's collections have grown to more than sixty-five thousand volumes, including the special collections. These include the Cape Cod History Collection of books, manuscripts, photographs, and microfilm, the most important collection of its kind in the United States; the Kittredge Maritime Collection, one of the finest maritime collections on the East Coast, notable for its concentration on Cape Cod sea captains and vessels; and the Lothrop Genealogy Collection, which is used by genealogists

> The death of a library,
> any library, suggests that the
> community has lost its soul.
>
> —Kurt Vonnegut

Heart of the Community: The Libraries We Love

Portraits of Daniel Davis and James Scudder Lothrop, Jr. overlook the Hooper room.

from all over the United States in examining their connections to Cape Cod history.

The archival collections are kept in a climate-controlled vault in the library's basement. This collection includes rare documents such as early deeds from many of the towns on Cape Cod, ship's logs, whaling journals, manuscripts, family histories, diaries, letters and other correspondence, cemetery records, photographs, historical documents, and maps and charts, as well as the collection of personal and research papers of author and historian Henry Crocker Kittredge. Historical materials related to the founding and development of the Sturgis Library are also kept here, as are original catalogs of the library.

⚜ ⚜

Kurt Vonnegut

Kurt Vonnegut is widely considered, as author Graham Greene stated, "one of the best living American writers." His novels include *Slaughterhouse-Five* and *Breakfast of Champions*. His family has lived in Barnstable since 1951. A former library trustee, he has written about the Sturgis Library with wry fondness. In *Where I Live,* a short story collected in *Welcome to the Monkey House* (1968) Vonnegut wrote:

> Not very long ago, an encyclopedia salesman stopped by America's oldest library building, which is the lovely Sturgis Library in Barnstable Village, on Cape Cod's north shore. And he

pointed out to the easily alarmed librarian that the library's most recent general reference work was a 1938 Britannica, back stopped by a 1910 Americana. He said many other important things had happened since 1938, naming, among others, penicillin and Hitler's invasion of Poland.

The reading room viewed from outside the library.

In his latest book, *A Man without a Country* (2005), Vonnegut praises the work of libraries and librarians in the age of the USA Patriot Act. "The America I loved," he writes, "still exists in the front desks of public libraries."

Barrington Public Library

Barrington, Rhode Island

Address: 281 County Road
                         Barrington, RI 02806
Date Founded: 1880
Date Built: 1917; 1984 and 2006 (renovations)
Architect: Martin and Hall; Donald Prout
                         Associates; Tappe Associates
Director: Deborah R. Barchi
Special Collections: Local History

Times change. When the Barrington Library Society formed in 1806, fiction was prohibited ("it worketh abomination and maketh a lie"). Eighty years later the library welcomed fiction with open shelves.

Reverend Samuel Watson, pastor of the Barrington Congregational Church, in 1806, helped to form the Barrington Library Society. Although there was a fee to join ($1 a year), and fiction was not allowed, the effort was the town's first step toward establishing a public library. For twenty years the Barrington Library Society provided books for its members, but gradually interest waned. Almost fifty years passed before Barrington's residents agreed to form their own public library. In 1880 leading town residents amassed a collection of two thousand volumes. By 1885 they had more than 6,600 books, 80 percent of which were fiction titles. When the Town Hall was built in 1888, the library was located there along with the high school, the Antiquarian Society, and a one-room jail. The library continued to grow, making changes in policy in the 1900s that allowed children to take

> ## What is more important in a library than anything else— than everything else— is the fact that it exists.
>
> —Archibald MacLeish

out library cards. With each new director came more changes. Emma Staples Bradford, the library's longest-serving director (1889–1939), initiated book classification and children's services and increased the library's collection to twenty-five thousand. Her successor, Susan Demory, introduced the card catalog, provided service to shut-ins, and oversaw another addition to the building. She also brought in the first nonprint media—a collection of phonograph records.

Bricks for Books

With growth in patronage came the need for more space. Additions to the Town Hall to expand the library had helped, but eventually the town realized the library needed a building of its own. A declining student population and a newer high school had dictated the closing of the Leander R. Peck School, which in turn opened an opportunity for the library. Dedicated in 1917, the school was constructed of brick from the brickyards in Barrington. (Bricks were handmade in the town in the 1600s; the Nyatt Brick Company was founded in 1848, and brick-making was a major industry until the 1930s, when the clay deposits ran out.) The town voted in 1982 to renovate the school.

In 1984 the new Peck Community Center and Public Library opened under the direction of Ruth Corkill. At the same time the old library became offices for the school administration.

An exterior view of Barrington Public Library.

Heart of the Community: **The Libraries We Love**

Patrons enjoying the library's ergonomic seating and flat-screen computers.

✿ ✿ Four in One

On a lower level of the building resides the Town Museum, sponsored by the Barrington Preservation Society. There you can find the recorded history of Barrington and displays of arti-

The children's room, decorated for the summer reading program.

facts. School children and researchers alike use the library and the museum, and the society sponsors ongoing projects such as recording oral histories and compiling publications of old photographs. The Community Center section of the Peck building also supports the Barrington Senior Center. With a variety of programs, a policy of governance, sufficient staff, and a proper facility, the Senior Center is a vital part of both the Peck building and the town. A fourth organization sharing the space is Tap-In (Touch a Person in Need), a volunteer agency located in the basement. It provides help to Barrington residents and the communities of East Providence, Warren, and Bristol.

Major renovations on the first floor in 2006 brought new ceilings, better lighting, more bookshelves, new carpeting and furnishings, a new teen room, service desks of cherry and granite, and a revamped reading room. The library remained open through the renovation.

The Barrington Library is the fourth-busiest library in the state. The library also leads the state in per capita use and per capita support. Director Deborah R. Barchi hears the heart of the community beating strong at the library, with its variety of programs for all ages, concerts, lectures, and, of course, its collection of 134,000 items, many of them works of fiction.

And that's no lie.

Heart of the Community: **The Libraries We Love**

PAGE

II

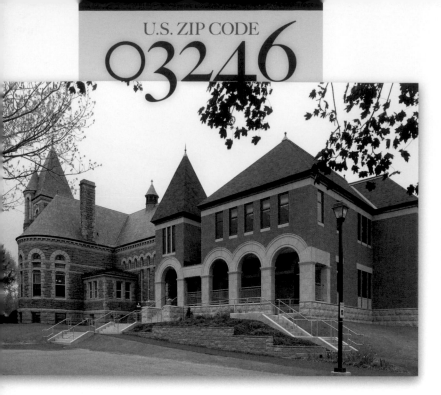

U.S. ZIP CODE
03246

Laconia Public Library
Laconia, New Hampshire

Address: 695 Main Street
Laconia, NH 03246
Date Founded: 1803
Date Built: 1903; 1957 and 2005 (renovations)
Architect: Charles Brigham; Prescott and Erickson (1957); J. Stewart Roberts Associates, Inc. (2005)
Director: Randy Brough
Special Collections: Local History; Civil War Collection

The year was 1803. In Washington, D.C., Thomas Jefferson authorized the Louisiana Purchase from France. In Vienna, Beethoven composed his Sonata for Violin and Piano, op. 47. And in Laconia, New Hampshire (then named "Meredith Bridge"), the Meredith Bridge Social Library was formed with just thirty members. As was the practice at the time, the library was privately owned and governed by affluent proprietors who paid annual membership fees. It was open on Saturdays from 3 to 6 P.M.

During the nineteenth century, as its collection grew, the library moved several times to various downtown buildings and finally to the vestry of the Unitarian church. In 1894 the city received a bequest of $150,000 from Napoleon Bonaparte Gale, a wealthy Laconia resident, to erect a building to house a public library and museum. Boston architect Charles Brigham was awarded the design job. Brigham designed the Christian Science Church (Boston), First Church of Christ Scientist (Boston), Fairhaven Town Hall (Fairhaven, Massachusetts), Millicent Library (Fairhaven), and other buildings, many of which are listed on the National Register of Historic Places. The building contract was awarded to E. Noyes Whitcomb & Company of Boston.

Now the year was 1903. At Kitty Hawk, North Carolina, Orville and Wilbur Wright made their first airplane flight. In Dearborn, Michigan, Henry Ford founded his car company. And in Laconia the Gale Memorial Library opened to the public. The building, created in the Romanesque Revival style, was constructed of red New Brunswick granite and gray Deer Island granite. The design included a three-story corner turret, several towers, carved woodwork, arched paneled doors, and a large circular stained glass skylight. In 1957 the library was enlarged, financed by the Gale Memorial Building Fund and a gift from the estate of Mrs. Martha Prescott, who felt that because her husband, the late Wilbur L. Prescott, had made his fortune in Laconia, the city should benefit from it. The two-story contemporary-style addition included a new children's room, staff room, and auditorium.

In 2004 the 1957 addition was torn down to make room for a 9,000-square-foot addition, and the original 1903 Gale building was renovated. The new Laconia Public Library was completed in 2005. The design includes a larger children's room, teen room, local history room, reference room, and a technologically advanced auditorium.

Fly Tying to Tie Dying

Since undergoing its new construction and renovation, the Laconia Public Library has offered bigger and better programs. Adult programs include the New Hampshire Humanities Book Discussion series as well as two senior citizen book discussion groups; One City, One Book, which is a program designed to bring people together to discuss literature and share views on

The Kiwanis Children's Room after the 2005 renovation.

The reference room and computer lab, showing 2005 renovations.

issues; Preview Forum, which is a nationwide program that uses media to spark community dialogue; workshops on a variety of topics such as knitting, journaling, fly tying, and jewelry making; local author programs and book signings; film screenings; cultural programs on Israel and Nicaragua; travel programs; and educational programs on subjects such as autism, fishing in New Hampshire, banned books, permaculture, and native orchids.

Teen programs include a monthly teen book discussion group as well as the Graphic Novel Club; a summer reading program just for teens; Dance Dance Revolution, which is an interactive music video game; film screenings; Yu-Gi-Oh, which is a strategic card game; workshops on jewelry making and tie dying; a poetry slam event; and an educational program on what life is like for teens in Israel.

It's Yoga, Baby

Programs in the Children's Department include weekly story times for various age groups as well as the monthly Family Bedtime story time; monthly book discussion groups; film screenings; baby yoga classes; magic workshops; a summer reading program; the Hear Me Read series; chess classes and annual tournament; and field trips to places such as Sturbridge Village and the Winnipesaukee Railroad.

The library has more than forty thousand books and nearly five thousand nonprint items in its collec-

tion. The library maintains book and audiovisual collections for adults, teens, and children. The Local History Collection consists of Laconia city directories and town reports dating back to the nineteenth century, Laconia yearbooks, a genealogy collection, New Hampshire town histories, and a local author collection.

The upper level book stacks with a view of the stained glass.

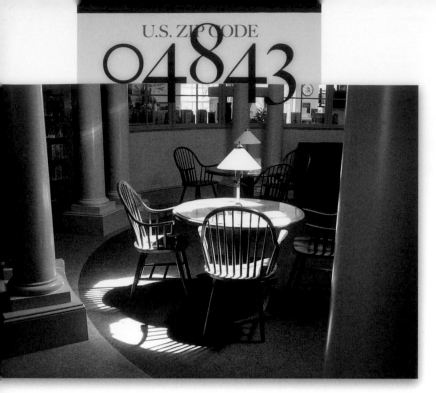

Camden
Public Library

Camden, Maine

Address: 55 Main Street
                      Camden, ME 04843
Date Founded: 1896
Date Built: 1928; 1996 (addition)
Architect: Parker Morse Hooper; Charles J.
                      Loring
Director: Andrea Jackson-Darling
Special Collections: Edna St. Vincent Millay Collection;
                      Art and Architecture Collection

Hometown girl Edna St. Vincent Millay, in the first lines of her poem "Renascence" (1912), could have been describing the view from the Camden Public Library, set between the wooded Camden Hills and Penobscot Bay:

> All I could see from where I stood
> Was three long mountains and a wood;
> I turned and looked the other way,
> And saw three islands in a bay.

Discovered by Europeans in 1605 when English Captain George Weymouth landed, the area was originally inhabited by the Penobscot Indians. In 1769 the first white settler arrived, and in 1791 the town was named "Camden" in honor of Charles Pratt, first earl of Camden and a colonist sympathizer during the American Revolution. Several woolen mills, including the Knox Woolen Company, prospered along the banks of the Megunticook River, and Camden was home to the H. M. Bean Shipyard, builder of the first six-masted schooner. By the turn of the century a number of the country's wealthiest families, attracted by the beauty of Camden, built estates there. Extending their generosity to the community, they contributed to the construction of the Camden Public Library, the village green, Harbor Park, the Camden Opera House, and the Camden Yacht Club. The library, designed by Parker Morse Hooper and Charles J. Loring, sits on land donated by Mary Curtis Bok Zimbalist. The cornerstone was laid in 1927, and a year later the library opened.

Fulfilling a Mission

The Camden Public Library's mission is to provide universal access to knowledge and lifelong learning through print, electronic resources, cultural activities, programs, and services. To this end the library offers collections of books, periodicals, and multimedia and collaborates with community groups to provide educational, informational, and recreational programs. The library's collection contains more than fifty thousand books and serial volumes, more than one hundred subscriptions, and more than five thousand audio/video materials. The original building has been restored to a reading room with tables and window seats, a large selection of periodicals, newspapers, and Maine books, and a computer for research and reference.

The library holds area historical documents, including a collection of works by Edna St. Vincent Millay, the first woman to receive a Pulitzer Prize for poetry. Born in Rockland, Maine, in 1892, Millay lived in Camden from 1903 to 1913. She was editor-in-chief of the high school magazine, *The Megunticook,* and wrote poetry, some of which was published in the children's magazine *St. Nicholas* and the *Camden Herald.*

Morris dancers on the lawn of the library. Courtesy of Ken Gross.

An exterior view of Camden Public Library in winter. Courtesy of Ken Gross.

Interspersed in the circulating collection are materials of historical and current women's studies, and on the third floor is the Ambrose C. Cramer Collection, an assortment of books with a concentration on European and early American art and architecture. Cramer was a Chicago architect. The adult collection, including books by Maine authors, is located mainly in the Centennial Wing, constructed as an expansion of the original space in 1996. The soundproof Children's Room is adjacent to the Juvenile Room, where Camden's youth can find materials and programs tailored to their needs. The Centennial Wing also houses a community meeting space and computer workstations for public use.

"The Jewel of Camden"

The library has an amphitheater and gardens for public use. In 1928 Mary Curtis Bok Zimbalist donated to the library land on which Boston landscape architect Fletcher Steele constructed an amphitheater using local trees and materials. It is a gathering place for community events such as the Ice Cream Social, which celebrates the culmination of the Adult Summer Reading Program. The Stroudwater Design Group of Yarmouth, Massachusetts, created a one-of-a-kind Children's Garden, filled with benches supported by granite books whose titles represent the literary contributions of Maine authors and illustrators.

The Jean S. Picker Memorial Garden was planted as a memorial to the late stateswoman, humanitarian, and world peacemaker. The garden is filled with flowers of varying shades of blue to complement the marine theme. Native plants such as lupine, sea lavender, blue flag, and wild roses flourish.

> The best of my education has come from the public library . . . my tuition fee is a bus fare and once in a while, five cents for an overdue book. You don't need to know very much to start with, if you know the way to the public library.
>
> —Lesley Conger

The Camden Public Library publishes a newsletter about programs and events, many of which are geared toward discovering the joy of reading. However, there also are music, dance, and stories in the Children's Room; the People's Poetry Project, which features writing workshops and a poetry reading; regular film showings; and featured artist presentations. Concerts, arts and lecture series, and children's story hours also are offered. Patrons can play chess, discuss the latest bestsellers, or swap songs at the Coffee House.

Although the library was originally funded in part by the wealth of several Camden families, the financial burden of its upkeep and expansion falls to the residents of Camden. When a transition endowment established in 1996 with the creation of the Centennial Wing needed supplemental money, the Camden Selectboard agreed that the town should provide the funds necessary to maintain the "Jewel of Camden."

Norman Williams Public Library

Woodstock, Vermont

Address:	10 The Green
	Woodstock, VT 05091
Date Founded:	1883
Date Built:	1884; 1999 (renovation)
Architect:	Wilson Brothers; Mark Mitchell
Director:	Debra Bullock Spackman
Special Collections:	Vermont History and Genealogy;
	Astronomy Books and Media;
	Health and Medical Reference

The title of Thomas Wolfe's novel notwithstanding, Dr. Edward Williams found that he *could* go home again. And when he returned home to Woodstock, Vermont, after twenty years away, in tribute to his father and the town he had his childhood home torn down and a library built in its place. Seven years after its completion, the library was so popular that Dr. Williams presented the library with $20,000 for a two-wing addition.

Three Careers

Dr. Williams practiced medicine in Northfield, Vermont, with his brother-in-law, Dr. Samuel W. Thayer, for two years before leaving the practice in 1851 to return to one of his first loves—railroad construction engineering. Thus it was that a country doctor helped build the railroad from Caughnawaga, Canada, to Plattsburgh, New York. Working with several small lines in New York, the Midwest, and Canada led to his appointment as Superintendent of the Pennsylvania Railroad System, where he assisted in developing the air brake, devising a uniform timetable adopted by all lines, and instituting block signaling.

Dr. Williams embarked on his third career—as a manufacturer—in 1870, becoming a partner and soon the president of Baldwin Locomotive Works of Philadelphia, the largest firm of its kind in the world. His position led to traveling throughout the world, election to the Royal Swedish Academy, and the amassing of a considerable fortune.

Meanwhile, Edward's father Norman became a member of a new book club in 1855, succeeding the Woodstock Library Society, founded in 1820. The group became the Woodstock Library Association and had a "library room" in the village, which accumulated 1,300 volumes over the years. The ladies ran tea and garden parties to help with funding the small, cramped room.

After the death of his parents, Edward and his siblings relinquished their shares in the family homestead for the creation of a public library. The Wilson Brothers, architects from Philadel-

I am excited about what's happening in my hometown and in libraries across the country. But I worry about whether our society will support public libraries so they can sustain this critical community service. In my view, investing in public libraries is an investment in the nation's future.

—Bill Gates

phia, designed the original library in 1883. Knowing the building was to be called the Norman Williams Public Library in honor of the family patriarch, the architects conceived a "Norman" style architecture of Romanesque nature—a bold choice for an old New England village.

Construction was completed in 1884. Because of the library's popularity, a double wing was added to the back of the building in 1901 to mirror the front.

In the 1980s the building was reroofed, and in 1999 the library underwent a major renovation. Architect Mark Mitchell of Barnard, Vermont, was in charge of designing the renovation. Expansion included remodeling the basement into a state-of-the-art space for children and teens and transforming the attic into space for administrative offices and the Vermont History Room. The usable space increased from five thousand to fifteen thousand square feet with the addition of a mezzanine level to house the reference collection, and the original reading room was restored with a gas fireplace, where one can read a book, newspaper, or magazine and enjoy a cup of coffee or tea.

A reading table on the mezzanine overlooking the first floor.

Quintessential Village

Woodstock has been referred to as "the quintessential New England village." Settled in 1768, this community of 3,200 has three covered bridges, several Revere bells, church towers that gleam against a Green Mountain backdrop, grand old houses edging the town green, and acres of farmland. It also has a year-round sports and events facility, the Woodstock Ski Touring Center, Marsh-Billings-Rockefeller National Historical Park (Vermont's only National Park), the Billings Farm and Museum, the Pentangle Council on the Arts, and, of course, the Norman Williams Public Library.

A grant from the Vermont Public Library Foundation has helped the library to provide free Internet access to registered patrons. The library receives some public monies, but more than 70 percent of its funding is provided by endowment and private contributions. Open six days a week, including three evenings, it has a collection of more than thirty-five thousand items and one of the highest per-capita items-loaned rates in Vermont. On a given Sunday afternoon patrons can attend lectures on a variety of subjects. They might find a musical performance or a presentation on native wildflowers. There's the Friends Film Series every Tuesday, sponsored by the Friends of the Library, featuring first-run, award-winning, and foreign films. And for those searching for their roots, the Genealogy Club meets every second Tuesday. The last Saturday of every month has a special program for kids, and Preschool Story Time is held every Tuesday morning. To end the day on a good note, Pajama Story Time is held every Wednesday evening. Day-care groups and school classes are encouraged to schedule visits. The library also offers a discounted membership to nonresident students.

From an old family homestead in a small village to a modern facility that welcomes all its villagers, the Norman Williams Public Library remains a place where you *can* go home again.

A covered bridge near the library.

Norfolk Library

Norfolk, Connecticut

Address: 9 Greenwoods Road East
                        Norfolk, CT 06058
Date Founded: 1889
Date Built: 1888
Architect: George Keller
Director: Robin Yuran and Rich Dann
Special Collections: Local History and Genealogy; Rare
                        Books on Hunting and Fishing

U.S. Senator Frederic C. Walcott of Connecticut, speaking in 1939 at ceremonies marking the fiftieth anniversary of the Norfolk Library, told an anecdote to illustrate the character of library founder Isabella Eldridge:

> Miss Isabella was accustomed to devote part of every morning when in town to watch the workings of the library and meet those who called. One morning she took a broom and was sweeping the front porch of its fallen leaves when an elderly man of pompous mien, a stranger, called and asked if there was a portrait of the founder.
> "Yes," Miss Eldridge said and showed him inside where her portrait hung.
> After admiring the portrait, the man turned to leave, thanked Miss Bella, and handed her a quarter with this farewell, "My good woman, you are serving a good cause and a noble woman." Miss Bella accepted the quarter and turned it in to the library fund.

That anecdote about service, humility, and the value of money still resonates. Isabella Eldridge established the Norfolk Library as a memorial to her parents, the Reverend Joseph and Sarah Battell Eldridge, and presented it to the town of Norfolk in 1889. Her hope was that the library would be a meeting ground for the community rather than just an institution, and it has maintained that character she gave it, serving not only as a storehouse of reading for instruction and pleasure, but also as a meeting site for groups. The library serves a population of 1,700 in Norfolk in northwestern Connecticut and patrons from outlying towns in Connecticut, Massachusetts, and New York. Norfolk is an eclectic mix of authors, writers, artists, and craftspeople.

Architect George Keller of Hartford designed the library. The Great Hall, additional stacks, and back alcove, also designed by Keller, were added in 1911. The Smith children's wing opened in 1985, made possible by the donations of Abel I. Smith, a Norfolk resident, and members of the community.

Who's Hoot in Architecture

The library is one of three libraries designed by Keller. In Gothic style, it features a turret, foliated gable carvings, gargoyles, stained glass windows by Maitland, Armstrong and Company, a barrel-vaulted ceiling, and stone fireplaces. Architectural highlights include the exterior, made of Longmeadow stone on the first floor with fish-scale tile shingles on the second floor. The original fluted Spanish tile roof, which had suffered from frost and fallen branches, has been replaced by asphalt shingles. Albert Entress of Hartford sculptured the gargoyle in the shape of an owl on the front porch. Another owl stands over the fireplace in the Great Hall and holds a book bearing the library's motto, "Inter Folia Fructus" (fruit among the leaves).

Norfolk Library. Courtesy of Christopher Little.

Mark Twain and Others

The library has welcomed a number of prestigious visitors, among them Samuel Clemens (Mark Twain), who donated a signed photograph of himself that hangs in the turret.

Stained glass windows by Maitland, Armstrong Company, c. 1888. Courtesy of Christopher Little.

His daughters Clara and Jean were visitors during the years 1904 through 1906. Clara first spent time in Norfolk while recovering from a nervous breakdown after the death of her mother, Olivia. Later Clara was joined by Jean and their father in the summer of 1905. In September 1906 Clara made her singing debut at the Eldridge Gymnasium with Samuel Clemens in the audience. The late author/philanthropist Brendan Gill of *New Yorker* fame was a supporter of the library, as was his friend James Laughlin, editor and chief of New Directions, publisher for such authors as Haydn Carruth and Ezra Pound.

years the group sponsored exhibits to showcase local artists; then introduced musical concerts and fund-raising to support those events. Each year the group donates hundreds of hours to library services and fund-raising projects such as auctions, author book signings, and the annual book sale. The proceeds support art exhibits, adults' and children's musical and literary programs, library interns, and the purchase of extra goods and services not included in the Board of Trustees' budget. The group squeezes every quarter raised for all it's worth. ("Miss Bella" would no doubt be pleased.)

Koffee Klatch for Kenya

The library provides cultural events, concerts, lectures, literary series, book discussions, and story hours. When children's librarian Eileen Fitzgibbons traveled with the American Friends of Kenya to the highlands of Thika to help build two libraries, creative fund-raising was required. She sponsored a two-week-long Kenyan Koffee Hour from 8 A.M. to 10 A.M. each weekday morning, opening the library early for muffins, coffee, and African tunes. The event was so successful that she raised more than $500 to help support the American Friends of Kenya.

Norfolk Library Associates

In 1974 a group of Norfolk women organized the Library Associates to promote and expand the library's services. In the early

Home Is Where the Heart Is

The Norfolk Library is the heart of the village and the pulse of the community. Known for its non-shushing atmosphere, the library welcomes children of all ages, conversation, laughter, and love of reading. Norfolk dogs know the library office well, where the biscuits are and where the water bowl is. Kids line up to get a special mouse stamp at the circulation desk when books are checked out. They look forward to special visits from their favorite authors such as Mary Pope Osborne who visited one recent summer's day; balloons and a special magical tree sported Magic Treehouse books, twinkling lights and a miniature tree-house with a rope ladder. One boy was heard to exclaim, "This is the day I've been waiting for my whole life!" With a collection of over 35,000 items, the library isn't just about books anymore. Cultural events abound and enlighten with salsa music, Yoga classes, literary discussions, poetry slams, films, concerts, international potluck suppers and more!

U.S. ZIP CODE

06770

Howard Whittemore Memorial Library

Naugatuck, Connecticut

Address:	243 Church Street
	Naugatuck, CT 06770
Date Founded:	1894
Date Built:	1894
Architect:	McKim, Mead, and White
Director:	Joan Lamb
Special Collections:	American Literature; Local History and Genealogy

It is a library built literally of granite but figuratively of iron.

In 1871 Naugatuck native John Howard Whittemore, Eban Tuttle, and Tuttle's son Bronson created the firm of Tuttle and Whittemore to produce castings made from malleable iron, a product much in demand by the railroads. Whittemore remained president of the company after it evolved into the Naugatuck Malleable Iron Company. He also had an interest in iron foundries in Chicago, Indianapolis, and Toledo as well as Connecticut. Believing that wealth ought to be shared with one's community, Whittemore commissioned the New York architectural firm of McKim, Mead, and White (creators of Old Penn Station, Columbia University, and the Metropolitan Opera House, among other buildings) to design two school buildings: the Salem School and seven years later the Naugatuck High School (now Hillside Middle School). He also commissioned a library that would serve as a memorial to his young son, John Howard, who had died in 1887. The library was built across from the town green, itself unique because it is the only one in Connecticut to include the public buildings facing it.

> Access to knowledge is the superb, the supreme act of truly great civilizations. Of all the institutions that purport to do this, free libraries stand virtually alone in accomplishing this mission.
>
> —Toni Morrison

A Thing of Beauty

John Howard Whittemore knew the value of beauty and the effect it has on the human psyche. He wanted the residents of Naugatuck to be not only proud of their library but also inspired by it. Today the library retains its beauty. Constructed of pink granite, it has buff-colored terra cotta panels above the windows and a continuous inscribed frieze. Through the fluted Ionic columns flanking the front doors, the first thing one sees is the front entrance rotunda, decorated with carved marble from Siena, Italy, and rich with paint and gilding. Cir-

Photo of John Howard Whittemore.

cling the walls of the rotunda are inscribed the words of poet Emily Dickinson, and on the floor beneath it is the library's insignia—a red and gold terrazzo tile medallion.

Originally the library housed 1,800 volumes; today it houses more than 47,000 adult books and 30,000 children's titles, 125 subscriptions, and more than 2,000 audio and video items. The original deed of gift stipulates that the library be governed by a board of trustees composed of five members, one from each of the local churches that were in existence in 1894.

Honoring History and Diversity

Naugatuck originally was a section of the "Mattatuck Plantation," now known as the city of Waterbury. Prior to being named Naugatuck, the area was known by several

Order No. 1496 A

$ 995.00

New York, September 15th, 1893

Mess Norcross Brothers :

You are hereby ordered to add to ~~deduct from~~ your Contract

dated May 18th, 1892, with Mr J. H. WHITTEMORE :

for General works, at of Public Library Building at Naugatuck, Conn.,

the sum of Nine hundred and ninety five — — — — — — — — — Dollars,

for furnishing and setting in place two bronze grilles, fifty two bronze rosettes, one bronze door frame and setting in place the bronze memorial tablet,

being in accordance with your estimate of August 14th, 1893

McKim, Mead & White

ARCHITECTS.

Amount of Contract,	$ 49,000.00	
Additions, $ 2,792.00		
Deductions, $ 128.00		
Balance to add ~~deduct~~,	$ 2,664.00	
Total Amount, . . .	$ 51,664.00	

Approved

OWNER .

Accepted *Norcross Brothers*

CONTRACTOR**S**.

Receipt from McKim, Mead, and White, architects of the library.

other names, the first being Judd's Meadow. This area was five miles south of Mattatuck Plantation, where two settlers bought land along the river. The acreage was named after Thomas Judd, one of the original settlers.

In 1702 the first mill built for textile carding and fulling (shrinking and thickening by moistening, heating, and pressing) was built along the banks of the river, and gradually more people were encouraged to settle there. In 1733 the General Assembly granted the growing settlement the right to govern itself and renamed it "Salem Bridge." By 1740 more than thirty families lived in Salem Bridge. In addition to the textile mill were a sawmill and a weaving establishment. The steep and rocky land wasn't especially good for farming, but the rushing streams provided the energy needed to turn the wheels that drove the newfangled mechanical devices.

By 1844, when the town was incorporated and renamed "Naugatuck," three hundred families called it home, and by 1893, with more than a thousand families, Naugatuck was becoming an industrial center. Nicknamed "the Rubber Town," Naugatuck was where Charles Goodyear opened the first factories to make rubber goods via the vulcanization process he had discovered.

Factories and mills sprang up along the Naugatuck River during the Industrial Revolution. The railroad that brought coal to the coast was completed in 1849, and the small mills and factories began to be replaced with larger ones. The mills and factories drew immigrants, who were looking for work, from England, Ireland, Germany, Italy, Portugal, Sweden, Poland, Lithuania, and Russia. The library still celebrates their history and heritage with culturally diverse programs. Free museum passes are offered to patrons, and the Readers Theater encourages local talent. The library offers free homebound service and hosts free blood pressure screenings provided by the Naugatuck Visiting Nurses Association.

The library also hosts programs to honor Naugatuck's war veterans. It celebrated the fifty-fifth and sixtieth anniversaries of D-Day and the fifty-fifth anniversary of Iwo Jima.

Painting of the library by Judy Jaworski.

Princeton Public Library

◆

Princeton, New Jersey

Address:	65 Witherspoon Street
	Princeton, NJ 08542
Date Founded:	1910
Date Built:	2004
Architect:	Nicholas Garrison, Hillier Architecture
Director:	Leslie Burger
Special Collections:	Paul Robeson Collection; Christopher Reeve Theater Arts Collection

If you listen carefully as you walk the floors of the Princeton Public Library, perhaps you will hear children's stories being read aloud in French, Spanish, or Japanese. Or "*Look! Up in the sky!*" Or maybe just, "Mommy, can we go get ice cream?"

When the Princeton Public Library opened a new facility in 2004, the community was immediately transformed. The number of daily visitors doubled, a teen center blossomed, and users of all ages flocked to the library for public art, tutoring, technology, coffee, and computers. An old institution had a new home, its third building in nearly a century. The library is located downtown, within walking distance of three public schools, and has become an important town commons. The library serves a diverse community, one in which fifty-four languages are spoken natively.

⚶ ⚶
Books by Gas Lamp

Voters approved funding for the Free Public Library in Princeton in 1909. Alongside rooming-house boarders, the library opened the following year in Bainbridge House, a colonial home owned by Princeton University. Residents enthusiastically supported the modest library: Some 600 people borrowed more than 7,000 books in the first nine months.

The library also inspired citizens to volunteer. Within months of its opening, local children raised money for the purchase of chairs. Subscription book clubs and town organizations donated hundreds of books, a gas lamp, window ventilators, a flagpole, and a "speaking tube." Librarians began providing books for dairy workers, schoolchildren, and "the men working on the railroad."

Princeton and U.S. history are woven into the library's history. The families of U.S. Presidents Woodrow Wilson and Grover Cleveland were among the early donors of books. The second library, built in 1966, was moved to a downtown location on Witherspoon Street, named after Reverend John Witherspoon, a signer of the Declaration of Independence who later served

as head of the College of New Jersey, which became Princeton University.

⚶ ⚶
Happy World

The new library has become the "community's living room." New and enhanced programs include a teen board, a human rights film festival, and services such as free ask-a-lawyer consultations. Public artworks are integrated throughout the building—ranging from a text sculpture of thought-provoking words etched into bluestone by conceptual artist Robert Barry to a seven-foot trumpeter swan on the third floor, inspired by E. B. White's *The Trumpet of the Swan,* by Mary Taylor.

Artist Ik-Joong Kang created *Happy World,* a thirty-foot-long mixed-media wall installation for the lobby. It features 3,700

A detail of Ik-Joong Kang's *Happy World*, a 4,000-item mixed media wall installation. Courtesy of Cie Stroud.

Heart of the Community: **The Libraries We Love**

Lining up for a mid-1950s story hour outside the library's first home, Bainbridge House.

tiles created by the artist, hundreds of which carry artifacts and words contributed by the community. When he discovered that fifty-four languages are spoken in Princeton, Kang decided to capture the town's international flavor by inviting children to write the word *library* in their native language and include these in the mural.

He also collected community artifacts such as sports memorabilia, Albert Einstein's playing cards, photographs, and a brick from the old library. All of these became part of *Happy World*, which visitors examine each time they enter the library.

⚘ ⚘
Hometown Heroes

Retired librarians remember how actor Christopher Reeve (1952–2004), who played Superman in four movies, ran up and down the library steps when he was a child. His life is honored by an annual lecture series on topics related to his interests in theater, political activism, stem cell research and paralysis. The li-

The main entrance of Princeton Public Library viewed from Library Plaza. Courtesy of Jeff Tryon.

brary also established the Christopher Reeve Theater Arts Collection, launched with a $5,000 donation from the Friends of the Princeton Public Library. Princeton native Paul Robeson (1898–1976) is remembered by the library with a collection and a bust by Antonio Salemme. Robeson was a true Renaissance man, well known as a Broadway performer and film actor, but also as a Columbia Law School graduate, New York City lawyer, American Professional Football League player, and a political and civil rights activist.

⚘ ⚘
Everyone Goes There

When library trustees asked patrons what they thought about their new library in 2006, thoughtful respondents ranged in age from eight years to seventy-eight. All had one thing in common: a love for their new community center. Wrote a seventy-year-old, "everyone goes there." Added an eight-year-old: "it's the heart of the community because it's close to the ice cream store!"

Heart of the Community: **The Libraries We Love**

Toms River Branch

Ocean County Library

Toms River, New Jersey

Address:	101 Washington Street
	Toms River, NJ 08753
Date Founded:	1924
Date Built:	1981; 2006 (renovation)
Architect:	Hillier Group
Director:	Elaine H. McConnell
Special Collections:	Local History and Genealogy;
	Morro Castle Files

Its beginning was decidedly singular: one Model T truck, one librarian and one assistant in a one-room cottage that was open one day a week.

The Ocean County Library was founded on 14 November 1924. Service began ten months later with a staff of one librarian and one assistant. Housed in a one-room cottage called the Logan Building on the grounds of the Ocean County Courthouse, the library had a book collection of 6,225 volumes and a Model T truck that was purchased for $997.

Back then the library was open one day a week. It served thirty-two schools and twenty-three adult stations (the rural, hard-to-get-to places in the woods) throughout Ocean County, New Jersey. For years the library used the Model T to deliver books to front porches, firehouses, and any other place where people assembled. In 1950 the first walk-in bookmobile was purchased, and by 1955 the library's twenty-year-old panel truck was replaced by two bookmobiles. Bookmobile service continued until 1995.

You do not really leave a library; if you do what it wants you to do, then you are taking it with you.

—Elie Wiesel

took place on 28 January 2006. The multimillion-dollar renovation added 50 thousand square feet to the library, which now features a 250-seat multipurpose room with stage, a twenty-station technology-training laboratory, a youth story and craft area with seating for forty, an art gallery, an exhibit room, and a silent study tower. The meeting room housed in the church will be converted into a gift shop and café.

Largest in the State

Today the Ocean County Library is a modern institution that encompasses twenty branches, hundreds of computers, and more than one million books, audio, video, and software titles. It is the largest public library system in the state, serving more than half a million residents. Located between the exploding metropolitan centers of New York City and Philadelphia, Ocean County is a textbook example of exurban growth—complete with its benefits and challenges.

In 1979 the Ocean County Board of Chosen Freeholders (the county governing body) purchased a Presbyterian church dating back to 1853 and broke ground on the property for a 54-thousand-square-foot library. The library, then known as the Toms River Headquarters, opened in 1981, and the church served as a meeting room that seated 150.

The grand opening of the newly renovated Toms River Branch

Community Sculpture Gallery

Inside the silent study tower on the second floor is *Buzzy*, a steel sphere, 30 inches in diameter, created in 1977 by sculptor Michael Allen Malpass of Brick, New Jersey, who died in 1991 at age forty-four. At the time Malpass created *Buzzy*, he was teaching welding at Pratt Institute in Brooklyn, New York. The half-inch steel rods were forged using traditional blacksmithing techniques and welded. "The activity of this piece gives a wonderful juxtaposition of noise mixed with the silence of this room," noted Chief Librarian Mary Malagiere, who was part of a library committee responsible for selecting the artwork from seven hundred submissions. A second Malpass work, entitled *O*, is placed in a niche outside the administrative area on the second floor.

Two soft sculptures that the library commissioned from Joanie San Cherico of Toms River hang in the lobby. The pieces, *Sandbar No. 1* and *Sandbar No. 2*, are abstract images of ocean shallows filtering sunlight and highlighted by sea foam. Also in the

Chris Freeman's *Woven Light/Flowing Fabric* lights up the Hugh B. Wheeler Reading Room. Courtesy of Chris Barnes.

lobby is *Reflections of the Ocean County Library,* an 8-foot bas-relief sculpture in bonded bronze created by Toms River sculptor Brian Hanlon. It shows images of people using the library and an open book with an excerpt of a letter from Thomas Jefferson to his friend John Wyche. Hanlon also created a bust of the late county freeholder James J. Mancini, which will be placed in the rotunda leading into the Mancini Hall program center.

Artist and designer Michele Oka Doner of New York installed the artwork floor in the atrium. The floor is made of glass-like terrazzo tile reflective of the ocean floor. Seventy-five cast bronze "floating" diatoms are embedded in the tile. A fiber-optic art piece of an asterism—a cluster of stars—was created on the ceiling of the atrium.

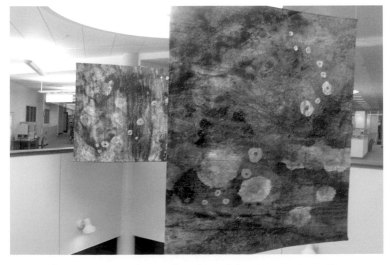

Sandbar No. 1 and *Sandbar No. 2* by Joanie San Cherico. Courtesy of Chris Barnes.

The Hugh B. Wheeler Reading Room is illuminated by an electric light sculpture called *Woven Light/Flowing Fabric.* Created by renowned neon-and-cold-cathode artist Christopher Freeman, this piece expands across the domed ceiling, bathing the Reading Room in a soothing blue light. "Light is a very important aspect of anybody's life," added Freeman. "It determines how we interpret our world."

"Connect People and Build Community"

The thirty-three municipalities that comprise Ocean County vary widely in median income, age distribution, and racial and ethnic makeup. With a vision to "connect people and build community," the library strives to provide services for all ages and populations and to be a catalyst for growth and change.

The library is committed to diversity and inclusion. The collections, programming, outreach, policies, and personnel practices reflect this commitment. The library has expanded the Spanish-language and African-American collections, has made bilingual staff available, has hired an outreach librarian, and holds culturally diverse programming on an ongoing basis.

Members of the staff are also involved in outreach, whether championing the library as cheerleaders, participating in a drill team with book carts, marching in parades, participating in health fairs and LGBT (Lesbian/Gay/Bisexual/Transgender) events, or mobilizing groups of people to celebrate the anniversary of Martin Luther King's "I Have a Dream" speech with a bus trip to Washington, D.C.

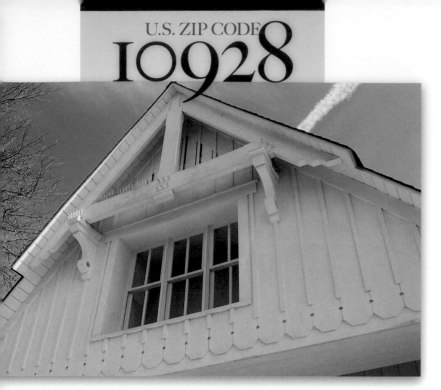

Highland Falls
Public Library

◆

Highland Falls, New York

Address: 298 Main Street
Highland Falls, NY 10928
Date Founded: 1896
Date Built: 1880s; 1954; 2001 (addition)
Architect: Conrad Remick (2001)
Director: Suzanne Brahm
Special Collections: Hudson River Art

He invested in steamships, railroads, and steel mills; she invested in minds.

The village of Highland Falls in the 1880s was a resort haven for many New York City residents, including Mrs. J. P. Morgan, wife of investment banker and financier John Pierpont Morgan. Mrs. Morgan, a respected member of the community, opened a small reading room and circulating library in the village, the first of three library buildings that have occupied the same site.

One Little . . .

In 1896 the Morgan Circulating Library established by Mrs. Morgan was chartered by the state of New York, and the Library Association was formed. In 1923 Mrs. Morgan sold the premises to the Library Association, and villagers took over its upkeep. Children went to the library after school to do their homework, a carpentry school was located on the premises, and Mrs. Morgan and her sister-in-law, Jenny Bigelow Tracy, held fund-raisers to help with the upkeep. The little white frame library in the center of the village served until 1952, when on a winter morning a fire broke out in the small electrical shop that was housed in the building.

One gets thrilled and frightened
at the same time in the presence
of a library because it reminds one
about one's past, present, and, most,
of the possibilities of the future.

—Bill Moyers

Two Little . . .

The library was so severely damaged it had to be torn down. Two years later a small red brick building was constructed on the site. The new library had a complete children's room in the basement, and the book collection was renewed and expanded.

Three Little Libraries

In the mid-1990s the library board recognized that the little red library needed to be larger. Because the library is a private association, taxpayers could not vote on a public bond—the community would have to raise the money on its own. A fund-raising campaign began with a party in 1997, and residents rallied to help their library expand. Conrad Remick, the project's architect, designed the addition to complement the turn-of-the-century buildings on Main Street. Ground was broken in 1999, and the building, constructed by John Flannery, was completed in 2001.

The New Little Library

Native Americans of the Algonquin tribe first inhabited the land where Highland Falls now stands, just outside West Point Military Academy along the Hudson River 50 miles from New York City. When the Dutch settled there in the 1600s, they named the place "Buttermilk Falls" for the turbulent brook that tumbled its way down to the Hudson River. A major thoroughfare for the settlement of New York State, the Hudson River during the Revolutionary War was the site of many forts, one of which was Fortress West Point. After the war West Point became the nation's first engineering school and home to the United States Military Academy. Some of the families currently stationed at West Point

A young patron reads in the in the library's Victorian Room. Courtesy of Tiffany French.

frequent the Highland Falls Library, and their children take part in the programs offered there. The area is also famous for the Hudson River School, a group of artists who painted romantic landscapes of the Hudson River Valley wilderness and of the newly opened West. Highland Falls Library displays examples of Hudson River School art as well as the work of local artists. Several walls are also open for the display of student artwork.

The exterior of the newest "little" Highland Falls Public Library blends well with the Victorian shops on Main Street—so much so that the library won an Honorable Mention Award for Best Building in 2002 from the New York Library Association. Inside, the library is inviting. The rooms are spacious and bright. The reading room has a brick fireplace for cozy reading in the winter and plush chairs, reading tables, and a sofa. The children's room features a parade of wild animals along one rounded wall and pint-sized tables and chairs. The reference area has a stained glass window, Victorian scalloped woodwork, and open reference stacks. The community room, with a vaulted ceiling and innovative overhead lighting, is a spacious area for holding programs.

The addition brought technology to the library—as a member of the Ramapo-Catskill Library System, it shares resources electronically with almost fifty other libraries. There are two terminals for circulating books and managing databases and two terminals for public use, including the Internet.

The library sponsors an art camp in the summer with a certified instructor. Sewing and quilting lessons are given, in the tradition of Mrs. Morgan's original training classes in "technologies." The new commu-nity room, besides hosting library programs, hosts senior citizens, community blood drives, and local civic groups. Concerts and recitals are held there as well. Programs for adults include a reading and discussion club, preschoolers have a scheduled story time, and the Friends of the Library Bookstore has a year-round book sale.

The newest little library has come a long way from the first. The Highland Falls Library now houses a collection of 30,108 books, 1,666 audio materials, 1,076 videos, and 40 serial subscriptions. It has never changed its status as a community service facility, however—Highland Falls Library is still a true heart of the community.

Photo of the old Morgan circulating library.
Courtesy of Highland Falls Historical Society.

Flushing Library

Queens Borough Library System
Flushing, New York

Address: Main Street and Kissena Boulevard
Flushing, NY 11355
Date Founded: 1858
Date Built: 1998
Architect: Todd Schleimann, Polshek and Partners
Director: Thomas W. Galante
Special Collections: International Resource Center; Han Collection on Chinese Culture

Whether its patrons say "melting pot" in Spanish, Yiddish, Afrikaans, Bosnian, Latvian, Marathi, or Thai, the Queens Borough Library System in New York City serves 2 million people in the most ethnically diverse county in the United States.

The Flushing Library, located in a vibrant multicultural neighborhood, is the flagship library of the Queens Borough Library System and the largest branch library in New York State. A substantial percentage of the borough population are immigrants, and the library offers programs, such as its adult learning center, to meet their needs. The library also is a focal point for downtown Flushing, and 1.7 million visitors entered the facility in 2005 to use computers, conduct research, check out materials, attend meetings, and participate in programs.

There is not such a cradle of democracy upon the earth as the Free Public Library, this republic of letters, where neither rank, office, nor wealth receives the slightest consideration.

—Andrew Carnegie

The library began in 1858 when the Flushing Library Association founded a subscription library, with members paying an annual fee of $2.00 (or $25.00 for a lifetime membership). It was the first library in the borough. After relocating several times the library almost closed in 1884 because of financial difficulties. A seven-year fundraising effort allowed the library association to purchase the First Baptist Church building on the corner of Main and Kissena in 1891. In 1902 New York City took over the library, bought additional land on the site with money donated by Andrew Carnegie, and built a new library behind the old one, which was later moved. In 1901 Carnegie had donated $5.2 million to New York City to build libraries. The Flushing library was one of eight in Queens. In 1957 the building was again replaced with a more modern facility. By the mid-1980s demand far outstripped space, and planning for the new Flushing library began, with the new building opening in 1998. The new facility quickly began attracting five thousand visitors a day, making it the busiest branch library in the state.

Exterior of original Carnegie building.

Metaphor for Learning

Metaphorically, the library's transparent four-story façade advertises learning: The glass curtain allows the facility's collections

A view of the library's 227-seat auditorium with a grand piano on stage.

and functional organization to be visually accessible from the street. The openness of the curtain-wall façade allows the public to see activity inside the library and invites the public in. The opposite façade is rendered with stone, its articulation alluding to the book stacks within and its opacity allowing perimeter shelving to be maximized. The 76,000-square-foot facility has a 227-seat auditorium, a multipurpose room for 150, conference rooms, exhibition areas, a quiet room for research, and state-of-the-art electronic facilities.

International Resource Center

A key feature of the library is the International Resource Center (IRC), housed on the third level and developed with the multicultural nature of the Queens and greater New York City community in mind. The IRC provides to the public, free of charge, one of the largest and most up-to-date collections of information on the peoples, cultures, and economies of the world. A special strength is information on global commerce and business. Among the special collections are the Han Collection on Chinese Culture, the International Business Collection, the International Fiction Collection, and the International Magazines and Newspapers Collection.

Since its founding in 1998 the IRC has expanded its collection in international languages. It now has material in fifty-one languages, including Afrikaans, Bosnian, Latvian, Marathi, Thai, and Yiddish. The In-

ternational Fiction Collection offers modern fiction in English and English translation.

The center also offers an eclectic mix of programs and exhibits. For example, in 2006 programs covered the water crisis in Bangladesh, Mao, Ayurvedic healing, and Internet censorship in China.

Adult reading room in Flushing's original Carnegie building, c. 1910.

U.S. ZIP CODE
11720

Middle Country Public Library

Centereach, New York

Address: 101 Eastwood Boulevard
Centereach, NY 11720
Date Founded: 1957
Date Built: 1971; 1986; 2003 (addition)
Architect: Hardy Holzman Pfeiffer Associates (2003)
Director: Sandra Feinberg
Special Collections: Business Resource Center; Family Education, Health and Medical Collection; Adult Literacy Collection

Middle Country Public Library (MCPL) wants its two buildings to be more than just two big boxes of books, thus it strives to be a community center for the sixty thousand residents it serves. It is the busiest library on Long Island, with an annual circulation of 1.5 million and 2,400 programs each year. The library offers twelve meeting rooms for hundreds of civic and business organizations, youth and senior groups, support groups ranging from bereaved parents to Alcoholics Anonymous, literacy tutoring, home schooling, cultural activities, and parent education programs. At any given time, all of the meeting rooms can be fully occupied, contributing as many as 1,800 visitors to the library.

An exterior view of Middle Country Public Library.

National Model for Family Place Libraries

MCPL is the national model for Family Place Libraries. Its programs for young children and their families have been replicated at urban, rural, and suburban libraries in more than two hundred communities across the country, affecting the development of family-centered services and shaping library spaces for families. With an interactive, drop-in Family Place space in each of its two buildings, the library attracts hundreds of fathers, mothers, grandparents, and caregivers each day. In partnership with a local family-support agency, the library initiated its Family Center to provide a social worker to assist families with special problems. In partnership with the National Association of Mothers' Centers, MCPL formed its Mothers Center, a peer-facilitated support group for mothers and young children, and helps ten other libraries do the same through the Family Place LI Network, which Middle Country Public Library administers. The library develops new models of library service to families, caregivers, and children: family literacy, technology, parent support, outreach to family home providers and new immigrant families, home-visiting programs, and intergenerational programs for parents, grandparents and children.

Resource for Business

The Miller Business Resource Center supports regional economic development and provides regional business research support through partnerships with a major business association and the local Industrial Development Agency. The center includes business, finance, law, adult literacy, and career information collections, computers, reading areas, meeting rooms, conference rooms, and offices for the business, career information, and adult literacy staff, as well as a shared office space used by its partners. The center provides office space for the local chamber of com-

Jim "Slim" Cooke's *Reading Garden Sculpture,* shown in front of the 2003 addition, complements the building's lobby.

merce, Smart Growth Initiative, and Small Business Development Center and serves as one of five regional centers for adult literacy services. Career counselors on staff offer one-on-one assistance to residents, and the annual Women's EXPO showcases more than seventy women entrepreneurs, attracting an audience of 1,600 to the library each October. Kevin E. McCormack, president of the chamber of commerce calls the library "unrivaled in its scope and value" for the business community.

Library for All Ages

The library also offers programs for seniors, including Senior Connections information and referral assistance, Lets-Do-Lunch-and-a Movie, an annual senior prom and New Year's celebration, dozens of cultural, craft, and game programs and activities, and the WISE (World of Information for Seniors and the Elderly) collection that houses information of special interest to seniors and their caregivers.

Teens are one of the library's newest target audiences. With three areas devoted to teens, including the Teen Resource Center now under renovation, the library offers activities such as Drama Improv, poetry slams, art programs, Anime Club, Science and Technology Club, Game Club, and teen dances and sleepovers. The annual Teen Battle of the Bands draws hundreds, and a first-ever musical offered teens opportunities to sing, act, dance, and create the scenery for a teens-only show.

The Museum Corner provides interactive, hands-on experiential learning for school children through changing exhibitions that help children explore the world—from art to architecture,

dinosaurs to dolls, the American cowboy to the early American schoolhouse—through more than forty themed exhibits during the past nineteen years.

Community resident Donna Kossack sums up the library's importance, saying, "It offers opportunities for everyone in the family to experience things they wouldn't have had a chance to try out."

On the Grow

In 2002 and 2003 the library completed a 107,000-square-foot, two-building expansion and renovation project, making it the largest public library on Long Island. Form follows function at the library, where architectural spaces reflect the activities taking place. Designed by architects Hardy Holzman Pfeiffer, both buildings are intended to reflect the "out-of-the-box" thinking of both the library staff and the community.

The project's principal architect, Robert Almodovar, said that the library's dynamic design reflects the library's innovative services and programs, making use of contemporary materials such as translucent window walls, metal shingles, ceramic tile, and clay tile blocks that in scale, size, and pattern reinforce the importance of what takes place in the interior.

The building's soaring, copper-roofed lobby has recently been complemented by the addition of the outdoor *Reading Garden Sculpture* by Long Island artist James "Slim" Cooke, whose sculpture is included in the permanent exhibits at the Smithsonian Institution in Washington, D.C., and the Museum of Modern Art in New York City. The sculpture is rendered in copper and designed to stimulate the imagination and reinforce the library's emphasis on building community and celebrating literacy.

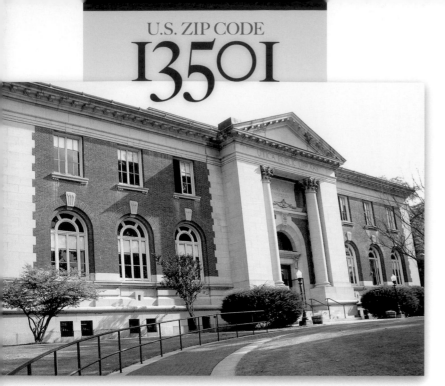

Utica Public Library

Utica, New York

Address: 303 Genesee Street
Utica, NY 13501
Date Founded: 1838
Date Built: 1904
Architect: Arthur C. Jackson
Director: Darby O'Brien
Special Collections: Local History and Genealogy

'Til periodicals do us part: The Utica Public Library is perhaps the only library in the nation to be cited as grounds for divorce. In his suit for divorce in 1912, Frederick Dager claimed that his wife spent too much time reading and studying at the Utica library.

However, in most other ways the library has been a builder—not a divider—of community. It is the central library for the Mid-York Library System and the regional resource center for all libraries in Oneida, Herkimer, and Madison Counties.

Utica's first library opened in 1825 as a private subscription library housed in the offices of attorney Justus Rathbone. In 1838 a public library opened and moved to several sites until the current library opened in 1904. The Thomas R. and Frederick T. Proctors donated the land, and W. P. White donated $1,000 to start the building fund. The building was designed by Arthur C.

> The library is not a shrine for the worship of books. It is not a temple where literary incense must be burned or where one's devotion to the bound book is expressed in ritual. A library, to modify the famous metaphor of Socrates, should be the delivery room for the birth of ideas— a place where history comes to life.
>
> —Norman Cousins

Jackson of Carrere and Hastings, the firm that had designed the main library of the New York City Public Library system. The building is a modified federal colonial with Palladian influences. The exterior is of Indiana limestone and New Haven brick. The entrance features a massive pediment supported by two stone piers and framed by Corinthian columns. A stone cornice crowns the building. A major renovation in 1988–1992 made the building handicapped accessible and added a new roof, floor and wall coverings, skylights, and drainage system.

A painting of the Battle of Oriskany, fought near Utica in the Revolutionary War. Courtesy of Cira Foster.

Battle of Oriskany

A prized possession of the library is *The Battle of Oriskany*, painted by Frederick Yohn in 1901. Oriskany is located near Utica, and the battle on 6 August 1777, was the one battle in the Revolutionary

Fireplace on the first floor of the library. Courtesy of Cira Foster.

War in which the combatants were all North Americans—loyalists and their Mohawk allies against the rebels and their Oneida allies. The painting depicts the wounded General Herkimer directing his rebel forces while seated at the base of a tree. It was one of the bloodiest battles of the war, and Herkimer later died of his wounds. Although the loyalists were victorious, the heavy casualties and looting of their camp led the Mohawks to withdraw, and the loyalists were forced to retreat north. The weakening of the force hampered the British strategy of capturing New York and thereby separating New England from the southern colonies. The painting has been reprinted numerous times and was used on a 1977 U.S. postage stamp.

☆ ☆
Petitioning for Survival

The library's place in the community was challenged in 1996 when the mayor attempted to eliminate the city's annual contribution to the library's operating budget. The Friends of the Library quickly mounted a petition drive to counter his attempt. That year the Friends of the Library was awarded the New York Library Association's Daniel Casey Library Advocacy Award.

Utica Library's first floor lobby. Courtesy of Cira Foster.

The library has long had a strong commitment to community service, with an emphasis on children. It was the original home of the Children's Museum of Utica, first housed at the library as the Utica Junior League's Junior Museum. Today it houses a genealogy and local history collection for researchers.

The library also participates in Weed and Seed, a Department of Justice program to eliminate crime and revitalize neighborhoods. Funds from this program support the library's twelve-station computer classroom, with classes and instruction offered at no charge to the public. The library also provides meeting rooms and art space where local artists can exhibit their works.

In recent times, the library has provided nearly six hundred programs attended by more than thirteen thousand children and their caregivers. These programs include a variety of Story-Time programs, after-school workshops, arts and crafts workshops, summer reading programs, homework help, tutoring, and art and poetry contests. The library has a special commitment to serving poor children through cooperative efforts with child-care and educational agencies, including Head Start, the Thea Bowman House, and the Neighborhood Center.

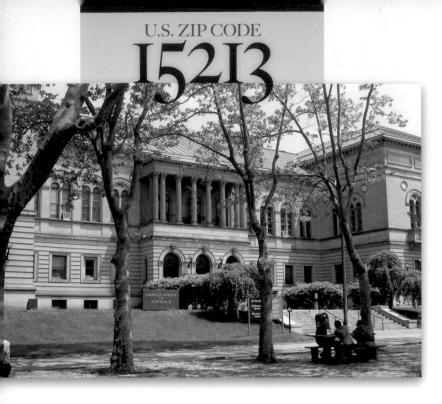

Carnegie Library of Pittsburgh-Main

Pittsburgh, Pennsylvania

Address: 4400 Forbes Avenue
Pittsburgh, PA 15213
Date Founded: 1895
Date Built: 1895; 2004 (renovation)
Architect: Longfellow, Alden and Harlow;
EDGE Studio
Director: Barbara K. Mistick
Special Collections: Pennsylvania History and
Genealology; Andrew Carnegie
Archives

> What can I say? Librarians rule!
>
> - Regis Philbin

This is the one that started it all. Industrialist and philanthropist Andrew Carnegie would fund the construction of more than 1,600 public libraries in the United States, but he made his first offer of funding to Pittsburgh in 1881. However, at first city officials turned him down because strings were attached: Carnegie required that communities provide a site plus 10 percent of the grant amount annually to fund the library's operating expenses. But Pittsburgh officials agreed to Carnegie's terms in 1890, and, five years later Pittsburgh's main library, a three-story Italian Renaissance structure, opened.

"Free to the People" since 1895

Established as a public trust in 1895, Carnegie Library of Pittsburgh serves Pittsburgh, as well as Pennsylvania's Allegheny County, with a history of leadership among the country's great public libraries. Through its nineteen neighborhood locations, including the Main Library and the Library for the Blind and Physically Handicapped, Carnegie Library of Pittsburgh is the region's most visited asset, welcoming close to 2 million customers in 2005. Each year the library provides more than six thousand free programs, classes, and other learning and training opportunities to customers.

Among all U.S. public libraries, Carnegie Library of Pittsburgh–Main offered the first fully organized children's department (1899), the first training class for children's librarians (1900), and the first science and technology department (1902). On 30 March 1979, the library was certified as a landmark property by the National Register of Historic Places.

Special Collections

Since 1895 the library has built an extensive collection of materials on the history of Pennsylvania. In 1928 the materials were consolidated into one unit, the Pennsylvania Department. The department has resources on Pennsylvania history, biography, law, economics, sociology, and demographics with an emphasis on Pittsburgh and western Pennsylvania.

Collections include:

- Andrew Carnegie Collection: Books, pamphlets, scrapbooks, and correspondence by or about Andrew Carnegie.
- Pittsburgh Photographic Library: More than 100,000 negatives and prints that are a visual history of the city of Pittsburgh from its origin through its industrial development and renaissance. The department also maintains a small circulating collection of pictures of Pennsylvania and Pittsburgh subjects.
- Genealogy and Heraldry: Family histories; census enumeration schedules of Pennsylvania, 1790–1920; a surname index file; Pittsburgh newspaper marriage and death notice indexes; city directories.
- Pittsburgh Clipping File: Circa 1900 to date, this file contains thousands of articles from local newspapers covering a variety of historical and current topics and personalities of the Pittsburgh area.
- Manuscripts: A number of collections consisting of original documents and personal papers reflecting the history of Pittsburgh.

Renovation

When renovation was planned in 2001, the main challenge was to provide a twenty-first-century library in a building constructed in 1895. The Capital Projects planning team envisioned a library

Carnegie–Main computer stations, set against the library's innovative glass-panel walls.

full of energy that was customer focused and provided a place for people to gather.

The first floor redesign turned the image of libraries upside down. The improvements represented a new way of thinking about libraries—everything focused on the customer. Focus groups told the library team that the physical structure of the library was too complex, confusing, and difficult to navigate. By creatively using signage, space, and staff, the library enables customers to make serendipitous connections from the first floor's new and featured book collections to other services and collections.

Take one step into the library, and you are invited to grab a cup of coffee, relax, and explore. The layout of the first floor is designed to encourage a circular flow of traffic with ease of motion and openness prevailing over barriers and walls. Reminiscent of retail bookstores, the library houses its own coffee and retail shop, quiet reading room, magazine, and large-print rooms. Creative displays that can be changed quickly are located in the front of the first floor to invite patrons to investigate additional areas throughout the library and to connect with subject specialists. The first floor also has an outdoor deck complete with a bamboo garden, which doubles as a venue for concerts. Since the renovations, circulation at Carnegie Library of Pittsburgh–Main has increased by 25 percent.

※ ※

Shush-Free Zones

Teens can count on not being "shushed" in the library's newly expanded teen space, which holds a variety of popular items in fiction, nonfiction, series, graphic novels, magazines, and music. Here teens can read, study, relax, and socialize at couches and tables or use the first group of personal computers dedicated to teen use—all reserved for them during after-school hours. The Teen Advisory Council helps direct teen programming, which ranges from Monday Movie Matinees to the weekly game of DDR (Dance Dance Revolution), a popular Xbox title. Since the redesign, circulation for teens has gone up 20 percent.

Carnegie Library of Pittsburgh is also one of the first libraries in the country to use electronic signage to provide an easier experience for customers. Throughout the first floor, large multimedia display beacons are located above each information desk and in and along glass panel walls. This signage system encourages customers to make new connections as interesting facts, images, quotations, and library events, services, and resources are revealed.

To help the community identify the Carnegie Library of Pittsburgh–Main as a destination, the library introduced a variety of programming opportunities. After Wordz, a series of after-hours jazz concerts, is held monthly during warm months on the new outdoor deck. The six-concert series, which features live music and refreshments, drew an estimated 1,400 in its first year. Music lovers also enjoy the library's monthly Sunday afternoon music programs, featuring local musicians of assorted music genres. Forty to sixty people attend these free concerts each month. The renovations also help the library reach new audiences through its monthly after-hours Film Series of independent films, which attracts an increasing number of viewers and film students from nearby colleges. And in 2005 the library hosted its first wedding.

U.S. ZIP CODE

16365

Warren Public Library

◆

Warren, Pennsylvania

Address:	205 Market Street
	Warren, PA 16365
Date Founded:	1831
Date Built:	1884; 1916
Architect:	Charles Delevan Wetmore (1916)
Director:	Patricia Sherbondy
Special Collections:	Pennsylvania History

It was an early form of multimedia: At the Struthers Library Theatre you could walk upstairs and read *Hamlet* and then walk downstairs and see it performed.

Through the contribution of Thomas Struthers, a local industrialist and philanthropist, the Warren Public Library was located in the Struthers Library Theatre building, where it provided service to the residents of Warren for thirty-three years. The original multipurpose Struthers Library building was opened in 1884. The theatre was specifically designed to provide financial support to the library, in addition to income derived from renting space in the building to the local newspaper, Masonic lodge, post office, and other businesses.

The main floor of the theater boasted an elegant auditorium and large stage. Early theatrical shows were replaced in the 1900s by vaudeville shows and motion pictures. The Struthers Library Theatre is the eighteenth-oldest operating theater in the nation.

The opening of the library—founded in 1831, chartered in 1873, and dedicated in 1884—was a heralded event on the "western frontier" of the United States. The community received letters of congratulations from notables of the day, including President Chester A. Arthur, physician and author Oliver Wendell Holmes, and suffragist Elizabeth Cady Stanton.

In 1915 the library moved to its present location, a new building that opened to the public in 1916, at 205 Market Street.

The library is distinguished by its architectural design, a neoclassical structure designed by Charles Delevan Wetmore, who designed hotel buildings in New York City and elsewhere. Wetmore was also one of the designers of Grand Central Station.

The exterior of the Warren Public Library features granite tablets created by Wetmore that enclose five inscriptions honoring literature, history, philosophy, biography, and religion. Charles W. Eliot, president of Harvard University from 1869 to 1909, wrote the inscriptions for the library.

The building was recently renovated to offer a modern, service-oriented facility. A highlight of the renovation is the Children's Room with an Allegheny National Forest theme, life-sized trees, and animals.

❧ ❧
Gem of the Allegheny

The Warren Public Library is situated in the historic district of Warren, which is located on the Allegheny River in rural northwestern Pennsylvania, which was home to the birth of the oil industry in the 1860s. In the late nineteenth century thirteen crude oil refineries were located within six miles of Warren. Warren is now one of the finest surviving Victorian communities in the United States.

Stuffed animals greet visitors to the Children's Room.

PAGE
36

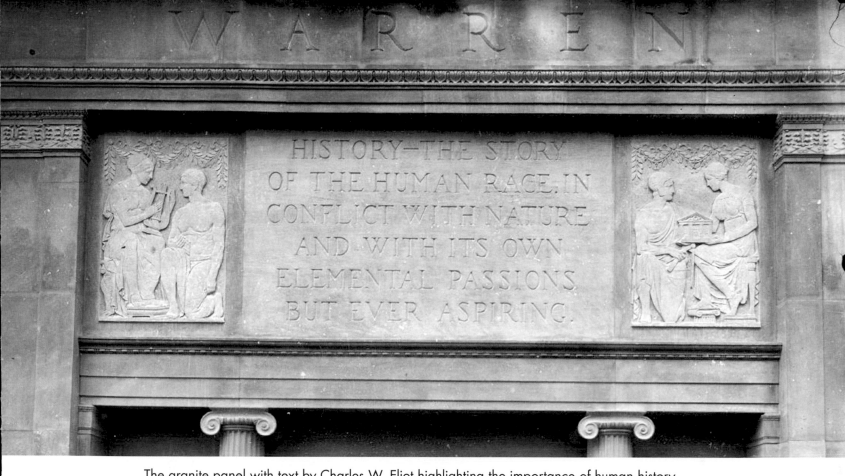

The granite panel with text by Charles W. Eliot highlighting the importance of human history.

The library has a collection of 168,742 items, a countywide library card, and an integrated automation system with an annual circulation of 250,818. Special collections include the 3,586-item Pennsylvania Collection with materials on local history and genealogy, development of early lumber, petroleum, and railroad industries, and materials relating to the Kinzua Dam and Allegheny Reservoir flood control project.

⊞ "The Warren Public Library has been a haven for me all of my life—security, quiet, knowledge, information, the start of wisdom."

✻ ✻

A Home Away from Home

Patrons clearly love their library. A sampling of their adoration:

⊞ "It is my second home! I come here for research, to introduce my grandchildren and others to the importance of reading, and to show them how to use a library. I would be lost without this library."
⊞ "So many times when I discover a new interest, it's like finding buried treasure when I find those books on the shelf."

> Book lovers will understand me, and they will know too, that part of the pleasure of a library lies in its very existence.
> —Jan Morris

Detail from one of the library's granite panels.

Darby Free Library
◆
Darby, Pennsylvania

Address:	1001 Main Street
	Darby, PA 19023
Date Founded:	1743
Date Built:	1872
Architects:	D. B. Price
Director:	Susan Eshbach
Special Collections:	Original Collection (1743)

When the Darby Free Library opened its doors, Thomas Jefferson was an infant revolutionary, Maria Theresa was newly crowned queen of Bohemia, and fines for an overdue book were counted in pence. Now, more than 260 years later, the Darby Free Library is still open for business. In fact, it still has some of those original books among its collection.

The year was 1743. On the tenth day of March a group of Quaker farmers and merchants in the village of Darby, Pennsylvania, met to organize the area's first cultural institution, the Darby Library Company. Twenty-nine townsmen signed an article of agreement founding what was then the second library in Pennsylvania and what is, in 2006, the oldest continuously operating public library in the United States.

An unrecorded amount of money was subscribed by the organizers for the purchase of books, and forty-five volumes at a cost of eleven pounds, ten shillings sterling were purchased. John Pearson was elected the first librarian, Joseph Bonsall secretary, and Nathan Gibson treasurer. With the assistance of botanist John Bartram, a member of the Darby Friends Meeting, arrangements were made to purchase the books in London. Funds for the purchase were transferred in the form of a bill of exchange to Lawrence Williams, to be paid on sight to Peter Collinson of London.

On 14 April 1743, the original library company minutes recorded a letter to Collinson written by Joseph Bonsall. The letter noted in part:

> There is a small number of us in Darby near Philadelphia who have formed ourselves into a company in order to purchase for our use a small set of books, with well-grounded expectations of our number increasing in a little time, and being advised by our friend and neighbor, John Bartram, to apply to thee to purchase these books, and in confidence of thy good disposition from the character he gives of thee to encourage such a decision we have thought fit there upon to send to and desire thee to do such an office of kindness for us . . .

✿ ✿
John Bartram:
Father of U.S. Botany

John Bartram was born on 23 May 1699, in Darby. He collected plants in the eastern United States, shipping many to gardeners in Europe. Considered the father of U.S. botany, he founded the 12-acre Bartram Botanical Garden on the Schuylkill River, about three miles from Philadelphia. He was one of the cofounders, with Benjamin Franklin, of the American Philosophical Society in 1742.

Peter Collinson was a businessman who was looking for an American plant collector who could supply the botanical needs of prominent Englishmen, who were eager to obtain new plant material from the colonies. John Bartram filled the bill, and the association between these two men made it possible for the new Darby Library to purchase and receive its original collection.

Portrait of John Bartram by Albert Hamson.
Courtesy of John Bartram High School.

Darby Library side view. Courtesy of Harold Borders.

The Original Collection

The books received and examined at a meeting of the library company on 5 November 1743, were:

1 Vol.	1738	*The Gentleman Instructed*
1 Vol.	1729	Puffendorf's *Of the Law of Nature and Nations*
8 Vol.	1736	*The Universal Spectator*
8 Vol.	1741	*The Turkish Spy*
2 Vol.	1718	Tournefort's *A Voyage into the Levant*
1 Vol.	1737	Whiston's *A New Theory of the Earth*
1 Vol.	1736	Addison's *Travels*
1 Vol.	1736	Barclay's *Apology*
1 Vol.	1738	Locke's *Some Thoughts Concerning Education*
1 Vol.	1738	*Religion of Nature Delineated*
1 Vol.	1741	Gordan's *Geographical Grammar*
1 Vol.	1743	Sherlock's *A Practical Discourse Concerning Death*
1 Vol.	1717	Whiston's *Astronomical Principles of Religion*
1 Vol.	1740	Maundrel's *A Journey from Aleppo to Jerusalem*
1 Vol.	1740	Dycke's *New English Dictionary*
1 Vol.	1733	Tull's *The Horse-Hoing Husbandry*
1 Vol.	1736	Blackmore's *Creation, a Philosophical Poem*
3 Vol.	1735	*The Independent Whig*
1 Vol.	1738	Wood's *Institute of the Laws of England*
2 Vol.	1730	Milton's *Paradise Lost and Paradise Regained*
2 Vol.	1702	Puffendorf's *The Compleat History of Sweden*
2 Vol.	1736	Raleigh's *The History of the World*
2 Vol.	1743	Lediard's *The Life of the Duke of Marlborough*

These books, with the exception of six of the eight volumes of the *Universal Spectator* and Dycke's *New English Dictionary*, are still in the possession of the library.

A New Building

In the early days of the library company, books were kept in the home of the librarian. Borrowers of books were required to re-imburse the library for one and one-half times the value of each volume not returned. Late fines ranged from three to six pence, depending on the value of the book. Company meetings were held in various members' homes at "two o'clock in the afternoon."

In 1872 a lot at the corner of Serrill (now 10th Street) and Main Street in Darby Borough was purchased from David Flickner for $1,000. Library members and citizens then raised $8895.54 to pay for the construction. D. B. Price was the architect and Charles Bonsall the contractor. First known as the Darby Library Hall, this is a two-story, front-gabled brick structure. The front façade is highlighted by a rose window situated prominently in the gable end. The front portal, up a flight of steps, has a full arch framing double doors. Two long narrow windows with full arch complete the symmetry. A bracketed cornice marches along the eave of the building.

The library now contains more than twenty thousand volumes of fiction, nonfiction, and reference books, plus audio, DVD, and videotapes. Information is also accessible through the Internet. Additionally, the library sponsors programs for children and adults throughout the year. The Darby Library is a member of the Delaware County Library System. With this affiliation patrons are able to access books from all over Delaware County.

Abingdon Branch

◆

Harford County Public Library
Abingdon, Maryland

Address:	2510 Tollgate Road
	Abingdon, MD 21009
Date Founded:	2003
Date Built:	2003
Architect:	Morris & Ritchie Associates.
Director:	Audra L. Caplan

Whether visitors view the fountain outdoors as they wind their way in, or view it indoors from the glassed-in reading area, this focal point of the Abingdon Branch of Harford County Public Library appeals to young and old alike as they use the library to gather, read, relax, and learn.

The library is situated between two elementary schools and surrounded by residential neighborhoods containing both single-family homes and townhouses. Sidewalks join the schools, the neighborhoods, and the nearby senior residence with the library. The grounds include walking paths and picnic tables, an outdoor amphitheater, and a pond complete with a wooden dock, fish, and a fountain. All of these amenities can be viewed from the magazine reading area of the library.

The building design, coordinating the circular theme from the shape of the building to the detail in the carpeting, offers both customers and staff comfort and convenience.

The Basis of an Oasis

The library building is interconnected with the pond, sloping terrain, and wooded area on the 15.2-acre site. The library was designed to be the focus of a greater community center, with an outdoor amphitheater, public meeting rooms, gallery space, and natural space that can be developed as gardens for the neighboring elementary schools. The natural materials covering the building exterior help the exterior blend into the landscape. The administrative wing is clad in stone, and the public spaces are finished in green-blue pre-aged copper panels. The east-facing glass at the building entrance is heavily tinted.

The exterior is designed to provide a progression of spaces and views for visitors. As customers enter the site they are directed to the center of the pond. The tree-lined entrance then turns, aiming customers toward the glass end of the building. In contrast, visitors next encounter the solid copper and stone east-facing wall. As they enter the landscaped parking lot they are nestled

between two wings of the building that create a sense of place. Then they walk up the round entry plaza next to the welcoming glass wall.

What Goes Around . . .

The design concept for the interior is a modern interpretation of the classic rotunda. Located at the heart of the building is the information desk with shelving, worktables, and computer stations radiating from that central point. This arrangement provides uninterrupted sight lines to the far corners of the building. The route to the children's area is defined by a low wall located on the outside curve of the rotunda, and the teen space is visible from the information desk but located at the opposite corner from the children's area to give the teens a feeling of independence. Their space received unique furniture and also faces the pond.

The Center of Community

The growing Abingdon community has a diverse population including seniors, preschoolers, stay-at-home mothers, and people of Korean, Latin American, Arab, and Vietnamese ancestry. The library strives to meet the needs of each group, whether that need is language learning, reading readiness, or large-print materials.

The Abingdon community's enthusiasm for this public library shows in the heavy use of the library. Drop-in story times are held twice a week, with between sixty and one hundred people at each one. Meeting rooms are booked by homeowner associations, scouts, college organizations, child-care administrators, and home-school groups. A mothers group meets in the morning before the branch is open to the public. The group is a sup-

The circular Ask a Librarian Desk echoes the library's design concept, a modern interpretation of the classic rotunda.

port system for social and educational interaction. Teens have after-hours parties focusing on themes such as Halloween or Harry Potter.

The schools use the library as a place to gather for many activities. During the recent holiday season, both a band and orchestra performed for the community. Students read in teams and earned books they donated to the library in a program funded by their PTA. Two elementary schools had a yearlong e-mail buddy program that culminated in a chance to meet for the first time at the Abingdon Library. A teen advisory group meets regularly to discuss books, play games including Xbox, and assist with programs for younger children and seniors.

Many author events are standing room only. Frank Cho, cartoonist and graphic novelist, brought in more than ninety people when he discussed his work. Leo Bretholz, author of *Leap into Darkness: Seven Years on the Run in Wartime Europe*, drew a crowd of 110 people to hear stories of his experience running from the Nazis. The Storyhouse Café, serving coffee and sweets, is a destination in and of itself. Customers can enjoy a drink and favorite snack either inside or outside on picnic tables.

The fountain, a focal point of the library, is also visible from the glassed-in reading room.

Heart of the Community: **The Libraries We Love**

West Avenue Library

Newport News Library System
Newport News, Virginia

Address:	West Avenue and 30th Street
	Newport News, VA 23607
Date Founded:	1891
Date Built:	1929
Architect:	Charles M. Robinson
Director:	Izabela M. Cieszynski

It serves one of the country's oldest areas and was at the center of one of the country's oldest social issues. In 1891 a subscription library association was formed by a group of young business professionals. On 6 July 1927 the Commonwealth of Virginia issued a charter of incorporation to a new library group, the Newport News Public Library, Inc., and within six months the new group had taken over the assets of the earlier group.

The new group wanted a new library building to replace the inadequate structure on 26th Street, where the library was temporarily housed. A building committee was formed, and by a vote of 2,285 to 827 the people of Newport News approved $45,000 in bonds to pay for the library. The library board contributed $6,200, and the Old Dominion Land Company donated land valued at $12,000 at the corner of West Avenue and 30th Street in the old downtown area. The cornerstone was laid on 11 April 1929, and West Avenue Library was officially opened on 14 October 1929—two weeks before the stock market crash. The building was the first in Newport News built to be a library.

Georgian Revival

The architectural style of the library, Georgian Revival, was prevalent in the United States from approximately 1895 to 1930. The building has the rectangular shape, symmetrical façade, dormers, cupola, portico, and symmetrical placement of chimneys that are Georgian Revival hallmarks. Mullions separate the glass in each window. The building resembles many of the colonial-era structures in Colonial Williamsburg and the College of William and Mary. Most of the repair work and interior renovation has had minimal effect on the appearance of the building.

Charles M. Robinson designed the building, as well as its neighbor, the Medical Arts Building. Robinson was a Richmond architect who designed many buildings for the Richmond School System, College of William and Mary, and other universities and school districts in Virginia. Robinson died in 1932; thus the library was one of the designs from his latter years.

Civil Rights

On 9 May 1949 W. Hale Thompson, a local black attorney, proposed to City Council that the library be opened to persons of all races. On 15 May 1949, City Attorney Harry L. Nachman recommended to the city fathers that any decision on Thompson's

Christopher Newport mural. Courtesy of John B. Warters, Photo Reflections.

Adult reading room. Courtesy of John B. Warters, Photo Reflections.

proposal be put off until the Supreme Court ruled on the constitutionality of race-restricted use of public facilities. However, within two months library branch No. 1 had been set up in a room of the Dorie Miller Center, known as the "Negro Recreation Building," in the predominantly black section of the city. Not satisfied with this halfway measure, Thompson returned to City Council on 27 March 1950 to again seek "unrestricted use of the Newport News Public Library for whites and Negroes."

Thompson, a local official of the National Association for the Advancement of Colored People, threatened to go to court if the library was not opened to blacks. The council refused, arguing that policies about the West Avenue Library were made by Newport News Public Library, Inc. and that the council merely approved them. At that point attorney William Davis Butts, representing Thompson, filed suit in the U.S. District Court for the Eastern District of Virginia against both the city and the board. On 8 July 1952, two days before the trial was to begin, the board of directors of Newport News Public Library, Inc. issued a statement, opening the library "to all adult inhabitants of the City of Newport News." The judge dismissed the case.

✾ ✾

The Landing of Captain Christopher Newport

In 1955 the library board proposed that "a mural depicting the landing of Captain Christopher Newport at Newport News Point on May 2, 1607" be commissioned and hung in the library for the upcoming Jamestown Celebration (Newport also carried settlers to Jamestown). The board approved a proposal from artist Allan D. Jones Jr. for a large mural to be installed at West Avenue. On the 350th anniversary of the landing, the mural was unveiled during ceremonies at the library. The 7-×-27-foot mural was executed in three panels. Displayed on the wall behind the circulation desk it serves as the centerpiece for patrons entering the library. The library was recently listed on the National and State Registers of Historic Places. For the 400th anniversary of the landing, the mural is being restored.

West Avenue Library serves the downtown area of Newport News, particularly employees of Northrop Grumman Shipyard and crew members whose ships are under repair on the Newport News waterfront. The library also serves as the telephone reference center and the program information line for the library system.

Cupola, West Avenue Library. Courtesy of John B. Warters, Photo Reflections

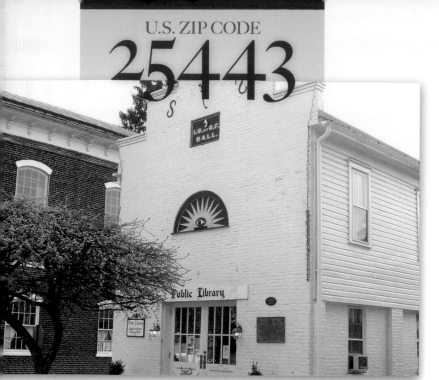

Shepherdstown Public Library

Shepherdstown, West Virginia

Address: German and King Streets
Shepherdstown, WV 25443
Date Founded: 1922
Date Built: 1800
Director: Hali Taylor
Special Collections: Human Rights Video Collection;
Rare Local History Books

When it was built in 1800, the market house that today houses Shepherdstown Public Library offered local farmers a sheltered place to sell their wares, and a centrally located spot for residents to buy farm-fresh products. During its long history, it has, in turn, been home to the fire department, the town council offices, a butcher shop, a school, and the local jail. A pigpen and a public whipping post were located in back. Today, it is the home of a thriving library that is literally and figuratively the heart of Shepherdstown. The building—the most distinctive in Shepherdstown and the one most frequently noticed by visitors—is West Virginia's longest continuously occupied library building.

In 1800 the building was a typical market house—a single story with large doors front and back. It stood in the middle of King Street with traffic passing on both sides—a location that allowed

sellers' wagons to drive in. The sides were open to shoppers and closed with wooden slats when not in use. Measuring 57 × 20 feet, it was an imposing building in early Shepherdstown.

From Market House to Library

In 1845, the Independent Order of Odd Fellows approached the town about building a second story onto the market house. They needed a meeting room, and as ritual demanded, it had to be on the second floor, with opaque windows to preserve the secrecy that surrounded their meetings. The brick front of the building was continued up and shaped to present a façade similar to that of the German Reformed Church and the whole was put under a new roof. A stairway was constructed on the rear exterior of the building to avoid interfering with the market entrance. This work was done in exchange for a 999-year lease between the town and the Odd Fellows, and the floor upstairs served as their meeting room until 1962, when the Woman's Club took over its lease for the library. The front of the second story features Odd Fellows symbols of the All-Seeing Eye of God in a sunburst and the Heart-in-Hand.

The Battle of Antietam, the bloodiest battle of the Civil War, was fought at nearby Sharpsburg, Maryland, in September 1862. The market house, like many other buildings in town, was used as a makeshift hospital during the battle. By the early 1900s, the market house had fallen into disrepair and many of the staid families tried to persuade other citizens to tear down the eyesore. The Odd Fellows firmly resisted and saved the building from demolition.

The Shepherdstown Woman's Club took over the bottom floor for a public library in 1922. The library was operated by the club, funded by donations, and staffed by dedicated volunteers for about fifty years.

Interior of the library. Photo courtesy of Hali Taylor.

The children's section of the library upstairs. Photo courtesy of Hali Taylor.

Despite limited and unpredictable funding, the library thrived and gathered a reasonably balanced collection of books. In 1948 the town was finally persuaded to remove the jail cells. The Woman's Club bought out the Odd Fellows' lease in 1962 and took possession of the upstairs for its children's department. In 1971 the Woman's Club turned the library over to the state.

⚘ ⚘

Not a Quiet Library

The library is an easy walk for residents of this small, pedestrian-friendly town. The library is not a "quiet" library. Residents consider it their community center and drop in to find out what is going on in town. Although the library does not own the building, town residents have resisted relocating the library because the market house has become firmly ingrained in public consciousness as "the library." The library has continued to serve the general public because the Shepherd University Library, where people go for a greater selection of reference materials, is located just down the street. Shepherdstown Public Library focuses on current fiction, biography, current events, cooking, gardening, home improvement, and its children's library collections.

The Friends of Shepherdstown Library play a huge role in raising awareness and funding for the library. Their fundraisers include a huge book sale; an evening of poetry, wine, and dessert; and the extremely popular dinner theater featuring the Rumsey Radio Hour—a live radio show with homegrown humor, music, stories, and poetry. They present educational programs such as "History Alive," which brings historical characters to life, including West Virginians Pearl Buck (writer), Mad Anne Bailey (frontierswoman), Belle Boyd (Confederate spy) and Mother Jones (labor activist).

The Shepherdstown Public Library's children's department houses an extensive collection of juvenile titles from picture books for the youngest child to young adult books in both paperback and hardcover. The library maintains a close relationship with local public schools, the Shepherdstown Day Care Center, the Shepherd University Nursery School, Project Excel, scouting groups, home schoolers, and various local private schools.

Children's programs begin with infants whose parents and/or grandparents bring them to the very popular lap baby programs. Two-, three-, and four-year-olds have their own programs, as do the elementary after-school visitors. The popular summer reading program begins after school is let out for summer vacation. Spanish classes are offered on Saturday mornings, and family movies are shown on the back of the library during the summer months, with free popcorn and old-fashioned ice cream for everyone.

All in all, not much call these days for the jail or the pigpen or the whipping post, although an occasional pot-bellied pig has been spotted upstairs.

Snow Flurry. Photo courtesy of Agnes and Alvin Freund.

Cabell County Public Library

Huntington, West Virginia

Address: 455 Ninth Street Plaza
Huntington, WV 25701
Date Founded: 1898
Date Built: 1980
Architect: Dean, Dean, and Kieffer
Director: Judy K. Rule
Special Collections: Grady Risen Real Estate Papers

The Cabell County Public Library is state of the art in West Virginia. In 1982 it was the first public library in the state to be automated with a computerized circulation system and online catalog. In 1996 it was also one of the first public libraries in the state to offer Internet access to the public and to have a website. In 1999 it became the first public library in the state to upgrade to a third-generation library automation system based on client-server architecture.

In addition to the main library, seven branches serve the county, and services are provided to libraries in neighboring Mingo, Putnam, and Wayne Counties. The library also is the former place of employment of children's author Cynthia Rylant, who wrote the 1993 Newberry Award–winning *Missing May* and created the two series Mr. Putter and Tabby, and Henry and Mudge.

> As a general rule, librarians are a kick in the pants socially, often full of good humor, progressive, and naturally, well read. They tend to be generalists who know so much about so many things that they are quite the opposite of the boring old poops they have been made out to be. Most of them are full of life, some even full of the devil.
>
> —Bill Hall

History

Planning for a library to serve Huntington began in 1897 and was formalized when a resolution to open a public library was adopted by the Ministers Association in 1898. In 1899 library supporters began collecting the books that formed the library's first collection, housed in a room leased in the Florentine Annex in late 1901. The library opened on 1 March 1902. That year Andrew Carnegie donated $25,000 for a new building, which opened in 1904 on the corner of Ninth Street and Fifth Avenue. In the late 1940s the city library became a county library, with branches opened in Milton and Barboursville, and bookmobile service was initiated to serve an even broader population.

Huntington Public Library, dedicated in 1904.

The current building, located across Ninth Street from the Carnegie building, was dedicated in 1980. In 1997 an expansion project increased the usable space in the building to more than 60,000 square feet. Meanwhile, branches were remodeled or built, bringing the number of branches to seven. With eight locations in the county, bookmobile service was no longer needed.

The Cabell County Public Library was established in its current form as a public corporation by a local law passed by the West Virginia Legislature that mandates funding from property taxes from the County Commission and Board of Education.

Looking down from the second floor reference desk onto the first-floor circulation area. Courtesy of Steve Christo.

❧ ❧
Hub of Regional Activity

The Cabell County Public Library is the center for a range of services and collaborations. It is the regional headquarters for twenty-eight libraries in six counties and is the subregional library for the blind and physically handicapped, housing more than forty-five thousand books on cassette. The library houses an Information and Referral department that serves as a clearinghouse and advocate for new social service agencies. The department was instrumental in the establishment of the Domestic Violence Center for Women and Coalition for the Homeless, which provides the multipurpose day shelter Harmony House as well as the rent-subsidized apartment complex Vanity Fair. For the county it houses the Tri-State Literacy Council, which utilizes twenty to twenty-five tutors to help about seventy-five adults improve their reading skills. It also hosts one of the longest-running book clubs in the area. The Brown Bag Book Club has met once a month for more than six years.

The library also supports local colleges, serving as the library for Huntington Junior College and supporting Marshall University's Department of Multicultural Affairs, College of Fine Arts, and Department of Music, as well as other departments, and offers free library cards to all students.

Beyond the county, the library has reciprocal agreements with other tri-state libraries, thus allowing Kentucky and Ohio residents to receive library cards. It also joins with academic and other public libraries, as well as state and local organizations throughout the tri-state area, to celebrate the literature of Kentucky, Ohio, and West Virginia at the Ohio River Festival of Books. In 2004 the festival featured more than one hundred authors and sixty workshops and programs. For two consecutive years the library has been the only facility in West Virginia participating in I Signed the Constitution Week. Patrons may sign a parchment scroll that is archived at the National Constitution Center in Philadelphia.

Musical groups entertain library patrons in May and December.

U.S. ZIP CODE
30606

Athens-Clarke County Library

Athens Regional Library System

Athens, Georgia

Address: 2025 Baxter Street
Athens, GA 30606
Date Founded: 1880
Date Built: 1992
Architect: Nix, Mann, Viehman
Director: Kathryn Ames
Special Collections: Athens History Archives, Genealogy, African-American History

At the Athens-Clarke County Library you can get locked in with your ancestors or read to an audience who will sit up and beg for more.

In the late 1700s Athens was a mere trading settlement named "Cedar Shoals" on the banks of the Oconee River. Then some of the surrounding land was purchased as a site for the first state-supported, chartered university in Georgia. Lots adjacent to the University of Georgia campus were sold and developed, and the area was renamed "Athens" in honor of the Greek city known for learning and culture. Athens was incorporated as a town in 1806.

In 1801 Clarke County was established by the Georgia General Assembly. Its population grew along with that of Athens, and in the 1800s agriculture, cotton, and textile production were major industries in the area. The first public library in Athens opened in 1880. It closed during the 1920s for lack of funding but re-opened in 1936 with support from the federal Works Progress Administration and the Women's Club. Today the Athens Regional Library System serves five counties with eleven branches

There is more treasure in books than in all the pirates' loot on Treasure Island . . . and best of all, you can enjoy these riches every day of your life.

—Walt Disney

and a collection of more than 370,000 items. The Athens-Clarke County Library is headquarters for the system and has been at its present location since 1992.

Paws for Applause

An example of the library's community outreach is the Read to Rover program. Young readers who have difficulty reading practice on canine listeners who themselves are in training to help the disabled. The dogs, to the children's delight, are rapt and nonjudgmental listeners. The Read to Rover program is the result of an alliance between the library and raiser-and-dog teams affiliated with Canine Companions for Independence. University of Georgia graduate student Rika Toll initiated the sessions. The program promotes reading, "which is what the library is all about," says Gail Firestone, the library's assistant director for youth services.

The library is also a place where patrons learn about their ancestors. The library's genealogical archives are housed in a temperature-controlled room. Patrons can attend lectures on preserving treasured personal documents or on compiling and organizing genealogical records. During the Genealogical Lock-In—A Night Owl Prowl at the Heritage Room, patrons spend the night locked in the genealogy room, researching to their heart's content.

Neighborhood children celebrate the inauguration of the Pinewoods Biblioteca with a traditional dance.
Courtesy of Stacey Overstreet.

A young reader and canine listener in the Read to Rover program.

Children of all ages come to have their imaginations tickled. Young children are entertained with storytelling, educated through animal encounters, and captivated by crafts. They can also meet authors, explore outer space, or watch a puppet show. Teens can learn chess, participate in crafts and games, watch movies, or share their talents in a coffeehouse atmosphere.

The program Live! at the Library presents musical concerts ranging from wind quartets to easy listening. The concerts, sponsored by the Friends of the Athens-Clarke County Library, are free. Or patrons can listen to an evening of classical poetry, get tips on improving their workplace, discuss world affairs, or get help with the newest Medicare plans. They can watch free international and independent films. They also can take workshops in computer use, join a book discussion group, or explore African-American and Native American history through printed material, videos, and online resources.

learning center was established. It is housed in a trailer in a predominantly Hispanic trailer park and serves seventy to eighty patrons a day, offering programs on health issues and job recruitment and cultural celebrations. Art, music, and reading programs are offered to young people, as are classes in English and Spanish. Tutoring is available for middle and high school students. Bilingual Internet classes are also offered. When a student completes the high school equivalency program called "Plaza Communitaria," a Mexican high school diploma is awarded.

The programs are designed to bring Hispanic and non-Hispanic residents together to learn about each others' language and customs. In a poem written by Antonio Deltoro and printed in the Biblioteca inaugural booklet, the ending lines speak to the idea behind the effort: "because for words, nothing is ever foreign."

𝄞 𝄢 Cultural Exchange

In 2004 the library was awarded a grant from the federal Institute of Museum and Library Services to meet three goals. One goal was to improve immigrant educational levels because the number of Mexican immigrants to the area has increased dramatically since 1990. A second goal was to increase the use of the library. A third goal was to provide an educational and cultural exchange between immigrants and the established community.

To these ends the Pinewood Biblioteca library/

Athens-Clarke County Library. Courtesy of Burke Walker.

Brockway Memorial Library

Miami Shores, Florida

Address: 10021 N.E. 2nd Avenue
                      Miami Shores, FL 33138
Date Founded: 1949
Date Built: 1949
Architect: Edwin T. Reeder
Director: Elizabeth Esper
Special Collections: Miami Shores Archives

The town has four thousand residents per square mile, and the library has six books per resident. The story of Miami Shores and its Brockway Memorial Library, however, goes beyond mere numbers. Miami Shores, located on Biscayne Bay, had its beginnings in the Florida land boom of the 1920s, separating itself from Miami proper in 1932 to incorporate as the village of Miami Shores. In 1943 George A. Brockway, an industrialist from Cortland, New York, who wintered in Miami Shores, gave funds to the village to have a library built on land donated by Bessemer Properties, a local corporation. Bearing Brockway's name, the building was designed to hold twenty thousand books. Today the Brockway Memorial Library has more than fifty-five thousand books as well as 151 periodicals and newspapers, more than 4,500 audio and videotapes, access to more than sixteen thousand e-books, and eight networked computers for patron use.

of reading tables and comfortable chairs. A recent addition to the south side of the building was designed to be in keeping with the original structure. Despite the addition, and changes in the décor through the years, the appearance of the library itself has remained much the same since it opened in 1949.

Brockway Memorial Library's mission is to fulfill the intellectual, educational, and recreational needs of the people of Miami Shores. It offers a puppet theater and Story-Time Fun for the younger set. For children ages eight through twelve there's the American Girls Club, the Brockway Book Club, and a summer reading program.

For teens there's a spot on the website called Teen Corner where teens are encouraged to share book reviews and their own writing. There's also a helpful homework link. In addition, the

Library Beautiful

Although occupying a mere 2.5 square miles and only ten feet above sea level, Miami Shores has a population of more than ten thousand people of diverse ethnic backgrounds. North Miami, with a population of nearly sixty thousand, is the nearest large city, and Miami itself (a population of more than 300,000) is approximately six miles away. Although small in area, Miami Shores is known as "the Village Beautiful," and its residents are proud, as well, of their library. Brockway Memorial Library, at the time it was constructed, was considered an outstanding example of "modern Florida architecture," according to then-Mayor Roy McKenzie. Built of limestone and brick, the long, low building has a front portico with leaded glass doors leading into an interior that features three fireplaces, hanging chandeliers, paneled book alcoves, and a scattering

Interior of the library, looking toward the main fireplace.

Heart of the Community: **The Libraries We Love**

A view of Brockway Memorial Library's porticoed main entrance.

library hosts a teen club, a teen advisory board, and, of course, all the latest and hottest teen titles.

❦ ❧
Preserving History

In 2001 the library raised more than $370,000 for a multimedia center, including $125,000 in grants from the State Library of Florida and a matching grant from North Dade Medical Foundation, for which the center is named. The balance was donated by library patrons and friends, and in 2002 the multimedia center opened, adding 2,500 square feet to the library and making room for videos and audio cassettes, reference materials, the Book Sale Room, and a room for storing the Miami Shores Archives. The new computer center has increased the number of computers available to the public and offers ten outlets for notebook computers; wireless connection is available throughout the library for laptop users. There is also a conference room for library meetings and programs and a reference room that contains more than 2,200 volumes of reference materials The library now has room to host cultural arts series and art exhibits and seasonal and holiday programs as well as guest presentations.

Miami Shores' history has its own special place in the library. A collection of artifacts, photographs, public records, newspaper clippings, and other material relating to the history of the area has been gathered and is being sorted and cataloged. The materials come from several sources, the most prominent being the collection of former Village Manager Lawton McCall. Dr. Thelma Peters, a historian who specialized in the history of the area, also donated her papers. Many of the materials date from 1925.

A view of the biography room.

As part of the fiftieth anniversary celebration of Brockway Memorial Library held in 1999, the materials that had been stored for years were moved to their permanent home in the library. The archives serve as a research tool for those who want to know more about the history of Miami Shores. The materials are kept in the North Dade Medical Foundation Media Center and are available to the public by appointment.

The Brockway Memorial Library, located on one of the village's main streets, is right in the heart of the village it serves. It is also in the hearts of its patrons. Say some happy fans, "I love my village library! It's my favorite place in Miami Shores."

U.S. ZIP CODE

33607

West Tampa Library

Tampa, Florida

Address:	2312 West Union Street
	Tampa, FL 33607
Date Founded:	1914
Date Built:	1913; 2003
Architect:	John W. Biggar; FleischmanGarcia
	Architecture
Director:	Joe Stines

To paraphrase Rudyard Kipling, "A cigar is only a cigar, but a good library is a Read."

West Tampa, founded in the swampland west of the Hillsborough River in 1895 as a suburb of Tampa, from 1900 into the 1920s was the center of the cigar industry in the United States. Cigar factories seemed to have sprung up on every street corner. Most of the cigar makers were immigrants from Cuba. One of the customs they brought with them was that of having *lectores* in the factories. *Lectores* were people who were paid to read to the other workers. They read from the *Tampa Tribune* (which they translated into Spanish) in the morning and from novels selected by the workers in the afternoon. Among the favorite novels were those by Balzac, Zola, and Flaubert. The news and novels then spread throughout the community as they were recounted by the workers to their families over dinner each evening.

The cigar workers honored the *lectores* by paying them the highest wages in the industry from their own wages. When the strike of 1931 ended the position of *lectore,* their novels were donated to the West Tampa Library.

America's libraries are the fruits of a great democracy. They exist because we believe that memory and truth are important. They exist because we believe that information and knowledge are not the exclusive domain of a certain type or class of person but rather the province of all who seek to learn. A democratic society holds these institutions in high regard.

—Robert Martin

A Neo-Classical Gem

The West Tampa Library was founded by a community of readers and listeners. It opened in 1914 on property donated by Angel Cuesta, a wealthy cigar factory owner. It was one of only thirteen Carnegie libraries built in Florida between 1900 and 1917 and was the first in Tampa. John W. Biggar designed the library in neo-classical style of red brick. In 1983 it was placed on the National Register of Historic Places. The building was expanded and renovated in 2003 by FleischmanGarcia Architecture. A 5,000-square-foot addition provided space for more books, CDs, DVDs, and computers. The beauty of the building, includ-

Sepia image of the original library.

Heart of the Community: **The Libraries We Love**

Artwork livens the stairwell area.

ing the long, arching windows, wood floors, soaring ceilings, and red brick exterior, was restored. The additional space made the library a center for children's programs, community meetings, and wireless Internet communication. The library today serves an ethnically diverse (African-American, Italian, Latino) population of about fourteen thousand, most of whom live within walking distance.

❧ ❧

A Center for Public Art

Public art was incorporated into the library as part of the expansion and renovation project. Visitors are greeted in the lobby by *Coming to Work, The Cigar Factory,* and *Main Intersection* by Dr. Ferdie Pacheo. The paintings depict historic West Tampa. The main reading room is enlivened by the stained glass windows of artist and author Synthia Saint James. Also, glass artisan Reggie Holder is at work on a colored and glass maquette (a usually small preliminary model). The 1989 Hillsborough County Public Art Ordinance allows the Board of County Commissioners to acquire works of art throughout the county. Community members volunteer for the Public Art Committee to help select artistically significant works for public places for all to enjoy.

A stained-glass work of art features books and readers.

Birmingham Central Public Library

Birmingham, Alabama

Address: 2100 Park Place
Birmingham, AL 35203
Date Founded: 1886
Date Built: 1927; 1984
Architect: Miller, Martin and Lewis; Kidd, Plosser and Sprague
Director: Barbara Sirmans
Special Collections: Southern History and Literature; Genealogy, African-American History, Map Collection

It has survived a shoe-box inception, a conflagration, and segregation. Now the Birmingham Public Library welcomes more than 500,000 visitors each year, making it the most visited site in the Birmingham area, surpassing all of the city's museums and parks. The library's vast collection of books, periodicals, videos, and audios is housed in two buildings: the Central Library and, across the street and connected by a skywalk, the Linn-Henley Research Library. The library has won awards for its genealogy collection and for outstanding service and was recognized for excellence by the Alabama Library Association Convention. Not bad for a place that began in a room that measured just fifteen by eighteen feet.

🙢 🙠
Of Fire and Fortune

The Birmingham Public Library originated in a renovated reception room in a Birmingham public school in 1886. Its collection contained three hundred books. Donations raised the number of books enough that, in an 1887 public school annual report, Superintendent John Phillips noted that the city of Birmingham needed a separate public library to house not only books, but also important papers pertaining to the city's history. By 1890 the fledging library's collection had grown to nearly two thousand books and could no longer be contained in the small reception room. In July of that year the school board, also looking to increase school space, rented the former Park Avenue Hotel owned by Christian Enslen. Renamed the Enslen Building, the property was remodeled into quarters for the both the high school and the library. At the same time the library was made available to the public for a small, yearly membership fee. In November of 1890 a formal reception marked its opening.

By 1902 the library had outgrown its space in the Enslen Building and was moved to the fourth floor of City Hall. The new quarters afforded space for a reading room, a small reference room, and a librarian's office; however, the rooms were located over the

city jail and adjacent to a large, open market, making quiet difficult to come by for library patrons. In 1907 Dr. Thomas Parke organized the Birmingham Public Library Association with a two-fold agenda—to encourage community support for a city library and to raise funds for a library building. Meanwhile, money was raised to refurbish the rooms in City Hall, and a professionally trained librarian, Lila May Chapman, was hired on a six-month contract to organize and catalog the burgeoning collection. One fire and thirty-eight years later, she was still there.

In 1925 City Hall caught fire. The library was decimated. In response to the disaster, libraries across the United States donated books to rebuild the collection, and community leaders

The Birmingham Library's children's department in 1927.

A mid-twentieth-century postcard view of the Birmingham Public Library.

campaigned to finally construct a separate library building. The funds were raised, and in 1927 from the ashes of the first Birmingham Library arose a massive limestone building fronted with columns, its edifice inscribed with the names of famous authors and artists and philosophers and its interior decorated with the murals of artist Ezra Winter.

Segregation and Renovation

The new Birmingham Central Public Library became a community focal point. Considered a model beaux arts facility, it featured electric clocks, three elevators, drinking fountains, a book lift, and art galleries. For decades the library served the city, but at that time Birmingham was a segregated city, and the library system was a segregated system. Separate facilities and services segregated the races until the civil rights movement in the 1960s brought a sit-in led by African-American college students. The library desegregated peacefully, and today a facility that once excluded African-Americans houses more than a million archival documents and photographs preserving the history of the U.S. civil rights movement.

Twenty years later, in 1984, a more modern building was constructed and named the Birmingham Central Public Library. The former building was renovated and renamed the Linn-Henley Research Library in honor of two Birmingham families instrumental in its restoration. In 2002 the Linn-Henley Research Library was recognized as being a site of state historical significance and will eventually be added to the National Register of Historic Places.

Branching Out

Branches of the Birmingham Central Public Library are located in every corner of the city, providing services and programs for adults, teens, children, and local businesses. In every branch patrons have full access to the library's half-million books, as well as audios, videos, computer software, music, and reference materials through the library's network. In addition, the library is part of the Jefferson County Library Cooperative, allowing patrons of libraries in neighboring municipalities to access the collections in the Birmingham Central Public Library. Though each library remains autonomous, each shares a sophisticated computer system and shared purchasing power.

The Birmingham Central Public Library has come a long way from its original tiny space—it is currently the largest public library in Alabama with twenty branches and two million items in its collection. It has a regional library computer center offering twenty computers and free training classes in basic PC and Internet skills. Its Literacy Branch targets high school children with its License to Read program, while middle school students are encouraged to sign up for WILD (Walking in Library Doors) cards. For adults there's the Brown Bag Lunch lecture and music program and an author and book program called Alabama Bound, which invites Alabama authors to the library for a day of informal one-on-one talks with patrons. The Linn-Henley Research Library has one of the finest collections of federal, state, and local government documents, regional history, and archival records in the southeastern United States. It is also noted for its genealogy and historic map collections.

37733

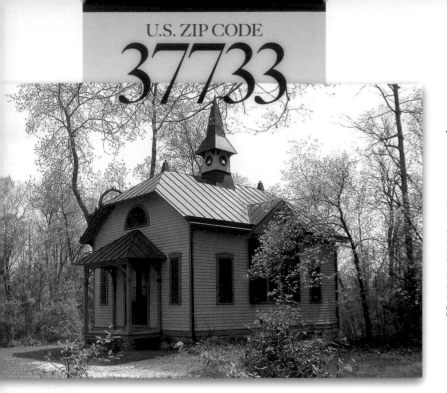

Thomas Hughes Library

◆

Rugby, Tennessee

Address: 5517 Rugby Highway
Rugby TN 37733
Date Founded: 1882
Date Built: 1882
Architect: Unknown
Director: Barbara Stagg
Special Collections: Victorian Library

Utopia has come and gone, but its library has survived.

Nestled among pines and oaks just south of the Big South Fork National Park lies Rugby, Tennessee, a utopian community founded by British author and social reformer Thomas Hughes, who wrote the 1857 bestseller, *Tom Brown's School Days.* The pride of Rugby, the Thomas Hughes Library, was built in 1882. Through Hughes's fame and influence, five thousand volumes were donated by thirty-eight publishers. Some two thousand more were donated by Rugby colonists and visitors, making the library at the time one of the largest in the South. During the height of the community experiment, the library was the focal point of intellectual and cultural life of residents, a resource for the literary and drama clubs that provided both expressive opportunity and pleasure to all.

"New Jerusalem"

Hughes dedicated the Rugby Colony amid great fanfare on 5 October 1880. He envisioned his new community as a place where those who wished could build a strong agricultural community through cooperative enterprise while maintaining a cultured, Christian lifestyle, free of the rigid class distinctions that prevailed in Britain. The idea for the colony grew out of Hughes's concern for the younger sons of landed British families. Under the custom of primogeniture, the eldest son usually inherited everything, leaving the younger sons with only a few socially accepted occupations in England. In the United States, Hughes believed, these young men's energies and talents could be directed toward community building through agriculture. The town site

Portrait of Thomas Hughes.

and surrounding land were chosen in part because the newly built Cincinnati-Southern Railroad had just completed a major line to Chattanooga, opening up this part of the Cumberland Plateau.

During the 1880s Rugby both flourished and floundered, attracting widespread attention on two continents and hundreds of hopeful settlers from Britain and other parts of the United States. By 1884 Hughes's vision seemed bent on becoming a reality. An English agriculturalist had been employed to help train new colonists. Some seventy buildings had been constructed on the town site, and more than three hundred residents enjoyed the rustic yet culturally refined atmosphere of this "New Jerusalem." Literary societies and drama clubs were established. Lawn tennis grounds were laid out and used frequently. Colonists and visitors enjoyed rugby football, horseback riding, croquet, and swimming in the clear rivers surrounding the village. The Tabard Inn, named for Chaucer's *Canterbury Tales,* soon became the social center of the colony. Rugby printed its own weekly newspaper, and general stores, stables, sawmills, boardinghouses, a drug store, dairy, and butcher shop were operating. During its heyday two trains a day ran to Cincinnati, providing a link to goods, services, and entertainment for all the Rugby colonists and the town's many visitors. Press in both the United States and Europe carried updates on the colony's progress.

Within five years, however, financial troubles, a typhoid epidemic, land title problems, and unusually severe winters gradually brought about Rugby's decline. The Tabard Inn burned in 1884, furthering the colony's decline. Thomas Hughes—whose aged mother, Madam Margaret Hughes, brother Hastings, and niece Emily lived in

Library interior, 1884. The collection and the furnishings remain virtually unchanged.

Rugby during its early years—managed to spend only a month or so each year in the colony. He poured more than $75,000 of his own money into the effort to create utopia in the wilderness. However, in spite of Rugby's obvious problems and failures, Hughes never gave up hope for the colony's future. In a letter to some of the remaining settlers shortly before his death in 1896, Hughes wrote, "I can't help feeling and believing that good seed was sown when Rugby was founded and someday the reapers, whoever they may be, will come along with joy bearing heavy sheaves with them."

By 1900 many of the original colonists had left, most for other parts of the country. Although Rugby declined, it was never deserted. Residents struggled over decades to keep its heritage alive and its surviving buildings and land cared for.

Victorian Time Capsule

The library itself grew in large measure due to Dana Estes, a leader among Boston publishers and a publisher of *Tom Brown's School Days*. His devotion to Hughes and his interest in social movements led him to recruit the publishers that contributed the five thousand books to start the library. The publishers' donations were representative of their idea of what an excellent public library should contain. Eventually two thousand additional titles were added. The collection also houses issues of various periodicals, including *Punch* and the *Illustrated London News*.

The Thomas Hughes Public Library was carefully tended. Its first official librarian, Eduard Bertz, a German scholar, designed a system of cataloging and organization that appears to be one of

a kind. The collection is rich with Victorian literature as well as books on science, agriculture, and the culture of the time. Since the demise of the Rugby experiment, the caretakers of Rugby have kept the library virtually unchanged—a time capsule of late Victorian intellectual interests and literary taste. Despite periods of heavy borrowing, virtually all of its seven thousand original volumes are still in the collection.

Online Resource Effort

Rugby and the University of Tennessee are initiating a project to make the collection open to the world in a way that will facilitate scholarly inquiry into the reading habits and intellectual climate of the utopian community at Rugby. Many items in the collection are available elsewhere but not the unique assemblage preserved in Rugby. A digitized catalog of the holdings and circulation record would constitute a valuable research tool for scholars. Potential researchers request information about the library's holdings several times each month.

The Thomas Hughes Library is available for scholarly research year round, and is shown daily to visitors from around the world. It stands as a testament to the place of libraries and literacy in public education in the nineteenth century as well as a record of the efforts of Hughes and his colleagues in the rural United States. The books are still on the shelves in the original catalog order, and all furnishings are still in place. The original building has been preserved by nonprofit Historic Rugby and community residents—all eighty-five of them—many of whom are descendants of the original settlers who hoped to create utopia.

Heart of the Community: **The Libraries We Love**

Benjamin L. Hooks
Central Library

Memphis Public Library and Information Center

Memphis, Tennessee

Address:	3030 Poplar Avenue
	Memphis, TN 38111
Date Founded:	1893
Date Built:	1893; 2001
Architect:	Looney, Ricks, Kiss; Shepley,
	Bulfinch, Richardson and Abbott
Director:	Judith A. Drescher
Special Collections:	African-American History; Local
	History; Memphis Music

For the visually impaired of Memphis, this library is the talk of the town.

In fact, the Benjamin L. Hooks Central Library is the only library in the nation with its own radio station. Since 1980 the station, originally called WTTL (West Tennessee Talking Library), has served the visually impaired population, providing news and information. The station, now called WYPL FM 89.3, continues that tradition, presenting daily readings of *The Commercial Appeal, USA Today,* and other newspapers and magazines as well as a variety of fiction and nonfiction books, author interviews, and specialty programming. A partnership with *Action News Five* also allows local news to be broadcast by radio. The library also has a TV station. WYPL TV18 is a government-access channel and produces more than thirty community interest programs each month on topics ranging from the blues to history to cooking and, of course, books.

History

What is now the Memphis Public Library and Information Center began as the Cossitt Library in 1893. Funded through a donation of $75,000 from the heirs of former Memphis resident and businessman Frederick W. Cossitt, the library sat on the public promenade overlooking the Mississippi River. The Cossitt Library expanded in 1905. In the mid-1920s the library began operating branches with the school system that were for public and school use. In 1935, during the days of segregation, the Vance Avenue branch was established as a full-service library for African Americans, replacing a storefront library that had been located on Memphis' famous Beale Street. During

the 1950s and 1960s Cossitt Library continued its expansion. The physical building in downtown Memphis went through a major renovation. The Goodwyn Institute, an astounding resource for business and technology materials, merged with Cossitt. As populations moved into suburban areas and demand grew for library services, a new Main Library was constructed and neighborhood branches were built in the suburbs.

For forty-six years the Main Library was a valuable community resource. However, with almost a half-century of use, the need for a new building was evident. Through a dynamic public and private partnership, a $70 million new Central Library was constructed in the center of Shelby County, and opened in November 2001. (Coincidentally, with over one hundred years of history, the Cossitt branch is still a vital part of downtown Memphis.)

Like many other urban areas, Memphis has become a melting pot of cultures and bustles with new development. However, Memphis also suffers some of the ills of other urban areas, such as illiteracy and socioeconomic disparities. The library, situated between one of the richest neighborhoods, Chickasaw Gardens, to the south and one of the poorest, Binghamton, to the north, is a bridge in the community. The library opened in 2001 with a mission to satisfy its patrons' need to know.

The Courtyard Frog, by artist
Sherri Warner Hunter.

Benjamin L. Hooks

The city council in 2004 named the library the "Benjamin L. Hooks Central Library" to honor the civil rights leader and longtime pastor of Memphis's Greater Middle Baptist Church. Hooks (b. 1925) was the first African American to serve as a criminal court judge in Tennessee and the first African American appointed to the Federal Communica-

Newly constructed in 2001, the library was renamed in 2004 to honor civil rights leader Benjamin L. Hooks.

tions Commission (FCC). His family owned one of Memphis's oldest black businesses, Hooks Brothers Photography, on Beale Street. He co-founded an African-American bank, Mutual Federal Savings and Loan Association, and was founding chairman of the National Civil Rights Museum. However, Hooks is probably best known as the former executive director of the National Association for the Advancement of Colored People (NAACP). As an African American growing up in Memphis, Hooks was not able to use the central library that is now named for him. During his lifetime the library system has grown from a segregated institution, in which blacks were relegated to a branch with worn books, to a system in which everyone has access.

❦ ❦
Something for Everyone

The library is a place where coffee (thanks to the café) and communication (thanks to wireless Internet access) flow. More than two hundred public-access computers help bridge the digital divide in Memphis. The computers are used by business professionals to conduct research, by grandparents to keep in touch with relatives, by students to play games after school, and by unemployed persons to look for work. A library card is not needed for computer access.

Programs that complement the resources on the shelves are presented almost daily. Themed activities include Family Activity Night, Wider Angle Film Series, Adult Enrichment Series book discussions with authors, and Sundays at Three local artist performances.

Three meeting rooms that can accommodate 350 people are

offered to nonprofit organizations at no charge. Politicians attend community forums in the meeting rooms to encourage dissemination of information. The Memphis Grizzlies basketball team has "adopted" a study room just for teens. Painted "Grizzlies blue" and decorated with all things basketball, the room is a haven for the high school set. The $70 million, 330,000-square-foot library also is the first public facility in Memphis to feature public art.

Memphis Grizzlies reading room.

U.S. ZIP CODE
40504

Lexington
Public
Library

Village Branch

Village Branch

Lexington Public Library
Lexington, Kentucky

Address: 2185 Versailles Road
Lexington, KY 40504
Date Founded: 2004
Date Built: 2004
Director: Kathleen R.T. Imhof; Betty
Abdmishani, Branch Manager
Special Collections: Spanish and Bilingual Books and
Audio-Visual Materials

Most libraries excel at bridging gaps—gaps between knowledge and resources, between generations, between the past and present. The Village Branch of the Lexington Public Library in Lexington, Kentucky, goes one step further: it bridges gaps between cultures.

The roots of the Lexington Public Library (LPL) date back to 1795, making it the oldest institution of its kind in Kentucky, and it served the city's largely native-born population well for many generations. In the early 1990s, thousands of Latin Americans began to immigrate to Lexington seeking work in the city's horse industry. As the number of Spanish-speaking immigrants grew, a small group of private citizens created a Spanish-language library at a neighborhood center. Space and hours of operation were limited, but volunteers supported the fledgling operation. Meanwhile, demand continued to grow for bilingual services and programming at the various branches of Lexington Public Library, and the large number of successful bilingual summer reading programs indicated the potential success of a new branch focused on bilingual services. The result was the Village Branch, which opened in 2004 in a 7,000-square-foot renovated storefront space on Versailles Road.

Location, Location, Location

Location was a key to the success of the Village Branch. The shopping center in which the branch is located places it within walking distance of the children and adults of Lexington's Cardinal Valley neighborhood, home to a diverse population including Anglos and African Americans as well as Latinos. The diversity of the Cardinal Valley neighborhood presented unique challenges to LPL, and the administration met those challenges head-on. While putting together the staff for the Village Branch, the

LPL administration looked for bilingual librarians and librarian assistants. As of 2006, all staff members can speak both English and Spanish. The staff has six native Spanish speakers, and when the first non-Spanish-speaking librarian was hired, the Library sent him to Spanish classes at the local community college and on a Spanish-immersion trip to Mexico. By making bilingualism a first priority, the LPL administration has made the Village Branch a welcoming environment for the majority of Lexington citizens, regardless of their first language.

The Village Branch has also addressed the needs of a bilingual population through collection development and multicultural programming. Approximately 40 percent of the collection at Village Branch is Spanish or bilingual material. The branch also hosts a number of popular bilingual programs, such as the Bilingual Café, the Bilingual Book Discussion Group, and Bilingual Boogie Bees. English classes taught by local literacy groups

A reading nook at the library.

Interior of the Village Branch, a 7,000-square-foot, renovated storefront space.

Bluegrass Literacy and Operation Read are offered at the Village Branch four days a week, and LPL offers computer courses in both English and Spanish.

Programming at the Village Branch is as diverse as the population the branch serves, and the Village Branch librarians have developed partnerships with a number of local groups in order to facilitate their programming needs. The Living Arts and Science Center has offered programs on topics such as astronomy, stop-motion animation, and cartooning. Other local businesses and social service agencies have given their time and energy to help present programs on topics from aikido (a Japanese martial art) to axolotls (a Mexican salamander). In the summers of 2005 and 2006, the Village Branch offered a children's program every weekday that the library was open.

The Village Branch also strives to help both school children and their parents with their school-related needs. Working in conjunction with local schools, the Village Branch offers a daily Homework Help program to assist local children, many of whom are learning English as a second language. Parents of school children also turn to the Village Branch for help with the translation of school-related forms and as a general source of information about other social services available to them.

✿ ❀

A Center of Community Life

Serving a tight-knit community makes "word of mouth" very important to the Village Branch, and for each person who gets help from the Village Branch, another four or five people are sure to hear about it. The synergy between courteous service and pa-

tron growth was never more apparent than in April 2006 when the branch put together a program for Día del Niño/Día del Libro (Day of the Child/Day of the Book). Though the event was advertised no more than any other library program, more than 1,200 patrons showed up for the festivities; the small storefront facility was packed with children and parents all eager to take part in the celebration.

To understand the success of the Village Branch, one needs to look not only at circulation statistics and door-count numbers, but also at the lively atmosphere that pervades the branch. Return patronage is no problem here: A surprising number of children and adults from the surrounding neighborhood use the library on a regular basis—some of them several times a week, some of them daily—and the sense of the library as a dynamic space for community service continues to grow. In addition to the information-rich programs on health issues such as AIDS awareness, Village Branch has hosted salsa dancing lessons, handicraft classes, and a Latino-style dance class for kids. While activities like these might not fit into the most staid ideas of what a library is, they have made the Village Branch a hit with the Cardinal Valley community. In this little storefront location that was once an auto-parts shop, a community has found not only a library, but a place to come together.

By tailoring services to fit their community, the administration and the librarians of Lexington Public Library have put together a dynamic new library for the people of Lexington, one that provides a diverse range of services for a diverse population. As a result, the residents of the Cardinal Valley neighborhood have turned out in large numbers and embraced the Village Branch. To these patrons, the Village Branch is more than just a library: It is a library they love.

U.S. ZIP CODE
44514

Poland Branch Library

Public Library of Youngstown and Mahoning County
Poland, Ohio

Address: 311 S. Main Street
Poland, OH 44514
Date Founded: 1935
Date Built: 2001
Architect: The 4M Company: Robert
Mastriana, Paul Mastriana, and
James Yoder
Director: Carlton A. Sears

The Poland Branch Library is located in Ohio's Western Reserve area, which Connecticut claimed as part of a sea-to-sea land grant. Although the states gave up their western claims in exchange for federal assumption of their American Revolutionary War debt, Connecticut retained the Western Reserve until selling it to investors in 1796 to raise money for a school system. Poland was called "town one, range one" of the reserve because it was the starting point for surveyors. The design of the library is an example of Greek Revival architecture of the Western Reserve, which echoed its New England connection. The library blends into the Historic Riverbank District and replaces a branch built on that site in 1965.

The Poland Branch Library opened in December 2001. It is a branch of the Public Library of Youngstown and Mahoning County system, which celebrated 125 years in 2005. Poland was the location of the system's first branch, dedicated in 1935 and located on the first floor of the Town Hall.

A Dorm Redux

Perhaps the most distinguishing historical feature of the Poland Branch Library is the Poland Union Seminary Dormitory. Poland, founded in 1796, was an educational center of the 1800s, with numerous private schools and colleges. The historic structure, built in 1846 as a home, became a dormitory in 1894. It is a functioning part of the library, and its design was incorporated into the library's exterior. Architects also preserved window stone surrounds from the 1965 library and placed these in the new library.

Poland Union Seminary's most famous student was William McKinley (1843–1901), twenty-fifth president of the United States. McKinley's family had moved to Poland when he was nine so he could attend the private school. Because the McKinley family lived in Poland, it was not necessary for McKinley to live in the dormitory; however, because he attended the seminary, he probably spent time with friends in the dormitory.

Operating in the Green

The Poland Branch Library features "green architecture," using a high percentage of materials from sustainable resources that are recyclable, affordable, and easy to maintain. The use of recycled materials and energy-efficient features has drawn the attention of national publications. For example, *Clem Labine's Traditional Building,* a magazine specializing in public architecture, published a feature in June 2002, noting:

> The new Poland Public Library . . . meets some very significant objectives for the community. The new library . . . not only serves as a local center of education, but also provides a gathering place for people of all ages. Additionally, the classic Greek Revival design of the building complements the Main Street setting and incorporates a historic landmark. Lastly, the innovative use of recycled building materials makes the structure an exemplar of "green architecture."

Environmental Design+Construction magazine also devoted several pages to the library in January 2002. "Environment, Education and Energy; it is not the three R's that we all grew up with, but the three E's that are now playing one of the largest roles in today's educational communities and the world. This is no more apparent than in Poland, Ohio."

Recycled materials are used in the library's siding, roofing, window frames and doorframes, wood flooring, carpeting, decorative surrounds, and landscape stone wall. The focus was on using products that are "Earth friendly." Architects wanted to use recycled materials but needed to ensure that the products met the highest quality standards. They studied information on testing and performance as they searched for exterior and interior building materials. The use of recycled materials was so important to the Mahoning County Recycling Division that it gave the library a $400,000 grant.

The library drew statewide attention when Governor Bob Taft

The Poland Library rear exterior, with atrium entrance. Courtesy of Al Teufen Photography.

came to get a first-hand look at the library as one of its first visitors in November 2001. Governor Taft praised the library, saying:

> I had to see for myself this one-of-a-kind library in Poland, and I am absolutely amazed at what has been accomplished here. You've found a way to use recyclable, environmentally friendly materials to build a highly functional library that's energy efficient. Now that's innovative and an extraordinary achievement. Congratulations, this truly is a landmark, both for the people of Poland and the citizens of Ohio.

The new building is 35,619 square feet; the 1965 building was only 4,600 square feet. The library now has room to grow. The design allows for a collection of seventy thousand items—75 percent larger than that of the previous building. Additionally, the library is fitted with the latest technology—an interesting contrast to its traditional style and furnishings. The main floor includes staff areas, children's and adult collections, videos, books on cassette, CDs, reference materials, a children's activity room, a young adult area, and a reading area that overlooks Yellow Creek. The lower level houses a meeting room, Friends of the Library Bookstore and Gift Shop, and Chapters Cafe.

The centerpiece of the library is the rotunda dome, which rises four stories. A decorated glass hallway leads between stacks to a periodical sitting room, which in turn connects two outdoor terraces that overlook Yellow Creek.

A highlight of the children's activity room is a puppet stage, designed as a front porch that mirrors the exterior design of the library. Use of natural lighting and energy-efficient insulated glass reduces the need for artificial lighting. As a finishing touch, the craftsmanship of local artisans is found throughout the library in its tables, chairs, bookcases, paintings and sculptures,

and ornamental iron railings reflecting the style of the area's historic bridges.

Built in 1846, the historic Poland Union Seminary Dormitory remains a functioning part of the library.

Heart of the Community: **The Libraries We Love**

Corryville Branch Library

◆

Public Library of Cincinnati and Hamilton County

Cincinnati, Ohio

Address:	2802 Vine Street
	Cincinnati, OH 45219
Date Founded:	1907
Date Built:	1907; 1997 (restoration)
Architect:	Edward L. Tilton; McClorey and
	Savage Architects, Ltd.
Director:	Frank Dugan
Special Collections:	Cultural and Ethnic Diversity

It's been up, and it's been down. Now it's up again, and the Corryville Branch Library is ready to begin its second century. In 1995, after years of neglect had reduced the library to little more than storage space, the community of Corryville decided to restore it and did such a good job that the effects are still rippling through the community.

❧ ❧

From Thriving to Neglected and Back Again

The North Cincinnati Branch, as it was then known, opened on 2 April 1907, one of nine area libraries built with funds provided by industrialist and philanthropist Andrew Carnegie. The Renaissance Revival-style building was designed by Edward L. Tilton and featured a stained glass dome supported by oak pillars. The branch was a linchpin of the Public Library of Cincinnati and Hamilton County during the early decades of its operation and often posted the highest circulation of all the system's branches. In February 1935 the total home circulation was 421,864 books.

However, by the late 1960s usage had dropped to fewer than thirty thousand items per year as the neighborhood experienced social, political, and economic upheaval. In 1970 the main floor was converted to a nonpublic area and later to a storage facility while the branch moved to the basement. In the early 1990s, in an effort to turn around this once-thriving community adjacent to the University of Cincinnati, a committee consisting of Corryville business owners, property owners, university representatives, city officials, and residents was formed. Through their efforts an urban design plan was developed to revitalize the area. As an educational, cultural, and recreational facility, the Corryville Branch and its renovation were key to this plan.

The Public Library committed $2.2 million to the restoration, which began in January 1996 under the direction of McClorey and Savage Architects, Ltd. The historic spaces and classical architectural details were preserved as the library was being renovated to meet the needs of the future, particularly for technology such as computers. The entire building is now devoted to public services. When the library reopened in 1997, it was renamed the "Corryville Branch" to better reflect the community it serves.

❧ ❧

Architectural Highlights

Architect Edward L. Tilton (1861–1933) was a native of New York who trained at the firm of McKim, Mead and White and at the Ecole des Beaux Arts in Paris. In 1890 Tilton established his own firm with partner

The children's room, with a plaster frieze of the Greek Parthenon.

The Corryville Branch, designed in the Renaissance Revival style of architecture.

William A. Boring, and together they designed the U.S. Immigration Station on Ellis Island, which won the Gold Medal Prize at the Paris Exposition in 1900. Tilton developed a specialty designing libraries across the United States, including the Pack Memorial Library in Asheville, North Carolina, the Springfield Public Library in Massachusetts, and the library of Emory University and the Knight Memorial Library in Providence, Rhode Island. Through his friendship with Andrew Carnegie's personal secretary, James Bertram, Tilton was well placed to obtain commissions to design Carnegie-funded libraries.

The Corryville Branch library features large stone columns flanking the entrance and doorway. A decorative stone pediment is topped by an *acroterion,* an ornament placed on a plinth at the apex of the pediment. As part of restoration, extensive cleaning and reappointment of decorative elements were completed. The two-toned tan brick exterior trimmed with limestone was cleaned and reappointed. To restore the look of the original building, the old shingle roof was replaced by a new tri-colored terra cotta roof.

The refurbished branch features an interior dominated by a large stained glass dome supported by a circle of carved oak columns. The dome, which was removed and thoroughly cleaned and reinforced before reinstallation, is surrounded by classical molding and floral ornamentation. Matching fireplaces with oak mantels are located in the two front rooms of the library. A plaster frieze from the Greek Parthenon, a decorative section of wall under the crown moldings, hangs in the children's room as it did when the branch opened in 1907. The original wood shelving lining the walls was refinished, and unique handcrafted architectural details were preserved and restored. The layout of the 1907 structure was reinstated with separate children's room and adult reading and browsing room; a central service desk is under the dome.

❦ ❧
Awards

The Corryville Branch Library renovation was a 1998 Ohio Historic Preservation Award recipient. The award is given for preserving Ohio's prehistory, history, architecture, or culture. The library also received the Cincinnati Preservation Award for preserving a historic cultural site that enhances the identity, beauty, economy, and quality of life.

The circulation desk.

Ohio Township Public Library

Central Library
Newburgh, Indiana

Address: 4111 Lakeshore Drive
Newburgh, IN 47630
Date Founded: 1916
Date Built: 2005
Architect: Veazey, Parrott, Durkin and Shoulders
Director: Steve Thomas
Special Collections: Local History

It's not just another pretty face.

Oh, sure, the building's form follows multiple functions. To maximize flexibility, most of the library's collection space is clear of columns, and the depth of the clear-span trusses is used to frame north-facing clerestories. The building rises from the plains like an ancient ruin, the capstones atop the exterior columns giving the building a Stonehenge look, and the fossilized leaf patterns in the carpet depicting something from dim days gone by. Dubbed by its architect an "artifact from the future," the Ohio Township Public Library System's central library aims to achieve a dialectic between the past and the present.

Inside, at the rear of the library café, a 9-foot-tall water wall provides white noise and a tranquil setting in which to read. A

28-foot stained-glass mural marks the entrance to the children's room. Winding its way through a forest scene, a river drops out of the mural into a glass waterfall that in turn runs under patrons' feet in an LED light creek. A wooden bridge over the creek leads into the children's room, where artificial trees mask support columns.

Tripping the Light: Fantastic

However, beneath all that beauty there is a brain. For example, when patrons enter the library, they enter the most modern of worlds. The library offers wireless Internet access and a Lutron lighting system. Motion sensors in the study rooms and restrooms turn the lights on and off automatically as patrons enter and leave.

The building's exterior, made from lightweight, high-performance autoclaved aerated concrete (AAC), is strong, low-maintenance, quiet, and well-insulated. AAC is made of fly ash, which is a waste product from coal plants. Rather than dumping the fly ash into a landfill, engineers have found a way to turn it into a building product that has a high R-value for insulation. High-performance Solarban window glazing is shaded on the

The library interior; stained glass by Sunburst Stained Glass. Courtesy of Bennett Photography.

Libraries are the real birthing places of the universe for me. I lived in my hometown library more than I did at home. I loved it at night, prowling the stacks on my fat panther feet.

—Ray Bradbury

Heart of the Community: The Libraries We Love

A fountain, a waterfall, and a water wall make the library a tranquil place, outside and in. Courtesy of Bill and Linda Bruns.

outside and fitted with light shelves on the inside to maximize daylight but minimize glare and direct heat gain.

The high-performance HVAC system features a heat-recovery chiller, low-temperature pulse combustion boilers with variable speed pumps, and integrated electronic controls for all building systems.

⚘ ⚘
Current Events

Solar panels on the roof provide all of the library's hot water, and photovoltaic cells in the roof provide some of the library's electricity. Electricity generated onsite is sold back to the utility company. The library's irrigation system uses water from a pond onsite, so it does not use fresh water to irrigate the grounds. The landscape features native plants and natural meadows. Resource-efficient materials, including cork, linoleum, and recycled content carpeting, were used throughout. Indoor air quality is assured by the use of low-VOC (volatile organic compounds) finishes and the under-floor air-displacement ventilation system. The building is designed to use the energy of a building half its size. Library patrons can learn about the building's performance by viewing a public monitor that displays the energy management system.

Because of these and other energy-efficient features, the library is the first Leadership in Energy and Environmental Design (LEED) public library in Indiana, a designation given by the U.S. Green Building Council to public buildings that are energy efficient and environmentally friendly.

The Ohio Township Public Library System has three branches with a service population of 31,002 in southwest Indiana. The headquarters of the system formerly was a Carnegie library built in 1916. In 1998 the board of trustees voted to build a new central library of 37,500 square feet. In 2001 the library system purchased 7.33 acres of land in the center of the township in Newburgh, where the greatest population growth was occurring. The library opened in 2005.

A sweeping view of the library's reading and computer areas. Courtesy of Bennett Photography.

U.S. ZIP CODE
47711

Oaklyn Branch Library

◇

Evansville Vanderburgh Public Library

Evansville, Indiana

Address:	3001 Oaklyn Drive Evansville, IN 47711
Date Founded:	1975
Date Built:	2003
Architect:	Veazey Parrott Durkin & Shoulders
Director:	Marcia Learned Au; Pamela Locker, Branch Manager

Winner of the 2004 Green Roof Award, the Oaklyn Branch Library is an environmentally friendly facility. Built into a hillside with a natural meadow roof and only one exposed façade, the views from inside are open and airy. Building materials reflect an earth conscious mindset.

The Oaklyn Branch is part of the Evansville Vanderburgh Public Library, which is made up of the central library and seven branches. The Oaklyn Branch was opened in an old school building in 1975, and the new building was completed in and opened to the public in 2003—offering large areas for collections, a computer lab, a public service area, a meeting room, café and courtyard spaces, and parking for up to one hundred vehicles.

Oaklyn serves the North East side of Vanderburgh County, one of the fastest growing areas of the community, with a county-wide population of 173,187.

✿ ❀
The Green Roof

Green roofs or vegetated roofing is a new development in sustainable building design which offer many social, environmental and economic benefits. In September 2002, a 17,250-square-foot Roofmeadow® green roof was installed on the new single-level Oaklyn Branch Library building. The new library is an earth-sheltered structure, blending the roof with the landscape on the

uphill side. This publicly accessible green roof was created as a native mesic meadow prairie blending into the landscape; irrigated with minimum evaporation; conserving energy; and requiring minimal maintenance. The roof's mesic meadow prairie plant community contributes to the restoration of prairie landscapes in this region. The green roof plants include: *Andropogon scoparious, Bouteloua curitpendula; Centaurea cyanus, Campanula rotundifolia, Carex annectans, Carex bicknellii, Coreopsis tinctoria, Elymus Canadensis, Liatris spicata, Phlox drummondii, Phlox pilosa, Sphaeralcea coccine,* and *Sporobolus heterolepis.* To support the weight of this intensive green-roof system, the architects provided a strong but lightweight steel/concrete composite roof deck.

From the nearby highway, the mature roof blends so seamlessly with the surrounding landscape that only the roof's dramatic LightBridge clerestory marks the library's presence. Daylight streaming into the central circulation axis through this clerestory is diffused by an ingenious CloudGate sculpture (which rotates after hours to become a security gate, enabling use of the forward public meeting room).

The Oaklyn Branch Library green roof has won several awards, including the American Institute of Architects 2003 Indiana Honor Award and the 2004 Green Roofs for Healthy Cities Award of Excellence for intensive institutional design.

CloudGate serves to diffuse daylight over the circulation desk and lobby of the library. Courtesy of Jerry Butts.

Comfortable lounge seating and custom CD bins are found in the adult and youth sections. Courtesy of Jerry Butts.

The Interior: A Community Center

The LightBridge clerestory that rises above the roof meadow has become a beacon to the community—a metaphor for the mission of the library visible for miles across the Pigeon Creek Valley. The library has become a vital community center with more than 35,000 patrons visiting each month and book circulation increasing three-fold.

The central clerestory, the high ceilings, and the dozen 11-foot-tall windows of the main eastern façade challenge the notion that earth-sheltered construction need be dark and cave-like; this library is the most day-lit of all seven branches in the Evansville system.

Stone veneer columns line the walls of the gallery, creating a solid base for the exposed wood ceiling to rest upon and spaces for art display cases and bookshelves. Maple wood millwork and furniture were chosen with a warm honey-tone stain to compliment the stone. The floor tile creates a grounded base with the use of slate-like porcelain tile in a warm earthy tone. Behind the circulation desk, where library employees stand much of the day, a natural cork floor was selected to help reduce strain and fatigue in addition to providing a soft surface to absorb sound.

The library's adult collection takes full advantage of the views outside. The window seats are dedicated to study tables and comfy lounge chairs while the tall book shelves line the back walls. The children's collections are located across the gallery space from the adult area for sound isolation and better control of the space. The gentle curves of the ceiling welcome the children into this space with a chasing rainbow of light. Programmable LED lights were used to add a spectacular dimension to this space with no exterior window.

Kimball, a local furniture manufacturer, built all of the custom-designed wood furniture; Euronique, a local millwork company, built the circulation desk and other millwork pieces. The millwork and furniture were carefully considered and created to ensure the library would function optimally while addressing the special needs of a contemporary library. For example, the wood end panels were designed to complement the soft-top curve of the computer carrels and the apron of the tables. The end panels also incorporated slat wall where books can be display outwardly.

In addition, the 2,100-square-foot enclosed patio built of Indiana creekstone provides a spectacular place to study, have a snack. or just hang out. With access just off the teen zone and the canteen area, the patio sees a lot of use.

The library provides much in the way of special adult programs as well as numerous ongoing children's events and programs. The comfortable, easily accessible meeting room hosts library events and provides space for the community to meet. In addition the room has been used as a polling place, a venue for tax-aid workshops, and a convenient location for neighborhood group meetings.

A study café is also available for the public to use for small meetings. The library book discussion groups meet here as well. This informal space—complete with diner-type booths and comfortable chairs—provides a warm environment where participants can enjoy refreshments. Oaklyn Branch has become the "third space" (home and work being the first and second) to many on the North East side of Evansville.

Clinton-Macomb Public Library

◆

Main Library

Clinton Township, Michigan

Address: 40900 Romeo Plank Road
Clinton Township, MI 48038
Date Founded: 1992
Date Built: 2003
Architect: TMP Associates, Inc.
Director: Larry P. Neal
Special Collections: Local History

The Clinton-Macomb Public Library has a place in history—literally. It is located at the intersection of Canal Road and Romeo Plank Road, where two early forms of transportation—the Clinton and Kalamazoo Canal and the Romeo Plank Road—met.

❧ ❧

Canals and Plank Roads

When Michigan became a state in 1837, one of the first major concerns of the new state legislature was how to transport settlers, goods, and services across the heavily forested peninsula. The few roads that existed were mainly muddy, narrow paths through the forests, swamps, and bogs. The legislature pushed to build three railroads and two canals and chartered private groups to build plank roads (sometimes called "turnpikes").

The crown jewel of the transportation system was a canal to be constructed from Lake St. Clair to Lake Michigan. It was named the "Clinton and Kalamazoo Canal" after the two rivers that supplied the water. Construction began in 1838 about one mile east of the library. Construction ended when funding ran out after several years of financial depression.

The plank roads (roads covered with a series of planks) fared much better. In Michigan 202 plank road companies were chartered. Because the plank roads connected many of the rural communities and farms, they were often referred to as the "farmer's railroad." Romeo Plank connected Mount Clemens and Romeo. Approximately 145 years later the Main Library was constructed on the historic site, apparently the only place in the state where a canal and plank road came together.

❧ ❧

A High-Tech Home Away from Home

Clinton-Macomb Public Library (CMPL) is a district library that serves a population of about 170,000 and strives to integrate his-

tory, friendly design, and technology. According to Kent Johnson, the lead architect:

> The design of the library presented a unique opportunity to create a building with strong symbolic presence within the community and reflects the culture and attitudes of the people it serves. While we felt it was our charge to create a symbol of civic importance, we were equally intent on developing interior spaces which are warm, friendly and inviting. For many people this facility will truly be a home away from home.

As did the canal and the plank road of yesteryear, history and the technology of today meet at the 84,000-square-foot Main Library, which is one of only a handful of libraries in the country with a materials-handling system, which allows returned items to be checked in and then sorted onto a cart automatically. The Main Library is also outfitted with stations that allow customers to check out their own materials. These stations, along with the sorting system, allow staff more time to assist customers. Other technologies implemented in the library include public wireless access, smart-chip enabled library cards, and radio frequency identification.

❧ ❧

Public Artwork

The Main Library is home to many works of art that have been donated by various residents and community groups. A mural, hand sketched and painted by local artist Dennis Orlowski, depicts the history of the site on which the Main Library is built. The mural includes the transportation theme of the Main Library by incorporating the plank road and canal all the way up to the steam engines and automobiles that once served the area. In addition to the mural the Main Library includes a public information rack that displays the First Amendment, bronze sculptures by artist Gary Price, a fieldstone fireplace, a Pewabic tile drinking fountain, an 1859 digitized wall map, and a rotating globe.

Mural depicting the history of the Main Library's location showing the plank road and canal.

The transportation theme also continues into the children's area with a variety of props including a fire truck and bus to allow children's imagination to soar.

Community Programs

The library strives to provide enriching programs for people of all ages. Children's programs bring in popular youth authors, clowns, and magicians to entertain children and to teach them the joys of reading. The Children's Services Department offers regular story-time activities for children up to age five to help them gain language acquisition, verbal skills, and early reading habits.

After children enter adolescence they still have an opportunity to get involved in library programs. The Teen Advisory Council (TAC) enables teens in grades six through twelve to have a voice in library programs, book discussions, and even in choosing some materials. Since the inception of TAC teen

The Globe, a donated work of art, hangs over the Main Library's grand staircase and popular materials area.

participation in library events—such as a teen karaoke night, game night, and the newest and most popular teen activity, Dance Dance Revolution—has increased.

Adults also are offered enriching library programs. With a background in local history and a room dedicated to the topic, the library lets adults weigh in on historical and even current events at library programs. The library partners with other organizations to offer programs such as exhibitions from the American Library Association on Frankenstein and Alexander Hamilton, and a film and discussion series on World War I from National Video Resources.

The Clinton-Macomb Public Library is a unique blend of technology and information on a historic site. The library's high commitment to technology, service, and community is appreciated by the customers who frequent the library and enjoy the art, ambiance, and materials. Just as the historic corner on which it stands was a gathering place years ago, the Clinton-Macomb Public Library still serves as a place where technology and community meet.

U.S. ZIP CODE
48076

Southfield Public Library

Southfield, Michigan

Address: 26300 Evergreen Road
Southfield, MI 48076
Date Founded: 1844
Date Built: 2003
Architect: Phillips Swager Associates
Director: Doug Zyskowski
Special Collections: Local History; Folktale and Fairytale

It began with just three hundred books. And now it has a Gizmo.

After Southfield township incorporated as a city in the 1950s, residents formed the Friends of the Southfield Public Library. They secured the old Brooks School, a two-story structure renovated to house the library's growing collection. In 1964 the library moved to the newly constructed Civic Center. By this time the collection had grown from 300 to 150,000, and a separate nonfiction level was added. Today the newest library building—located in the civic center complex and constructed of glass, steel, brick, and limestone with a glass tower—is a reflection of the steel and glass corporate offices across the street and the more sedate brick structures on its other side. Its tower, designed to be a metaphoric beacon of enlightenment, is a Southfield landmark.

The library's mission is simple: to provide information and encourage reading. Members of the library staff make public service their first priority. There's a drive-up window so that patrons can pick up or drop off books without leaving their car, wireless Internet access throughout the library, two computer labs and hands-on computer lessons, express check-out stations, a books-by-mail service, notary services, free access to ELLIS (English Language Learning Instruction System), a self-guided, interactive English language course, and a call-ahead book request service. Collections include Folktales and Fairytales, large-print materials (and low-vision computer enhancements for patrons with limited vision), foreign language books, magazines and newspapers, literacy primers and workbooks, and current bestsellers.

A book-themed sculpture graces the front of the library.

Spacemen and Gizmos and Dragons, Oh, WOW!

The children's room on the first floor, named "Worlds of Wonder" (WOW), features a tree house, a space station, Story Book Castle (complete with dragon), and the Gizmo, a fantasy creature device featuring a collection of telescopes for children to peer through. Bright colors decorate the various worlds, and pictures referring to each area are inlaid in the carpet (a space shuttle for the space station, a crown for the castle, a leaf for the Readers' Treehouse). The first of three fireplaces offers a cozy place to read in the winter. Story phones are located in the Storybook Castle so that the youngest patrons can hear stories on demand. For

The gleaming glass tower of the library is a Southfield landmark.

teenagers an area called "Club Q&A" provides a social setting that complements the more utilitarian research and study areas. There are café-style booths, each with its own TV/DVD/video player recessed in the wall, individual flat-screen computer stations, three study tables, a lounge area, and a collection of young adult books, CDs, and magazines. The library has more than 150 public computers, color photocopiers and printers, the Imaginarium Children's garden, an observation deck on the second level, and a fountain terrace. The elliptical Southfield Room juts out from the third level and appears to be floating above the Tower Lobby. A spiral staircase leads up and up. Looking down, one sees quotes by famous authors inscribed in the swirling terrazzo floor. At the Book Ends Café patrons can enjoy a cup of something cold or hot. Each floor has small-group meeting rooms; the auditorium and meeting room have advanced audio-visual capabilities. Sculptures and prints decorate every area.

> Whatever the cost of our libraries, the price is cheap compared to that of an ignorant nation.
>
> —Walter Cronkite

"Discovery Is Key"

"The idea of discovery is key," says library director Doug Zyskowski. Patrons often discover something about the building each time they tour the library, and a variety of new programs, art and exhibits, and events is scheduled for each season. Book clubs, guest speakers, public meetings, educational and cultural programs, discussions, and classes are ongoing. The library strives to promote literacy and lifelong learning by offering programs in library skills. Partnerships are developed with local schools, and the library's collections complement those of local academic institutions.

Entry to the library lobby.

Heart of the Community: **The Libraries We Love**

West Bloomfield Township Public Library

West Bloomfield, Michigan

Address: 4600 Walnut Lake Road
West Bloomfield, MI 48323
Date Founded: 1934
Date Built: 1984
Architect: TMP Associates
Director: Clara N. Bohrer

The West Bloomfield Township Public Library began as a community service project in 1934 when members of the Keego Cass Women's Club—a group of mothers, grandmothers, and other civic-minded women—obtained books to open a library in one of their clubhouse rooms. In 1937, the club petitioned West Bloomfield Township to take over operation of the library, and in 1938 voters approved establishing and funding a township public library located in Town Hall. (The levy at that time was .25 mill—one-tenth of a cent).

By the late 1940s the library's collection had grown to more than 11,000 volumes, and the .25 mill property tax was no longer enough to maintain library services for the growing township. Voters approved raising the levy to one mill.

funding to the library on a consistent basis, so in 1974 the library took the Township to court. In a landmark case, the Oakland County Circuit Court ruled that the library is a separate entity from the Township and has the right to levy and receive a mill of property tax.

In 1984, the Main Library opened a 16,000-square-foot building at the Civic Center and expanded it to 25,000 square feet in 1988. West Bloomfield Township continued to grow. In the mid-1990s, the library initiated a two-year strategic planning process, which led to a successful 1997 ballot request for $10.8 million to renovate and expand library facilities. Today, the library is one of the busiest in Michigan—the destination for more than 3,000 West Bloomfield residents each day, with more than half being children.

Where There's a Mill, There's a Way

In 1958, several Township residents donated 1.5 acres of land south of the Town Hall on Orchard Lake Road for a new library. The Library Board, with help from the Friends of the Library, purchased another half acre. In 1963, the new West Bloomfield Township Main Library on Orchard Lake Road was dedicated and won a national architectural award.

The population of West Bloomfield Township continued to grow. Its farms, apple orchards and summer cottages disappeared as homes and schools were built. The library had outgrown its Orchard Lake building. In 1973, the West Bloomfield Township Board purchased 99 acres off Walnut Lake Road as the site for a civic center complex that would include a new library building.

The library lost three millage (taxation) elections requesting building funds. Undaunted, the Library Board began saving money from the operating budget for a library building fund. However, the library became enmeshed with the Township in a battle over funding. According to Michigan Public Act 164, public libraries are allowed to be their own taxing authority and are guaranteed one mill. The Township was not providing this

Great Beginnings

Because West Bloomfield residents place a high value on education, the library has created prominent space where youth and

The West Bloomfield Township Public Library.

Heart of the Community: **The Libraries We Love**

The Friends Terrace is a place to enjoy tranquil and natural surroundings while reading or using the library's wireless technology.

families can read, learn, and grow together. Library staff listen closely to what parents, teachers, and other caregivers want for their children and continually look for ways to enrich the library experience for young babies to young adults.

The design of the youth services room is based in current research on brain development and learning strategies. The library dedicated significant resources to create an innovative environment that stimulates children's growing minds through purposeful interaction with their parents and other caregivers.

In 2001 the library was selected as one of only twenty organizations nationwide to participate in a program to develop techniques and materials that parents can use to nurture language and literacy skills in babies, toddlers, and preschoolers. Library staff incorporated knowledge from this project into the library's own emergent literacy initiative aimed at parents, teachers, and caregivers. Grow Up Reading™ @ the West Bloomfield Township Public Library provides techniques and materials that parents and others can use to help children in kindergarten through fifth grade become fluent readers. The library's Learningscape structure for babies and toddlers integrates colors, textures, and shapes into a learning zone that stimulates brain development. The branches of the Reading Tree shelter a puppet stage used for dramatic play and creative expression. The Activity Center has a full schedule of story times, puppet shows, book clubs, and programs for babies, toddlers, preschoolers, and elementary students.

However, the emphasis on literacy and learning doesn't stop at the library's doors. The library reaches out to school principals and teachers, parents and child-care providers, and community organizations with resources that support reading and learning. These resources include meetings with school professionals;

book talks and other programs for elementary, middle, and high school students; story times at child-care facilities; kits that are distributed to pediatricians to promote the importance of reading to young children; and mailings to new parents that discuss how to read to their infants.

From its own tiny beginnings, The West Bloomfield Township Public Library has grown steadily into one of the most-used institutions in the community—and one with a far-reaching impact.

The activity center is always busy with educational programs to stimulate children's interest in reading and learning.

Howell Carnegie District Library

Howell, Michigan

Address: 314 West Grand River
Howell, MI 48843
Date Founded: 1875
Date Built: 1906; 1991 (renovation)
Architect: Elijah E. Myers; Osler/Milling
Architects
Director: Kathleen Zaenger
Special Collections: Howell Area Archives

When Howell, Michigan, built its library in 1906, local farmers helped raise it from the ground up—literally. They brought in fieldstones to donate as building material. Indeed, farmers have always been important to Howell: The town was founded by four farmers and their families in 1835. Within fifteen years the town had four church buildings and a school. Soon after that women residents began to organize a library.

> The closest we will ever come to an orderly universe is a good library.
>
> —Ashleigh Brilliant

Carnegie Bequest

The Ladies Library Association of Howell established a lending library in 1875. It was located in a rented house on the back of the square where the present library now stands. By the end of the nineteenth century the facilities were too small to handle the growing collection of books. A request for funding was made to Andrew Carnegie, who donated $15,000. The Classical Revival-style library was designed by architect Elijah E. Myers, who was hired by the Howell Township Board in 1902 for $300. He also designed the Michigan State Capitol in Lansing and the Texas State Capitol in Austin. The front entryway is dominated by a pedimented portico supported by four limestone half-columns centered by an arched double-door entry with a fanlight transom and limestone surrounds.

Howell's 8,000-square-foot library was constructed on a site donated by the McPherson brothers, four prominent Howell citizens. The

The children's room.

square that the library stands on is a full city block located on Grand River Avenue at the west end of downtown. The avenue was along the main route between Grand Rapids and Detroit. On 19 November 1906, Howell residents were invited to tour their new library. As the story goes, the fieldstones that local farmers donated were such excellent examples of rocks broken by glacial action that for many years after the building was completed, a geology professor from the University of Michigan brought classes to study them

In October 1988 voters approved a levy to operate a district library approximating the boundaries of the Howell School District. Voters also approved a bond issue to restore and expand the library building. In 1991 the library was renovated, and an expansion of 22,000 square feet quadrupled the size of the building. In June 1993 the library and Osler/Milling Architects were given an award for Excellence in Recognition of Distinguished Accomplishment in Library Architecture from the American Institute of Architects and the American Library Association. The library serves a population of approximately 42,000.

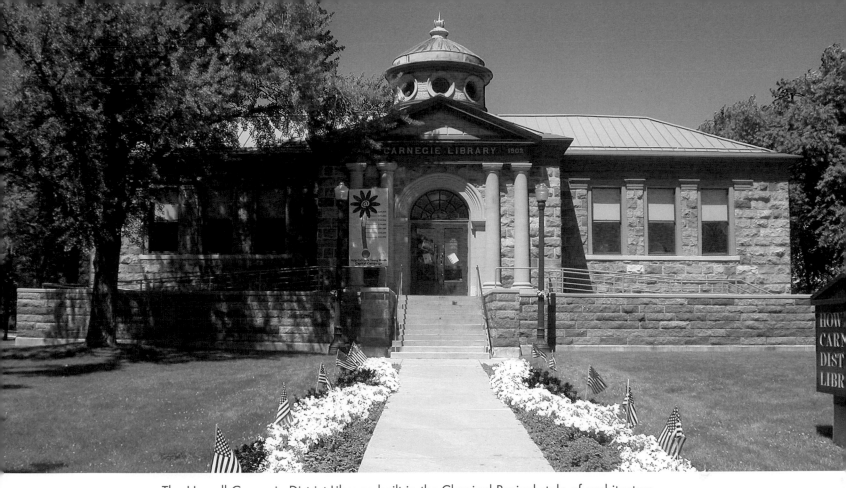

The Howell Carnegie District Library, built in the Classical Revival style of architecture.

Bubbles in a Summer Day

Outside the library, on the lawn, residents have parties and picnics and listen to concerts on warm summer evenings. Inside the library residents make use of many programs and resources. Programs include weekly book-group meetings, teen programs and children's story time sessions. On the lower level of the library the Howell Area Archives collects, organizes, and maintains printed items, memorabilia, photographs, and written materials of historical significance to Livingston County. Articles about Ty Cobb's visit to the Howell Opera House, locations of Native American burial grounds, Civil War records, a collection of historical photographs of Howell, genealogical information, cemetery records, obituaries, and accounts of the Underground Railroad are among the items of local interest.

Front Lawn Landmarks

In 1906 the Howell Women's Club donated a fountain on the front lawn of the library. The fountain was removed for about two years in the late 1960s and then was restored in 1970. In 1977 the original cement figures were replaced by more durable ones. Also on the front lawn is a Civil War historical marker erected by Waddell Women's Relief Corps in memory of Waddell Post 120 and all veterans of Livingston County who served in the Civil War 1861–1865. It includes the inscription "They fought to save us a Nation." The Centennial Vault Historical Marker—with a time capsule to the people of 2076 placed in 1976 by the Howell Bicentennial Committee in commemoration of the U.S. Bicentennial—is also located on the lawn. Howell's downtown has been named a National Historic District for its nineteenth-century architecture, much of it, such as the library's, restored and preserved for the future.

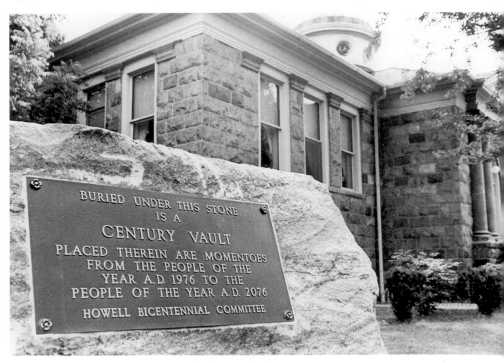

The century vault built in 1976 includes a time capsule to be opened in the year 2076.

U.S. ZIP CODE

52001

Teen Zone

Carnegie-Stout Public Library

◆

Dubuque, Iowa

Address:	360 West 11th Street
	Dubuque, IA 52001
Date Founded:	1900
Date Built:	1902
Architect:	John Spence and W. S. Williamson
Director:	Susan Henricks
Special Collections:	Genealogy

One hizzoner made the pitch; one hizzoner made the donation; and a lot of women made the most of their chance to vote.

The first library in Dubuque began as a subscription library when a group of businessmen held lectures to raise money for books that would encourage a "system of healthy reading" for the public. Their initial attempts in 1857 netted 150 books contributed by Dubuque attorney J. S. Blatchley, who had a library in his law office.

❧ ❧

The Power of Speech

Those 150 books had increased to about 14,000 by the time the group of businessmen reorganized itself into the Young Men's Library Association. The association collected annual dues and, to raise more money, held the aforementioned series of public lectures. Such literary notables as essayist and poet Ralph Waldo Emerson, antislavery speaker Charles Sumner, editor/author J. G. Holland, showman P. T. Barnum, and author Edwin Whipple drew crowds.

At the beginning of the twentieth century Mayor Jacob Rich (who also was director of the Young Men's Library Association) approached Andrew Carnegie, the steel magnate and philanthropist whose company had provided the steel for the East Dubuque Bridge, for funding. Carnegie agreed to contribute $60,000 to build the library in Dubuque with the stipulation that the city provide a suitable location and pass a tax levy to support the library. Former Mayor Frank B. Stout donated a plot of land in memory of his father, and 73 percent of the voters approved the levy in a special election (although women would not have the right to vote for another two decades, they participated in this election and approved the levy by a ratio of 30 to 1). The Young Men's Library Association donated its assets of $25,000, a library board was appointed, and construction of the library began in 1901.

In October 1902 the Carnegie-Stout Public Library, named for its two biggest benefactors, opened to the public with a three-day

reception. The building was designed in the classical Beaux Arts style with columned entrances, plasterwork, oak woodwork, and three skylights. The mammoth front doors opened to a long hallway flanked by reading rooms. Miss Bessie Sargent Smith was elected librarian and was paid the grand sum of $1,000 per year. The opening was billed as the social occasion of 1902, and most of the town's residents attended.

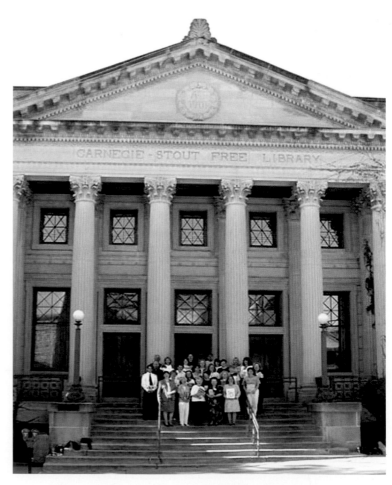

Library staff members pose with their favorite books in front of the historic part of the library.

The library's historic rotunda capped by a skylight.

Transition

For fifty years the library grew. The emergence of such entertainment technologies as radio, television, and motion pictures did not lessen people's need for a place to find information readily or simply to read a book at their leisure. In 1953 the library underwent a renovation that included modernizing its interior décor, covering the chairs in bright colored leather, and installing linoleum floors. In 2005 plans were made to return the building to some of its original splendor. Those plans, now being implemented, include using the second floor again to shelve and circulate materials, and uncovering windows and skylights that had been obscured. Space is being added to house the growing collections of materials and the library's computers.

The Carnegie-Stout Library celebrated its hundredth birthday in 2002. Again the entire community was invited to attend the rededication ceremony. A ribbon was cut, refreshments were served, and patrons posed for their photo with story-book characters.

Information Resource Center

The library now has a collection of 300,000 items and more than 37,000 registered borrowers. Carnegie-Stout's mission has always been to serve as a resource center to meet the informational and recreational needs of its users. To promote reading and lifelong learning the library has developed programs such as computer classes, movies, story-time activities, children's yoga, read-aloud times, book fairs, a chess club, adult book discussion groups, and

guest lectures. The library is computerized and offers lap top computers for circulation in the library and wireless access to the Internet. The library web page leads patrons on a virtual tour of the library and its catalog and services, and offers homework help, links to other libraries, and web resources. The library also houses a collection of genealogical documents, histories, maps, and old newspapers on microfilm.

Director Susan Henricks says the library strives to be a cultural center in partnership with the community. Programs that reach out to young people are a high priority. Young adults have their own collection of books, and a young-adult librarian plans programs for teens. Library hours reflect patron needs, a "personal librarian" concept includes an e-mail address to which patrons can send questions and requests and have the research done by library staff, and the TeleCirc system allows patrons to manage their library accounts by telephone.

Children gather at the landmark mural in the story hour room.

T. B. Scott
Free Library

◆

Merrill, Wisconsin

Address: 106 West First Street
Merrill, WI 54452
Date Founded: 1891
Date Built: 1911; 2001 (addition)
Architects: Claude and Starck; Frye Gillan
Molinaro
Director: Bea Lebal
Special Collections: Local and Regional History

The early years of T. B. Scott Library were shaped largely by two men. Both men were born in Scotland in the first half of the nineteenth century. Both men became wealthy U.S. businessmen. Both men endowed the public library in Merrill.

Thomas Blythe Scott, for whom the Merrill library is named, made his fortune in lumber and railroads on the Wisconsin frontier, served as a Republican state senator from 1872 to 1883, and was elected as Merrill's first mayor. When he died he bequeathed $10,000 to the city of Merrill to establish a public library. For its part, the city was to provide suitable quarters within five years. The city councilmen, who wanted a new city hall, proposed housing the library in the same structure. A turreted red brick Victorian building was completed in 1889, and the library opened in March of 1891 with a very respectable collection of two thousand volumes. It was one of the first twenty public libraries in the state.

After twenty years in the cramped, irregularly shaped rooms of city hall, the library needed its own separate structure. The library board applied to Andrew Carnegie, who gave hundreds of grants to cities across the United States and Europe for the construction of public libraries, and in 1911 the new library opened. It was built in the spare Prairie style—just three percent of the Carnegie libraries were so styled. An addition was constructed in 1969, then replaced in 2001. The library is listed on the National Register of Historic Places.

🐿 🐿
The Women's Study Class

In Merrill, as in many communities across the United States, study clubs for upper-

North side of the 2001 addition. Courtesy of Fry Gillan Molinaro Architects, Ltd.

> The three most important documents a free society gives are a birth certificate, a passport, and a library card.
>
> —E. L. Doctorow

and middle-class women became popular during the late 1800s. These volunteer service and study clubs had a close relationship with public libraries. Members of the Study Class of Merrill, a group of women who organized in 1887, all supported and used the library and were registered as "special privilege" members. The husbands of seven of the women served on the library board during the first decade of its operation, and Janet Russell, a charter member of the group, became the first librarian.

🐿 🐿
Intrigue in the Library?

Minutes of the T. B. Scott Library Board serve as a detailed historical record of the many deliberations and decisions made through the years. The library minutes books sometimes contain intriguing cryptic remarks, such as this one from the minutes of 14 June 1938: "A letter was read from the secret service division regarding use of library by counterfeiters." The letter no lon-

Mrs. Max Van Hecke, board secretary, receives H. V. Kaltenborn check from board member Norm Chilsen in 1945.

ger exists, and the minutes don't elaborate—leaving a mystery for the ages.

⚘ ⚘

Small Library, Big Impact

T. B. Scott Library is one of the few libraries in the state to have twice been named Library of the Year by the Wisconsin Library Association (WLA). In 1976 the library was cited by the WLA "as an outstanding example of what a library can do and be in a small community."

The library once again received the coveted award in 2002, for "creatively and energetically 'growing' services and facilities for their community and its changing needs over the past 111 years to stand as a model library for Wisconsin and excellent example of how even a relatively small library can show vision and leadership in the development of library services, both locally and regionally."

⚘ ⚘

A Community Resource for More Than a Century

H. V. Kaltenborn, who was raised in a house across the street from the original T. B. Scott Library, began his career as a war correspondent, sending weekly reports on the Spanish-American conflict to his hometown newspapers. He went on to become a pioneer in radio journalism and one of the most famous announcers of his day. In 1945 he sent a check for $2,000 to the library board to establish a book fund. The accompanying letter states, ". . . as a youngster I profited so much from the books I was able to get out of the library that I want to help others enjoy the same advantage."

A current patron recently wrote, "The definition of a heart, to me, is something that keeps a body alive . . . this library is a place that keeps the mind and body growing . . . How could you not love such a place!"

Study Class of Merrill; librarian Katherine Barker seated at right, 1908.

U.S. ZIP CODE
55108

Saint Anthony Park Branch Library

◆

Saint Paul Public Library

Saint Paul, Minnesota

Address:	2245 Como Avenue Saint Paul, MN 55108
Date Founded:	1917
Date Built:	1917
Architect:	Charles H. Hausler
Director:	Melanie Huggins; Rose Ann Foreman, Branch Manager
Special Collections:	Local Authors Collection

It's three blocks from the University of Minnesota, two miles from the Mississippi River, and an unknown distance from Lake Wobegon.

The Saint Anthony Park Branch Library is part of the Saint Paul Public Library in much the way Saint Anthony Park is part of Saint Paul. Located in the northwestern corner of the city, Saint Anthony Park was named after the Village of Saint Anthony in Minneapolis and annexed to the community of Saint Paul in 1887. The area is a mixture of tree-lined residential streets, a com-

The interior of the historic portion of the library. Courtesy of Theodore E. Roseen and the Friends of the Saint Paul Public Library.

mercial area, and an industrial area. Many of its inhabitants are students, faculty, or employees at the Saint Paul campus of the University of Minnesota.

The Saint Paul Public Library began as a reading room started by the Young Men's Christian Association in 1856. In 1863 the association merged with the Saint Paul Library Association and the Mercantile Library Association to form the Saint Paul Library Association. The Saint Paul Public Library was established in 1882 with a collection of 8,051 books housed in the Old Market Hall. The library collection grew rapidly to 158,000. Construction of a separate library facility had

> A library is not a luxury but one of the necessities of life.
>
> —Henry Ward Beecher

been approved, but before it was completed, a fire destroyed most of the collection. Eventually the new library was finished, a new collection was established, and the library blossomed. By 1917 a branch library was needed to serve the burgeoning population. Today the Saint Paul Library has twelve branches and a bookmobile.

✿ ✿

Oldest Branch

Opened in 1917, the Saint Anthony Park Branch Library is the oldest branch in the Saint Paul Public Library system. It is listed on the National Register of Historic Places and is one of the last of the Carnegie libraries, built at a cost of $25,000. Local architect Charles A. Hausler designed it in the Beaux Arts style so common to Carnegie buildings. Constructed of brick and sandstone, it features arched and recessed windows, a double set of steps leading to the front entrance, a wide sandstone frieze, terra cotta cornices, and molding and dentals with inserts of tiny bronze-colored balls. Remodeled in 1957, the library was restored in 1986, and in 2000 an addition that matches the character of the original building was built in the rear to house the children's area.

The Saint Anthony Park Branch Library numbers among its patrons several prominent people. Saint Paul resident Garrison Keillor has written of the library:

> The Saint Anthony Park Branch Library . . . is a magnificent building that fills one with a sense of light and grace. You cross the grass and ascend the steps and pass through the little foyer with its community bulletin board and there, next to the librarian's counter you contemplate a world of choice . . .

The Saint Anthony Park Branch Library. Courtesy of Theodore E. Roseen and the Friends of the Saint Paul Public Library.

❧ ❧
Justice Was Served

U.S. Supreme Court Justice Warren E. Burger frequented the library, as did Minnesota Governor Elmer L. Andersen. Professors from the university as well as authors and artists use the library. Its collection includes 140 titles from seventy-five Saint Anthony Park authors. Erin Hart, Shannon Olson, Maurice Kilwein Guevara, William Kent Krueger, Nicole Lea Helget, and actress Linda Kelsey have all presented there.

In addition to being a place to find information, attend an event, or simply enjoy a good read, the Saint Anthony Park Branch Library serves as a community center. The Saint Anthony Park Library Association is one of the oldest public library support organizations in Minnesota. It was formed in the 1920s and still supports the library and library-hosted events. The annual Saint Anthony Park Arts Festival has been held on the library grounds for thirty-seven years. In the 1930s a sewing circle met at the library to make maps—tactile maps for the blind—so that people who were sight-impaired could more easily navigate the city. The Maps for the Blind Project earned nationwide attention. The 1940s brought the establishment of the Saint Anthony Park Historical Association, an organization whose members explored and preserved the community's history. They held their meetings at the library and became so successful that they expanded to become the Ramsey County Historical Association, serving the entire county. In the 1950s the Community Interest Center was created to connect area churches, schools, and community organizations. Members met at the library for two decades.

Saint Anthony Park Branch Library maintains one of the highest volume circulations per square foot of any Saint Paul library.

It offers classes in the Internet and in library catalog and database management and hosts a book club, a summer journaling workshop, and cultural workshops.

The Virginia Sohre grant allows the Saint Anthony Park library to purchase $20,000 in children's materials each year. The grant was established by a beloved library neighbor who truly loved children and wanted them to discover a wonderful world of books.

Young patrons enjoying the children's area of the library. Courtesy of Theodore E. Roseen and the Friends of the Saint Paul Public Library.

Brookdale Library

◆

Hennepin County Library System

Brooklyn Center, Minnesota

Address:	6125 Shingle Creek Parkway
	Brooklyn Center, MN 55430
Date Founded:	1981
Date Built:	1981; 2004 (renovation)
Architect:	Buetow and Associates (2004)
Director:	Amy Ryan
Special Collections:	Assistive Technology; Job and Career
	Information

"The public library is an institution so pliable that it bends to every growing need of community life; so susceptible to social needs, so eager to render all possible service, that it must by virtue of its own nature reach out beyond the city borders," said Gratia Countryman a century ago. She could hardly have imagined how far-reaching her words would be.

The Brookdale Library in Brooklyn Center, Minnesota, is part of the Hennepin County Library System, which was founded in the 1920s by Countryman, who was director of the Minneapolis Public Library. From its early years delivering books by "book wagon" to rural residents, Hennepin County Library today circulates more than 12 million books and other items annually via twenty-six libraries, Children's Readmobiles, and outreach services. Customers access its website more than 200,000 times each week.

Following many years of service by a bookmobile, the Brooklyn Center Library was built in 1965, and demand for library service in the area grew. In the 1970s, a tiered concept of library service was planned, and the Brookdale Library opened as the second of HCL's three "area" libraries in 1981.

Meeting Twenty-First Century Needs

In 2004, the library reopened following a two-year, $19 million renovation that essentially reinvented the library, ushered in twenty-first century technology, and configured the library as part of Hennepin County's Brookdale Regional Center complex that also includes a Service Center, District Court, Human Services, and other County offices.

The library serves one of Hennepin County's most culturally diverse areas—approximately 160,000 people live in the area and speak more than ten native languages. Many members of the community are longtime library customers who are at home at

the library, while others have recently emigrated from countries that don't have a public library tradition and are unfamiliar with its services; therefore, when planning the community-based facility, staff sought community input. Suggestions from service organizations, schools, faith-based institutions, and individual community members helped shape the space and the services.

A New Kind of Neighborhood

Rather than arranging the collection of 165,000 books, magazines, and reference materials in the traditional way by format, then subject, the new library arranges them in "information neighborhoods" focused around high-interest subject areas geared to meet the needs of specific customer groups. The areas are identified by user friendly, intuitive design cues derived from the area's history and cultures, such as color schemes, carpet patterns, and large graphics and signage. Within each "neighborhood" are reference books, circulating books, magazines, and newspapers. Computers have home screens with databases and websites related to the subject. A winding interior boulevard called "Mainstreet" connects the areas and provides spots for sitting and gathering areas for quiet or group conversations.

High-Tech Is High Priority

Residents said access to technology was one of their highest priority needs. The library is now equipped with 134 public access computers that are continually in use. Meeting rooms are equipped with programmable lighting systems, state-of-the-art projection systems, audio, video, and digital media, and connections to LAN, WAN, and Wi-Fi workstations. Study rooms are equipped with computers. There are even self-service options, including Express Checkout, Express Reserve Pickup, and an

The library's Job and Career Information Center.

automated drive-up book drop. Friendly librarian "stations" have replaced the reference desk, the Teen Neighborhood features a cybercafé-style computer zone. plus books and music for teens. Creative interior design includes fiber-optic constellations embedded in the multipurpose Star Dome room, fiber optic stars twinkling on the floor in the entrance rotundas, and a children's area with a floor-to-ceiling hand-painted puppet castle, a 20-foot dragon book bin, and a whimsical, 32-foot-tall animal sculpture.

The library offers something for every age group from infant to senior citizen, in support of HCL's vision of "a future where everyone is an eager and engaged lifelong learner." Computer services in the Job and Career Neighborhood enable customers to search and apply for jobs. A computer lab offers tutorials. The training room holds classes in using the catalog, the Internet, and online databases. Baby Storytime—for children from birth to twenty-four months—stimulates infant senses with books and music. An after-school program for children in grades three through five is a collaboration between several school districts, the city, and community organizations.

Business classes for Hmong men and

A whimsical animal sculpture by artist Christopher Tully is a community landmark. Courtesy of Buetow & Associates and Wheelock Photography.

women and an International Teen Club are facilitated by the library's outreach liaison for the Hmong community. Conversation Circles are held each Thursday night to help new immigrants practice their language skills. Multicultural performing arts programs, author talks, and summer children's programs such as Guys Read book discussions and puppet and magic shows are offered. At Paws to Read sessions, children can strengthen their reading skills and have fun by reading aloud to a certified therapy team of Animal Humane Society volunteers and pets trained to work with young readers.

"Our" Library

The April 2005 issue of *American Libraries* included Brookdale Library in its Library Showcase, and Loren E. Abraham of the American Institute of Architects featured the library in an article entitled, "Hennepin County Brookdale Regional Center: Reimagining the Relationship Between Human Beings and Their Environment." The mayor of Brooklyn Center said of the new facility, "We could not be happier with *our* new library."

U.S. ZIP CODE

58501

Bismarck Veterans Memorial Public Library

◆

Bismarck, North Dakota

Address: 515 N. Fifth Street
Bismarck, ND 58501
Date Founded: 1917
Date Built: 1963; 1989 and 1996 (additions)
Architect: Ritterbush Brothers; Arnie Hanson;
Warren Tvenge
Director: Thomas T. Jones
Special Collections: Local History; Lewis and Clark

Libraries receive donations for their collections from various sources: Sometimes it's the long arm of the law, sometimes it's the open hand of largesse.

In 2004 the Bismarck Veterans Memorial Public Library received two hundred CDs—by artists ranging from Mozart to Mellencamp, Kravitz to Coltrane—as part of the settlement of a 2002 price-fixing lawsuit against eight CD manufacturers and retailers. The settlement required the music companies to donate $76 million worth of CDs to libraries and schools.

More recently one grateful library patron donated his late wife's collection of CDs, tapes, and videos—more than one thousand items—to the library. "The Bismarck Public Library," Carl Vender said, "was the place where, if you couldn't find my wife at home, it would be the first place you would look."

After his wife, Millie, died, Vender, with the help of his sons Charles, Bradley, and Michael, donated her collection. "One of her favorite things to do while she worked on crafts was to listen to books on tape," Vender recalled. "She could be seen walking through many parts of the town with her headphones, getting her exercise, and enjoying the sights of the city while listening

From your parents you learn love and laughter and how to put one foot before the other. But when books are opened you discover that you have wings.

—Helen Hayes

to books." "The boys learned the value of the library from Millie," he said.

Library director Thomas Jones remembers seeing Millie with her sons. Now grown son Michael and his wife, Maria, continue the family tradition by bringing Carl and Millie's five-year-old grandson, Gabriel, to explore the library. "Part of the satisfaction of giving," Vender said, "is knowing your donation will benefit not only people today, but also build a foundation for the future."

In fact, the Bismarck library began with donations. Soon after the city was founded in 1873, a group of Bismarck women established a reading room. By 1915 the Bismarck Civic League and the Commercial Club (forerunner of the Chamber of Commerce), with guidance from the State Library Commission, undertook a book drive, resulting in a lending library of 1,500 books housed in the Commercial Club rooms.

❧ ❦

The "Ayes" Have It

Interest grew, and the Andrew Carnegie Foundation was asked for a grant to fund construction of a "real library." Bismarck was offered $25,000 if the city would provide a minimum upkeep of $2,500 annually. In 1916 A. W. Lucas, president of the City Commission, proposed the plan to the commission, and its members

Library front entrance.

The main floor of Bismark Veterans Memorial Public Library.

decided to ask the voters. Voters approved the library by a vote of 374 to 70. The city then donated the site at the corner of Thayer Avenue and Sixth Street, and the Commercial Club began collecting books for the new Bismarck Public Library, which opened in 1917 with a collection of four thousand items.

The first library board members were prominent Bismarck residents: C. B. Little, C. L. Young, Otto Holta, George F. Will, and Agatha Patterson. In 1933 a trained children's librarian was hired, and in 1938 a trained catalog librarian was hired. The operating budget in the 1940s was less than $20,000. The Carnegie Library building served the city through the 1950s but became inadequate in size for the growing city.

In the early 1960s the city began planning a new 16,000-square-foot, three-level facility to be located farther north on Sixth Street. Financed through a $240,000 bond levy and named to honor the area's World War II and Korean War veterans, the Veterans Memorial Public Library opened in 1963 with a collection of 100,000 volumes. The building served for a number of years, services expanded, and the library became an active place with expanding attendance and need for more space.

In 1976 Burleigh County contracted with the library to operate bookmobile services to rural schools and communities. The staff, collection, and bookmobile are housed in the library. The bookmobile currently makes sixty-one stops monthly and utilizes one full-time librarian and one part-time assistant.

In 1989, after almost ten years of meetings and planning, the newly remodeled and enlarged Bismarck Veterans Memorial Library opened with 70,000 square feet, more than tripling the size of the old building. A new parking lot was constructed on the west side of the library, and the front of the library now faces Fifth Street. The library encompasses the entire block.

Grants and a Grand

The library offers the public four meeting rooms (one being a 240-seat recital room with a grand piano and large-screen VCR), a video conferencing facility, and nine single- and multiuser private study rooms. It also houses the Missouri River Room, the library's rare materials collection; the Grants Resource Center; a library training center where courses are taught to the public; and a media reviewing room.

Many electronic resources and databases are available to the public. These include an online catalog along with full-text newspaper and magazine databases, genealogy, community information, health, history, music, and antiques resources and databases. The library has fifteen dedicated search stations for online catalog access and thirty-seven public access computers for Internet searching, e-mail, database research, and word processing. Wireless Internet access is available to laptop users in most areas of the library.

Since 1993 Bismarck Veterans Memorial Public Library has been a member of the Central Dakota Library Network (CDLN), a resource-sharing and automated consortium of fifteen libraries. CDLN also cooperates with other state libraries and systems and shares more than 466,000 items with its system, SirsiDynix's Horizon Information Library System.

Library-sponsored teen programs, children's story hours, book discussions and group meetings, Internet users, and other patrons help keep the library busy. Plans are currently underway to remodel an area of the library and build a 600-square-foot coffee shop that will be leased and operated by an independent vendor. The youth services area is also slated for redecoration.

Darby Community Public Library

◆

Darby, Montana

Address: 101½ South Marshall
Darby, MT 59829
Date Founded: 1956
Date Built: 2004
Architect: Ron La Rue and the Roundwood Engineered Structures Dream Team
Director: Amy Lee Fannin

You might call it a "branch" library: The Darby Community Public Library (DCPL) is constructed of small, round logs called "roundwood."

After the wildfires of 2000 that burned more than 350,000 acres in the Darby area and more than 840,000 acres in the state of Montana, the U.S. Forest Service devised ways of using underutilized forest products through the National Fire Plan and contacted members of the DCPL Board of Trustees to ask if they would be willing to use the roundwood method of construction. The board was delighted to be part of an effort to improve forest management, reduce fire hazards on the forest floor, and help to improve the watershed and wildlife habitats while reducing the danger of wildfires to communities adjacent to U.S. National Forests.

The library also was delighted to showcase the innovative roundwood construction method as a way to help the sagging timber industry discover a marketable use for small-diameter logs. Indeed, roundwood construction has gained recognition as observers from all over the United States and several foreign countries have visited the library.

※ ※

Library of Logs

Nature answered the call for the Darby Library's innovative construction materials, but the impetus for the building came from the call of nature: The library project began merely to provide librarians and library patrons with a restroom. Eventually, however, the project snowballed into a complete state-of-the-art library, replacing a sixty-five-year-old log building that measured only 500 square feet and had no plumbing. The new library has a children's room, computer room, community meeting room, and reference area that blends into the main library and reception desk. It has become the center of community activities—and, yes, it has restrooms.

Several local civic and nonprofit groups, such as Alcoholics Anonymous, Adult Education, Veterans of Foreign Wars, Library

Board of Trustees, Literacy Volunteers of the Bitterroot, and the Senior Citizens Club, use the community room. This room has become a commons as members of the community hold small meetings and gather to discuss local issues.

Interior view of roundwood contruction.

Heart of the Community: **The Libraries We Love**

The new Darby Community Library replaced a 500-square-foot log building.

State-of-the-Art Computer Room

The library's computer room is state of the art. Many students, seniors, and other residents who do not have the economic means to own personal computers use the computers for research and e-mail. Seasonal workers and out-of-state and foreign visitors who travel through the area also use the computers.

Preschoolers use the children's room during the school day, and children of all ages use it after school, looking through the stacks or using the children's computers, which have multilevel software programs. The room also has a wide selection of parenting books that adults can read as their children read their own books.

The library opened in September 2004, built without debt for $950,000 through a partnership with the U.S. Forest Service and other private, city, county, state, and federal entities. The library is located sixty-four miles south of Missoula in the Bitterroot Val-

ley of western Montana. It is a district library for a population of 4,200 living in a 780-square-mile area, most of which is national forest. The number of cardholders has more than doubled during the past year.

Many patrons have commented, "I can't believe that this beautiful library was built here in the little town of Darby."

The library fireplace.

> I'd be happy if I could think that the role of the library was sustained and even enhanced in the age of the computer.
>
> —Bill Gates

Heart of the Community: The Libraries We Love

Batavia Public Library

Batavia, Illinois

Address: 10 S. Batavia Avenue
                     Batavia, IL 60510
Date Founded: 1882
Date Built: 2002
Architect: Engberg Anderson Design
Director: George H. Scheetz
Special Collections: Windmills; Local History

Windmills are old, particle accelerators new, and the twain meet in Batavia, where Mark Twain just happens to greet its public library patrons.

The library's slogan, "Knowledge for the City of Energy," links the cities past, present, and future with energy. Batavia once was home to six windmill factories, and indeed, the library now owns an historic windmill, one of fourteen Batavia-manufactured windmills that are on display around town. In 2006, the library published *Windmill City: A Guide to the Historic Windmills of Batavia, Illinois.* Daniel Halladay, inventor of the first self-governing American-style windmills, and John Burnham, president and co-founder of the U.S. Wind Engine & Pump Co. (one of the leading windmill manufacturers in the United States), were active in the Batavia Library Association.

Now Batavia is home to the U.S. Department of Energy's Fermi National Accelerator Laboratory (Fermilab), and the Tevatron, the world's most powerful particle accelerator. The library sponsored and hosted a World Year of Physics 2005 celebration in collaboration with Fermilab, Illinois Mathematics and Science Academy, and SciTech Hands On Museum. Dr. Leon M. Lederman, Nobel laureate (physics, 1988), was the featured speaker at both the World Year of Physics 2005 event and the library-sponsored Books Between Bites program.

A Peripatetic Past

Batavia Public Library began as a library association circa 1867. Members paid a $5 lifetime membership fee and a yearly tax from which books were purchased. These books were kept in an upper room in the Harvey Building on South Batavia Avenue. The association adopted a "free library plan" in 1873, which allowed users (including nonmembers) to check out materials free of charge. The library then moved to the Buck Building. In 1882, Batavia Public Library became a tax-supported public library, as a direct successor to the Batavia Library Association. By 1888 it had out-

> A public library is the most enduring of memorials, the trustiest monument for the presentation of an event or a name or an affection; for it, and it only, is respected by wars and revolutions, and survives them.
>
> —Mark Twain

grown its quarters and was moved to the new Van Nortwick Block on Wilson Street. Following the wishes of her late husband, Don Carlos Newton, Mary M. Newton presented the property at One North Batavia Avenue, the red-brick Levi Newton homestead, to the library board in 1902. In 1921, the Levi Newton home was razed to extend Wilson Street, and the library board purchased the Don Carlos Newton property on Batavia Avenue.

The Batavia Public Library District was formed in 1975. In 1981, a new library building was constructed at the corner of Lincoln Avenue and Wilson Street. The library moved west from the Newton House to its new facility, which ushered in a new level of library services and materials. Batavia soon experienced explosive growth to its east and west. The library board purchased property at the corner of Wilson Street and Batavia Avenue in 1998. To serve a population of approximately 23,000 and still growing, voters approved by referendum the construction of the current 54,000-square-foot building. On 27 January 2002 the newest Batavia Public Library was dedicated.

The new library, which was designed to complement the historic downtown, resembles historic buildings made of limestone from the city's quarries. Batavia's quarries supplied stone for the rebuilding of Chicago after the great fire in 1871.

A windmill built in the early 1900s on the lower east side of the library.

A Community Meeting Place

The library is a welcoming place to gather, exchange ideas, and participate in cultural events. It sponsors educational and entertaining programs, as well as summer and winter reading clubs for readers of all ages. The library cosponsors numerous community-wide programs, including the Books Between Bites lunchtime lecture series; annual One Book, One Batavia events (the 2006 program included a visit from author Lois Lowry); and the Batavia Library Writers Workshop. Since opening, the library's meeting rooms, available free of charge to not-for-profit organizations, have been in high demand. Located on two main streets, the library is easy to access, and the interior is inviting, comfortable, and spacious.

An Art Center

Stained-glass windows that commemorate the library's sixty-year sojourn in the historic Newton House were moved to the new building. Exhibit space for local artists is available throughout the year, and young patrons display their distinctive collections in the youth services department. A permanent collection of original paintings by local artists, representing Batavia landmarks, is on display. *Fox River Ice-Skating,* a painting by illustrator John Falter, inspired by the Fox River at Batavia, graced the cover of the *Saturday Evening Post* of 11 January 1958. In cooperation with the Batavia Woman's Club, which owns the original painting, a larger-than-life reproduction was installed in the library in 2006.

Oh, and about Mark Twain. He presented a lecture in Batavia in 1869, sponsored by the Laconian Literary Society, which co-founded the Batavia Library Association. Twain's visit is commemorated by a statue located on a bench at the library entrance—one more way in which the library pays tribute to its historic place in the life of the community.

John Falter's painting, *Fox River Ice Skating,* inspired by the river that runs through Batavia. Courtesy of the Batavia Woman's Club.

Heart of the Community: **The Libraries We Love**

Ida Public Library

Belvidere, Illinois

Address: 320 N. State Street
Belvidere, IL 61008
Date Founded: 1885
Date Built: 1913
Architect: Grant Miller
Director: Connie Harrison
Special Collections: Local History and Genealogy

Sometimes a little change can maintain the status quo: When members of the Belvidere Ladies Library Society needed money to keep their library going, they collected it one dime at a time.

The society organized the town's first library sometime before 1850—before the town had a railroad or a daily newspaper. The library's collection was kept in a bookcase in the home of Mrs. Carolyn Jocelyn, an Episcopal clergyman's widow who taught school in her home. In 1853 the society's name was changed to the "Belvidere Library Association," possibly because men had joined the society. One hundred subscribers bought stock at five dollars a share and set up in the Alex Neely building on East Lincoln Avenue. Unspecified trouble with the acting librarian resulted in the demise of the library until 1874, when the Belvidere Ladies Library Society reorganized in a store owned by Kittie Jenner on

North State Street. From there the library moved to the post office and from there to a former office building of the Waterman Lumber Company. The women went from door to door to raise funds to keep the library alive. They also hosted dime sociables, with the proceeds going to the purchase of books and library upkeep. They also hosted lecture series, parlor dramatics and festivals, spelling bees, and recitations.

First Lady of the Library

One of the prominent supporters of the Belvidere Ladies Library Society was Ida Fuller Hovey, the youngest daughter of General Allen C. and Nancy Benjamin Fuller. Born in Belvidere in 1859, Ida died of consumption at the age of twenty-four but not before she had endeared herself to many and used her musical talents to help raise money for the library society. Shortly after her death her father offered $5,000 to the city to found a library in her honor. The city accepted, and a room on the second floor in the newly constructed City Hall was furnished. Mary Crandall was appointed head librarian. On 25 July 1885, the Ida Public Library was opened for public inspection, and a few days after the opening, the first book was checked out.

The library quickly outgrew its space in City Hall. In 1909 the library board sought financial help from philanthropist Andrew Carnegie, and in 1913 the Ida Public Library had its own home on North State Street. With its interior archways, high ceilings, stained glass windows, and red tile roof, the new library offered space for patrons to read and study as well as a separate room where women's organizations could hold exhibits of artwork or crafts. Circulation rose, a telephone was installed in 1918, and in 1919 "the building committee took up the matter of electric lights."

In 1927 the board voted to join the American Library Association, and in 1939 the Juvenile Vacation Reading Project began. The 1940 and 1950s brought the installation of fluorescent lights and an upstairs washroom. The library collection continued to

Adult fiction and reading area in the original Carnegie building.

Library mural painted by Belvidere High School art students.

Books are a delightful society.
If you go into a room filled with
books, even without taking them
down from their shelves, they seem
to speak to you, to welcome you.

—William E. Gladstone

grow, as did the number of patrons. In fact, by the 1980s space was again a problem. The Ida Public Library celebrated its one hundredth birthday in 1985 with the promise of a new addition. With the aid of a state grant, the library constructed a 10,000-square-foot addition that included a larger circulation desk area, more shelving space, a study area, a children's department, an audio-visual room, and a staff lounge. The grace of the old building was retained amid the modern features of the new one.

Jewel of Belvidere

After the addition was completed, the library also expanded its services. Public-access computers were installed, a website created, and an online database initiated. A community meeting room was established. The Children's Story Hour became a regular feature, and summer reading groups continued. The Hispanic Outreach Program was launched, and the library joined with the Illinois Literacy Council and local schools to encourage literacy. A history and genealogy room became a repository for local information.

With more than seventy-three thousand books, a collection of video and audio materials, and three hundred subscriptions, today the Ida Public Library, dubbed the "Jewel of Belvidere" in a newspaper article following the completion of the addition, serves a population of twenty-five thousand.

The children's room.

Heart of the Community: **The Libraries We Love**

Rock Island Public Library

◆

Main Library
Rock Island, Illinois

Address:	401 19th Street
	Rock Island, IL 61201
Date Founded:	1872
Date Built:	1903
Architects:	Leonard M. Drack, Drack & Kerns
Director:	Ava Ketter
Special Collections:	Local History

Its godfather was the lumber king, not the steel baron, and its first librarian liked the job so well that she stayed for sixty-four years. The Rock Island Public Library is the oldest public library in Illinois. Although public libraries in Elgin and Chicago had been organized earlier, they opened later. With its two branches—the 30/31 Branch and the Southwest Branch—the Rock Island Public Library serves a community of thirty-nine thousand. The library opened on 25 November 1872, in a small, rented room in the Mitchell and Lynde Building (now the National City Bank). It had begun in 1855 as an association library: Members were required to pay an annual fee of $3. The venture failed after two years, and the library was revived in 1865 as the privately funded Young Men's Literary Society. The society sponsored lectures by luminaries such as Ralph Waldo Emerson and used the proceeds to purchase books. The society operated until 1872, when the state of Illinois authorized communities to assess taxes to support public libraries.

The *Rock Island Argus* newspaper was a key supporter of the library and also pushed for Sunday hours on the belief that city libraries are intended for the masses. In the era of six-day workweeks, Sunday was the only free day for a majority of the working class. The *Argus* editorialized that "a taste for reading is the highest blessing heaven can confer," noting that reading "lifts one above the trodden clod." Despite some resistance, the library board approved keeping the library open from 2 to 5 P.M. on Sundays.

The current building was opened in 1903 and was at first called "Rock Island's Temple of Literature." The building featured Carthage marble in the foyer and steps, golden oak, decoration in the Italian Renaissance style, and a skylighted rotunda. The building has been updated and refurbished several times. In 1986 a large addition included a sculptural fountain on the north side. The library also was renovated at the same time with the goal of recapturing the authenticity of the original building. The dome was reopened and illuminated from underneath, and original oak doors and brass fixtures were refurbished. The marble foyer at the main entrance was opened to its original appearance.

❦ ❦

A Weyerhaeuser—Not a Carnegie—Library

Following the lead of many other communities, the library board had contacted Andrew Carnegie about an endowment for the building. Carnegie reportedly responded: "Any town that has Frederick Weyerhaeuser need not ask a library from me." Weyerhaeuser (1834–1914) and his brother-in-law and partner Frederick Denkmann were the lumber kings of the United States. Weyerhaeuser had settled in Rock Island in 1856 after immigrating to America from Germany several years earlier. In the high-water time of the spring, the Mississippi River near Rock Island was choked with logs rafted in from Wisconsin. Weyerhaeuser was generous, lending the board $50,000 and donating another $18,000 while Denkmann added $2,500. Weyerhaeuser's insistence on a fireproof building that "would be an ornament to our city" prevented cost-cutting measures that would have compromised the building's classic beauty. When timber in the region dwindled, he founded the Weyerhaeuser Company in Washington State in 1900.

Portrait of the library's benefactor, Frederick Weyerhaeuser.

Brass and oak stair railing, an example of the library's Italian Renaissance–style decoration.

Renaissance Revival Design

In 1901 the library board examined four sets of designs and selected that of local architects Drack & Kerns. Leonard M. Drack's Renaissance Revival design included the balanced symmetrical façade, smooth stone walls, and architrave-framed windows. The front façade is enhanced by four sets of double Iconic columns rising to span the first and second floors. The entryway features a heavy pediment with scrolls and brackets. Names of twelve well-known (and lesser-known) poets adorn the frieze, including Shakespeare, Virgil, Dante, Longfellow, and Emerson. The exterior is of canyon gray Berea sandstone from the Cleveland quarries in Ohio, which has weathered over the years to a warm buff color.

Ellen Gale: An Amazing Record of Service

The career of the library's first librarian, Ellen Gale (1853–1948), spanned from the Civil War Reconstruction era to the incidents leading up to World War II. She served as head of the public library for sixty-four years and as librarian for the Young Men's Library Association for four years prior to that. When she retired in 1937 her tenure

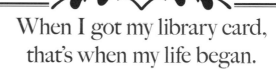

When I got my library card,
that's when my life began.

—Rita Mae Brown

was longer than that of any other head librarian in the nation. In fact, the *Municipal Yearbook* for 1935 listed her as having served longer than any municipal employee in the United States.

Miss Gale went to work for the library at age fifteen in 1868. Although she had no formal library training, she educated herself by attending conferences and visiting other libraries. In 1881 she was one of the founders of the Western Library Association, the first library association in Illinois. She was an early advocate of library services for children. When it became clear in 1895 that the library needed to supplement the public schools, she purchased more juvenile books. By 1902 more than 27 percent of the library's holding were children's books, and the 1903 building included a children's department. In 1909 she began services to schools.

Today, the library is a member of the Prairie Area Library System and houses more than 200,000 volumes as well as items undreamed of by Miss Gale: CDs, videos, DVDs, and free Internet access.

A photograph of Miss Ellen Gale, former director of the library.

U.S. ZIP CODE
65301

THIS MEMORIAL IS THE GRATEFVL
ACKNOWLEDGEMENT OF THE
PEOPLE OF SEDALIA, TO
ANDREW CARNEGIE,
FOR HIS GENEROVS GIFT
OF THIS BVILDING.

Sedalia Public Library

◆

Sedalia, Missouri

Address: 311 W. Third Street
Sedalia, MO 65301
Date Founded: 1895
Date Built: 1901
Architects: Mauran, Russell & Garden
Director: Pam Hunter
Special Collections: World War I Veteran Profiles;
Sedalia Newspapers From 1866

If at first you don't succeed at establishing a library, try, try again.

The town of Sedalia certainly did try, try again. And again. The first attempt at establishing a library was undertaken by a group of the town's leading residents in 1871. They offered lectures and other entertainment as well as books lent for a fee, but the venture failed for lack of funds. The books were donated to the Queen City Seminary and destroyed in a fire. In 1879 several local civic-minded women bought a few hundred new books and had a year of success before their library closed. Subsequent attempts to create a lasting library also failed. In 1894 the idea of a free public library was placed on the town ballot but was voted down for lack of canvassing. The next year, however, brought success: The measure finally passed.

Events happened quickly after that. A board of directors was appointed, and a tax was levied to provide for the establishment and maintenance of the library. Additional books were purchased, and the collection, numbering more than two thousand, was housed in the natural history rooms of the courthouse, where the first library association had been quartered. Donated furniture made the rooms comfortable, and the library kept its doors open six days a week.

❦ ❧
Carnegie to Missouri: "Show Me"

In 1899 the county court ordered the library's board of directors to find a new facility. Board member D. H. Smith, thinking this would be the end of yet another library attempt, wrote to industrialist and philanthropist Andrew Carnegie for help. Carnegie's secretary, James Bertram, replied that if Sedalia agreed to provide a building site and spend $4,000 a year for maintenance of the library, a grant of $50,000 would be forthcoming—the first Carnegie library grant awarded in Missouri. A site was chosen at Third and Kentucky Streets, and construction commenced. In 1901 the new Sedalia Public Library opened. On 29 July 2001, the

library celebrated its centennial. Its oak woodwork still gleams, the glass floor behind the checkout counter still fascinates, and although the library has been updated to twenty-first century technological standards, the stern visage of President Andrew Jackson, painted in 1824, still keeps watch.

❦ ❧
Harmony and Hard Work

One of the remarkable aspects of the Sedalia Public Library was the way in which the board of directors and the architects cooperated. "The building was planned and designed in an ideal

The library's upstairs lobby, showing
skylight and woodwork details.

Heart of the Community: **The Libraries We Love**

Stately fireplace in the reference area.

way, the library board and the architects working steadily, hand in hand, to achieve the best results. Free interchange of thought, free criticism, and withal a hearty co-operation have produced a building adapted to its every purpose . . ." wrote Faith E. Smith in an article for the December 1901 edition of *The Public Library Bulletin*. At the dedication F. M. Crunden of the St. Louis Public Library also remarked on the ". . . complete harmony between the architects and the library board."

This positive working relationship produced a building that is both beautiful and functional. The library, constructed in classic Greek style, is built of white terra cotta and limestone and a red tiled roof. Four limestone columns flank the entrance steps. Inside, the front entrance leads to a main hall flanked by rooms on either side. The floor is made of marble. The second story features a rotunda and a room with seating for four hundred.

Through the years repairs and improvements have been made, and the library's collection has grown from two thousand books to more than seventy-three thousand, with 143 subscriptions and three thousand audio and video items. Close to 100,000 people come through the doors each year. Outreach services, offered even in the earliest days, continue to serve patrons unable to get to the library. There is a thriving children's department, although

The front entrance to library with "Free to All" over the door.

now computers are available for schoolwork, whereas a hundred years ago scrapbooks of old newspaper articles were used as the basis for essays. Preschool story hour is popular, as are the summer and winter reading programs. Computers with Internet service are available to the public, and one can browse through the past in the Genealogy and Local History Room. Among the library's treasures are rare copies of Sedalia newspapers dating back to 1866, a set of Royal Canton China used by President and Mrs. Rutherford B. Hayes on a visit to Sedalia in 1879, and the portrait of President Andrew Jackson painted in 1824 by Philadelphia portraitist Robert Street. The library is listed on the National Register of Historic Places.

Sedalia is probably best known for its state fair, but any tour of downtown is likely to include a visit to the library. The first fair was held the year the Carnegie library opened and is regarded as a measure of the state's economic health and a recording of the history of the state's agriculture. Similarly, the Sedalia Public Library might be regarded as a measure of how strongly the heart of the city is beating, because as Faith Smith put it in 1901, "In all the work of the library, the supreme endeavor is to understand the interest and needs of the community"—something the Sedalia Public Library has been doing for more than one hundred years.

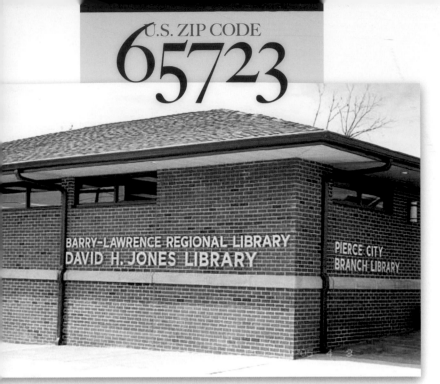

BARRY-LAWRENCE REGIONAL LIBRARY
DAVID H. JONES LIBRARY

PIERCE CITY
BRANCH LIBRARY

Pierce City Branch Library

Barry-Lawrence Regional Library District
Pierce City, Missouri

Address:	101 N. Walnut
	Pierce City, MO 65723
Date Founded:	1986
Date Built:	2001; 2003 (rebuilt)
Architect:	Richard Werner
Director:	Carmen Archer
Special Collections:	"Pierce Empire" newspaper on
	microfiche, 1876–1902

It's an ill wind that blows no goodwill.

When a tornado destroyed the Pierce City library in 2003, emergency funding and insurance money replaced the building, but the goodwill of people from around the world replaced the books.

For years the town's collection of books had been housed in the old Harold Bell Wright Church high on a hill. Books lined the shelved walls and the pews. In 2000 a donation from former Pierce City resident David H. Jones, now a lawyer living in Springfield, Missouri, allowed for the renovation of an old garage on a corner of Main Street, and the library moved there. The building became part of the Barry-Lawrence Regional Library District, allowing the library to greatly expand its collection and to add computer stations and an automated circulation system.

Town without a Library

Not long after the renovation was completed, a tornado swept through the town and destroyed most of the downtown area.

The library after the tornado hit.

Nothing was left of the library except a pile of rubble. What books the tornado did spare the ensuing rains ruined. Newspapers reporting on the tornado called Pierce City "the town without a library" and printed stories describing the destruction and requesting donations from authors, publishers, book dealers, and book lovers countrywide.

The Silver Lining

After the tornado hit, a group of Pierce City residents met at the Harold Bell Wright Church to discuss ways to rebuild the little library they'd lost. They organized as the Friends of the Library, met with the Barry-Lawrence Regional Library supervisor for guidance, and began collecting books. Judy Bowman, secretary of the group, had moved to the area from Mazon, Illinois (via Humbolt, Kansas), just a year before. When members of her quilting group back home e-mailed after the tornado asking what they could do to help, Judy told them that although emergency funding and insurance money would replace the building, they needed help replacing the books. Donations began arriving, the first from Mazon, and as word spread through the Internet and the media, people all over the country sent books or money or both.

Judy stored the first of these books in her basement. When word reached Marli Murphy of the *Kansas City Star,* she wrote about the library's plight in her Sunday column. An avalanche of books followed. Other newspaper stories spurred further action. Eventually more than twenty thousand books were collected. Volunteers from the Chamber of Commerce spent hours sorting and storing the books. Duplicates were sent to other libraries in the system, to the Veterans Home in Mt. Vernon and the library in Sarcoxie, Missouri. More than a thousand new paperbacks were sent overseas to the 203rd Battalion of the National Guard stationed in Iraq. Others were sent to a missionary project in Kwajalen in the Marshall Islands, and some found their way to schools. Even Santa got into the act, distributing books at Christ-

Curious George at a computer in the children's room.

mas, and bookshelves were set up at the bank and the beauty shop so that patrons would have books to read until the library could be rebuilt. Even after the request for materials stopped, donations kept coming. Schools and organizations across the country held book and penny drives. Authors donated signed copies of their books. On one day, Judy Bowman reports, deliveries arrived in trucks from FedEx, UPS, and the post office, as well as on a tractor-trailer truck carrying a pallet of books and two other trucks carrying smaller loads.

At the groundbreaking ceremony, what had been heartbreak became hope as six golden shovels broke ground for the new David H. Jones Library, aided by a second donation from Jones himself. A state-of-the-art facility would include a community meeting room as well as room for more than fourteen thousand new books, DVDs, and other items. When construction was completed in February of the next year, Jones cut the ribbon to open the new Pierce City Branch of the Barry-Lawrence Regional Library.

Mapping the Kindness of Strangers

The 1,300 residents of Pierce City will not soon forget the devastation of the tornado. Nor will they forget the goodwill of many people across the United States and overseas. Judy Bowman constructed a quilt-panel map bearing hundreds of buttons, each representing a shipment of books from twenty-one countries and forty-nine of the fifty U.S. states. She recalls a man from Paris, France, seeing her working on the quilt. He made a donation and then wondered just where she would put his button. Judy also put

together seven scrapbooks containing every letter received with a shipment of books. The map and scrapbooks are on display at the library. At the dedication ceremony, trustee Carol Hirsch dedicated the new library to the freedom of opportunity it offers every person seeking self-education. Added Missouri State Librarian Sara Parker, "The role of the library has remained the same—to take care of the small children and teach them how to read and love books; they take care of the information needs of adults, and they enrich our lives when we are seniors and have some leisure time to read."

Children's program at the library.

Johnson County Library

Central Resource Library
Overland Park, Kansas

Address:	9875 W. 87th Street
	Overland Park, KS 66212
Date Founded:	1952
Date Built:	1995
Architect:	Gould Evans Associates
Director:	Mona Carmack
Special Collections:	Assistive Technology Resources;
	Genealogy

In the nineteenth century Johnson County, Kansas, was an outpost on the Santa Fe Trail and home to Wild West legends such as Wild Bill Hickok before he was dealt his "dead man's hand." (The Central Resource Library is actually situated on a street that coincides with the original Trail.) Such legends of the Wild West quickly went the way of saloons and spittoons, but Johnson County remained a rural area until a post–World War II development boom. Today Johnson County is the most populous county in the state and a suburb of Kansas City.

Economic Engine

The Johnson County Library (JCL) system is comprised of thirteen facilities, one of which, the Central Resource Library, opened in 1995 and has won architectural and library awards. Constructed from an existing building (reducing costs considerably), the Central Resource Library has a soaring design that mirrors the county's role as the economic engine of Kansas.

The Johnson County Library is emblematic of community building in postwar suburban Kansas City. Although the county was nearly one hundred years old when the library system was founded in 1952, new residents moving into building-boom housing in Johnson County after World War II found little infrastructure awaiting them—including public libraries. However, community leaders successfully campaigned for a referendum, the library system was founded, and today it serves 380,000 people.

The Central Resource Library is one of the few physical symbols of the sprawling county's identity. (Johnson County contains twenty-one incorporated cities.) The library's branch facilities are focal points for neighborhood life, and the referendum for the Central Resource Library's funding in 1992 garnered

72 percent approval. Most residents know where the library facilities are, and 84 percent of library district residents are cardholders. The library ranks at or near the top of its population category (250,000) of the Hennen's American Public Library Rating Index (HAPLR Index), which measures factors such as funding, staffing, and circulation.

Building Community

Community building continues to be a focus of the library. An example is the library-sponsored Community Issues Forums, which provide residents with opportunities for dialogue about issues such as health care and prescription costs, regionalism and metropolitan urban planning, race relations, transporta-

Staff librarian helping library patrons.

Heart of the Community: **The Libraries We Love**

Exterior view of the library at night. Courtesy of Mike Sinclair, Gould Evans Associates.

tion, economic development, and education. These forums have earned such respect that a county commissioner asked the library to adapt a series of sessions for community vetting of a county strategic planning issue.

The library's collaborative approach has earned it "a place at the table" in the community, and solutions beneficial to all parties evolve. The library collaborates with other government, nonprofit, educational, and commercial institutions serving common clientele, especially the underserved. Most of the library's outreach services to those who cannot come to the library emanate from these collaborations. For example, the Johnson County Library is the hub for several content-based partnerships that distribute information via the Internet, including JoCoHealth.net, a partnership that offers Web-based health resources, including resources for the uninsured and underinsured and which is used primarily by professionals; JoCoFamily.net, a partnership with the courts and Corrections Department, among others, that offers resources to at-risk children and their families, including full explanations of the juvenile justice process; and JoCoBusiness.net, the Web face of JCL's business resources and business programming, which have been community assets, especially for small businesses, for twenty years.

The library has won national library awards for its public leadership, innovative services, literature programming for developmentally disabled adults; and literature programming for teens in the juvenile justice system.

Outreach librarians facilitate the two literature-based programs for youth in the justice system. Read to Succeed (RTL), serving residents of the Johnson County Juvenile Detention Center, is supported by a deposit collection. Changing Lives Through Literature (CLTL), a national alternative sentencing

program, consists of a series of literary discussions based on books that present problems, solutions, and consequences that allow the participants an objective view of familiar situations. Judges and probation officers are part of the CLTL discussions as well. The program has consistently lowered recidivism, compared to national averages—as participants see their own lives in the stories they read. As one teenager commented about the program, "It allows you to think in different ways and express your feelings." Corrections staff and judges deem the programs "very, very beneficial"—an evaluation that could no doubt be given for all the services the library provides to the Johnson County community.

Johnson County Library. Courtesy of Mike Sinclair, Gould Evans Associates.

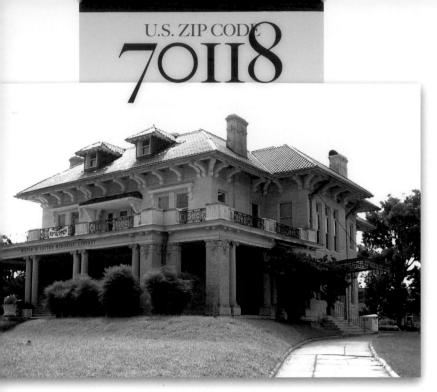

Milton H. Latter Memorial Library

◆

New Orleans Public Library
New Orleans, Louisiana

Address:	5120 St. Charles Avenue
	New Orleans, LA 70118
Date Founded:	1948
Date Built:	1907; 1985 (renovation)
Architect:	Favrot and Livaudais; Samuel
	Wilson Jr.
Director:	Missy Abbott

Before serving the uptown community of New Orleans, the stately, century-old mansion housing the Milton H. Latter Memorial Library was the home of a noted New Orleans family and later an elegant retreat for a silent screen star. It has stood the test of time, including the ravages of Hurricane Katrina.

❦ ❦

First, an Elegant Home

Set in an entire city square of ground, the mansion was built by Mr. and Mrs. Marks Isaacs, proprietors of a New Orleans department store that bore their name. The Isaacs commissioned architects Favrot and Livaudais to design the house. They hired George Glower to construct the mansion, which a Chicanos-based firm decorated. Local craftsmen, Petit and Boh, hand crafted the Flemish-style woodwork of the mantels. The mirrors and chandeliers were imported from Czechoslovakia. The mahogany for the paneling and staircase came from South America. Local artist John Geiser painted the Dutch murals and German mottoes in the Blue Room. The two front rooms have fresco ceilings signed "De Rudder, Paris 1858" which was imported from France. These ceilings originally graced a mansion in the French Quarter. The wall panels of cherry-red damask are from the original Louis XIV French Parlor.

In 1912 after the death of Marks Isaac, Frank B. Williams purchased the house. His son, Harry Williams, was a well known aviator. He was vice-president of the Weddell-Williams Air Service Corporation which builds many of the world's fastest planes. Harry Williams married the silent film star Marguerite Clark in 1918 at the height of her career. He brought his bride to New Orleans to live in the mansion his father bought, and she gave up her silent film career for marriage.

After Harry Williams's death in a plane crash, the mansion was sold to Robert S. Eddy, who filled the house with magnificent furnishings and oriental rugs. Owner of a number of racing

> When you read to a child, when you put a book in a child's hands, you are bringing that child news of the infinitely varied nature of life. You are an awakener.
>
> —Paula Fox

tracks, Robert Eddy and his wife held week-long parties for their friends during the racing season.

❦ ❦

The Latters Realize Their Dream

The Eddys sold the house to Mr. and Mrs. Harry Latter in 1948. Their dream was to transform the mansion into a public library as a memorial to their son, Milton, who lost his life at Okinawa during World War II. The Latters purchased the house for $100,000 and donated $25,000 for alterations. The city spent an additional $15,000 converting the mansion into a facility unique at that time in U.S. library history. The city formally dedicated the building on 31 October 1948.

❦ ❦

A Renewed Community Treasure

When the library was in need of extensive restoration and renovation in the early 1980s, the Latter family again rallied to help. Shirley Latter Kaufman donated a significant amount of money to begin renovations; funds raised in a city bond issue supplemented

The circulation desk at Milton H. Latter Memorial Library.

Kaufman's gift. After two years of restoration and redecoration, Latter Memorial Library reopened in July 1985.

The principal rooms of the library's first floor were restored as closely as possible to their original design and used as reading rooms—allowing library users to experience the atmosphere of the private, luxurious residence. The former service areas were converted into the a red, white, and blue children's reading room. The library's second floor contains the adult reading room and open stacks for some 50,000 volumes. To make the building handicapped accessible, an outside entry-ramp and an elevator were installed.

Storytime, Salons, and Surfing the Web

The library has hosted a popular children's story time and a book salon for grown-up readers. Community programs range from health information for seniors to a look at the racy side of New Orleans's colorful history. To supplement its five public access computer terminals for Internet use and word processing, the library has added Wi-Fi for laptop users.

Past and Present

Today Milton H. Latter Memorial Library exists not only as an information and education center, but as a reminder of more

elegant and gracious times on St. Charles Avenue. Although the library needed some roof repairs after Hurricane Katrina in 2005, it was spared the devastation faced by most of the other New Orleans library branches. (Eight of the twelve branches were completely ruined by wind, water, and mold.) The Latter Memorial Library's reopening in early 2006 was a welcome sign of recovery to its patrons.

The "Green Room," now used as a reading room.

Eureka Springs
Carnegie Public Library

◆

Eureka Springs, Arkansas

Address:	194 Spring Street
	Eureka Springs, AR 72632
Date Founded:	1910
Date Built:	1912
Architect:	George W. Helmuth
Director:	Jean Elderwind
Special Collections:	Local History

Even a town with healing springs needs a well of words.

Eureka Springs is named for the springs whose curative waters drew settlers in droves to the Ozark Mountain wilderness in the nineteenth century. In 1856 Dr. Alvah Jackson was the first white person to locate the springs. During the Civil War he founded a local hospital and treated patients with water from the springs. Later he sold the water as "Dr. Jackson's Eye Water." A friend of Jackson, J. B. Saunders, in 1879 claimed that the water had healed his crippling, neurological condition. He began promoting the city to people across the state, and Eureka Springs boomed. The town was established in 1879, and in just a few months the population had swelled to more than ten thousand. By 1881 the city was the fourth largest in Arkansas.

Interest in the springs slowed to a trickle as the public turned its attention toward science and technology and away from the healing power of the water. However, the city continues to draw

> When I was young, we couldn't afford much. But, my library card was my key to the world.
>
> —John Goodman

tourists to its arts and crafts boutiques, a Passion Play, Victorian homes, UFO conferences, motorcycle rallies, and literary festivals.

❦ ❦

A Library of Their Own

In 1912 a library building was completed after Andrew Carnegie, at the request of a visitor to the springs, donated $12,000 to build the structure, and R. C. Kerens, a Eureka Springs investor, donated the land. Listed on the National Register of Historic Places, the Classical Revival-style building is an architectural gem. Constructed of limestone from local quarries, the imposing structure has a grand stone staircase leading to the entrance, which is flanked by Doric columns.

In the early 1900s fewer than 7 percent of Arkansans had access to free public libraries. Through the perseverance of the local library board, headed by Benjamin J. Rosewater, the establishment of the Carnegie library made Eureka Springs one of the first communities in the state to offer its residents a library.

At first the Eureka Springs Carnegie Public Library was open for a mere three afternoons a week. It depended heavily on memberships and donations for income, but the Carnegie "open shelf" policy, whereby a patron could browse among open bookshelves rather than have to ask a clerk to fetch a book from closed stacks, drew more and more patrons. By 1921, the library was open six days a week. Progress was slow but steady. Library patrons and

Andrew Carnegie's portrait rests on the library fireplace, with others who helped bring the library to fruition. Courtesy of Doug Stowe.

Eureka Springs Library, constructed from locally quarried limestone. Courtesy of Doug Stowe.

other concerned residents held fundraisers, and the collection of library materials grew.

✿✿
Community Support and Service

The library became part of the Carroll County Library Department in 1956, allowing it to receive county tax funds for maintenance and operation. In 2002 county residents voted to double the amount of county property tax that supports this library and other libraries in the county. Although the building has remained relatively unchanged, with the increase in funding the library was able to add services and expand its hours. It now offers a Library Guild for grades five through twelve, preschool craft programs, and high-speed Internet access. It also frequently hosts local art shows, a foreign film series, and a summer film series for children. The Wednesday Morning Story Hour is now in its twenty-fifth year.

Through the years, many noted writers have used the library—including Eureka Springs resident Irene Castle (author and part of the immortal dance team, Vernon and Irene Castle), and more recently, Ellen Gilchrist, Donald Harington, and Crescent Dragonwagon.

✿✿
Expanding Horizons

Today, although the city's population has declined to approximately 1,900, the library is still a vital part of the community.

With a circulation of well over 53,000 and a host of scheduled lectures, programs, and classes, the staff and volunteers of the library stay busy. The library's mission statement says much about the library's role in the community: "To build strong communities by promoting the joy of reading, the love of knowledge, and the excitement of discovery through materials, personal services, programs, and equipment equally accessible to all."

The library's public service desk. Courtesy of Doug Stowe.

Heart of the Community: **The Libraries We Love**

Grace M. Pickens
Public Library

◆

Holdenville, Oklahoma

Address: 209 E. 9th Street
Holdenville, OK 74848
Date Founded: 1901
Date Built: 1934; 1985 (renovation)
Architect: Unknown
Director: Fran Cook

It took many a slice of pie, but it wasn't a piece of cake.

In 1901 the Ladies of the Twentieth Century Club wanted to establish a library for Holdenville. Club members held fundraising events, such as a book reception at the opera house, Latin classes, and pie suppers. The women also collected one hundred books and a used globe, and opened the library in a room above the Taylor and Hamilton Building. In 1902, the library moved into two rooms above the law office of Frank L. Warren, who offered the space rent free. However, by 1929 the small library, now located at City Hall, had become cramped, and the Ladies of the Twentieth Century Club sought a larger space and money to fund it. A resolution to provide a tax fund for the library's first year was approved. Mayor Fred Treadwell appointed a library board, and the federal Works Progress Administration began construction of the library building on land on the corner of Oak and 9th Streets donated by Judge and Mrs. Warren. Rock for the building came from the old city water works, and the water tower that stood on the land was donated to nearby Atoka.

☆ ☆

By the Grace of Pickens

The library served the city from 1934 until 1985, when space again became tight. A fund drive raised $62,000, which was matched by a grant from T. Boone Pickens Jr. He also set up a twenty-year trust fund for the library, the interest of which could be spent on books. Although actor Clu Gulager was born there in 1928, and baseball pitcher Dizzy Dean was another well-known resident, Pickens is perhaps Holdenville's most influential native. His father leased oil and mineral rights in Texas. T. Boone Jr. made his money in oil, too, and by 1981 his company, Mesa Oil, had become one of the largest independent oil companies in the world. The library is named for his mother, Grace M. Pickens, who taught school in Holdenville and ran the Office of Price Administration during World War II, rationing gasoline and other goods for four counties.

Later more money was needed to upgrade the collections, bring the library into the technological age, and update the building to code. Grant after grant—thirteen in all—was applied for and awarded for a total of more than $1 million. The library now had a parking lot, a handicapped ramp, and sidewalks.

☆ ☆

Hot Air, Cold Cash

Today the library has a collection of 22,000 books, 1,000 videos, and 260 audio cassettes. At least thirty thousand people visit each

Portrait of Grace M. Pickens.

Heart of the Community: **The Libraries We Love**

PUBLIC LIBRARY
A D 1934
ERECTED UNDER
PRESIDENT ROOSEVELT'S
RECOVERY PROGRAM
AND WITH GIFTS FROM THE
CITIZENS OF HOLDENVILLE

Cornerstone on the Grace M. Pickens Public Library.

Patrons in the computer area.

since 2000. The library has also launched a recycling/fundraising program for empty inkjet cartridges that can be recycled and re-manufactured. The library's summer reading program receives between two dollars and twelve dollars for each cartridge and one dollar for each cell phone turned in.

The Grace M. Pickens Public Library has become what the Ladies of the Twentieth Century Club must have envisioned more than a hundred years ago: a place where people can expand their horizons into the twenty-first century and beyond.

year, and twenty thousand articles are circulated. The library provides a public computer area, a meeting room, a youth section, a children's department, and a public work area. The library sponsors a summer reading program and the Sonic Junior Balloonist Program, a two-hour workshop for ten- to fourteen-year-olds that teaches them history, math, and science while they learn to build and fly model hot air balloons. The program has provided free educational workshops in Oklahoma, Texas, and Kansas

The richest person in the world—
in fact, all the riches in the world—
couldn't provide you with anything like
the endless, incredible loot available
at your local library. You can measure
the awareness, the breadth and the
wisdom of a civilization, a nation,
a people by the priority given to
preserving these repositories of all that
we are, all that we were, or will be.

—Malcolm Forbes

76443

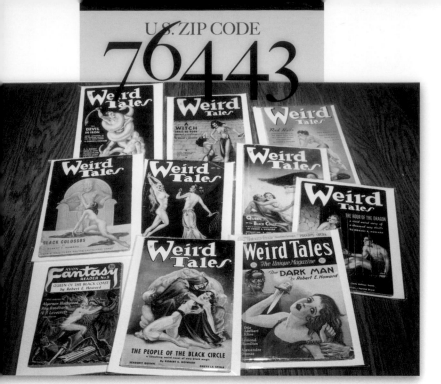

Cross Plains Public Library

◆

Cross Plains, Texas

Address: 149 Main Street
Cross Plains, TX 76443
Date Founded: 1979
Date Built: 1912
Architect: Unknown
Director: Cherry Shults
Special Collections: Robert E. Howard Collection

> ## Defend your local library as if your freedom depended on it.
> —John Jakes

In a small town in Texas the librarian meets the Barbarian. The Cross Plains Public Library houses a collection of original manuscripts written by native son, Robert E. Howard, creator of Conan the Barbarian and many other fictional characters. Securing that collection is not the little library's biggest achievement, however. Unlike most libraries in the United States, the Cross Plains library is not owned by a local government entity, nor was it built with funding by industrialist and philanthropist Andrew Carnegie. Instead, the library is owned and operated by the Friends of the Cross Plains Library, a private, nonprofit corporation. The city and county provide only about 20 percent of the annual budget, and members of the community, former residents, and local businesses donate the remainder.

The Cross Plains Public Library is located in the smallest of the three towns in Callahan County, but it is the largest library in the county, the only one that is open every weekday, and also draws patrons from three neighboring counties. Cross Plains has a population of fewer than 1,100, and the county population is about 12,500. In an area where jobs are scarce and the economy has been in a slump since the local oil boom ended in the 1930s, the Friends and volunteers have worked to make the library a center of learning for all.

Making Cross Plains a Better Place to Live

In March 1978 the residents of Cross Plains held a town hall meeting to decide how to make Cross Plains a better place to live. One suggestion was to create a library. Volunteers formed the Friends group and spent weeks soliciting financial support from Cross Plains school alumni, current and former residents, the city of Cross Plains, and Callahan County. In October of 1978 the Friends were able to purchase a building. Volunteers helped renovate the building, repair the leaky roof, build shelves, and

provide the necessary furnishings. Two volunteers attended a workshop on how to manage a library, individuals and publishing houses donated books to fill those wide, open spaces, and in February 1979 (just eleven months after the idea was proposed), the library opened. Two years later the Cross Plains Public Library became a member of the Big Country Library System, which provides many educational benefits as well as funds for the purchase of books.

Promoting Learning and Culture

Open Monday through Friday from 1 to 5 P.M. with a collection of thirteen thousand books, the library promotes learning and culture in the local community. Grants were obtained to set up a computer system for automating inventory, to provide an on-line catalog accessible through the library's website, and to provide three Internet-capable computers for public use. No fees are charged for any services except printing and photocopying, and there is no geographic restriction on who can use the library and check out materials.

The library has several programs to make learning fun for children—all staffed by volunteers. About twenty years ago volunteers developed a preschool program called "LAP" (Learn About . . . Program) to help children ages three through five learn skills they will need to be ready for kindergarten. Recently added is a Lapsit program for children to age three; parents attend with their children and learn how to encourage early brain development with music, finger play, and stories with colorful

Cross Plains Library's preserved 1912 storefront. Courtesy of Ginny Hoskins.

pictures. In summer the reading program, the Read-Aloud Café, provides lunch, stories read aloud, and related learning activities for primary and elementary students. For the last seven years K–12 students have participated in a writing contest that the library sponsors.

Three times a year the Friends bring a regionally known author to speak at Meet the Author evening. Attendance varies from 40 to 150 (in a town with a population of fewer than 1,100). The library is working on an Oral History project, recording interviews with long-time residents and making the materials available for researchers—or those who just like to read about the "old days." The materials are also stored at Texas Tech University as part of its Southwest Collection. The library has a genealogy group, and its members are raising funds to purchase the archives of the local newspaper on microfilm and to purchase a microfilm reader and computer dedicated to genealogical research. Classes in basic computer skills are offered on an as-needed basis, and the library provides space for Central Texas Opportunities to offer GED classes.

Thanks to a gift from the heirs of Clara Nell Spencer, a local teacher, the library has in its collection the complete Newbery and Caldecott award-winning books, updated annually by Mrs. Spencer's heirs. Because one of her children died of polio, her heirs asked that the library create a display covering the history of the polio epidemic in the area, and volunteers have gathered information and photographs about the epidemic. A few years ago the Friends purchased the building next door to the library, as well as the vacant lot adjoining it. The lot has been developed into a small park, and the Friends are raising funds to renovate the building for the new children's library. When that is done, there will be an area for the display on the polio epidemic.

The Howard Legacy

Of special note is the Howard collection, including some of his original manuscripts, many books (including several first editions), numerous biographical works, and publications about Howard's writings. Another local nonprofit organization, Project Pride, purchased and restored the Howard home, and the library works with them to sponsor Howard Days every June. Serious scholars come from around the world to visit the Howard House Museum and to view and research the library's collection of manuscripts, books, and comics.

Robert E. Howard first editions. Courtesy of Ginny Hoskins.

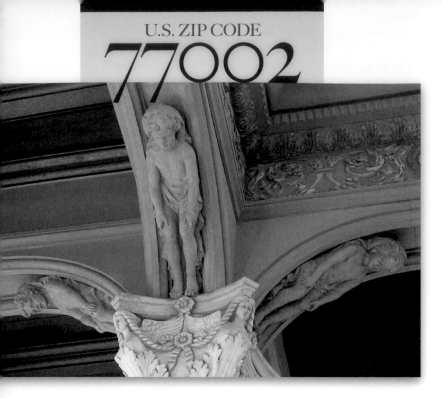

Houston
Public Library
◆
Julia Ideson Building
Houston, Texas

Address:	500 McKinney
	Houston, TX 77002
Date Founded:	1854
Date Built:	1926
Architect:	Cram and Ferguson
Director:	Rhea Brown Lawson
Special Collections:	Local and State History

In 1897 it was no place for a lady. A half-century later it was named after one.

In 1854 the Houston Lyceum was founded to instill culture among community members. It was a men-only organization that sponsored lectures and debates, collected dues and donations. Senator Sam Houston was one of the many who donated books. By 1878 the lyceum had thirteen hundred volumes and a dozen magazine subscriptions in its collection. In 1884 the lyceum was designated a depository for U.S. government documents, and in 1887 women were allowed to become members.

🐿 🐿
From Lyceum to Library

After women began to swell its numbers, the lyceum in 1897 moved its collection to three rooms on the fourth floor of the

Photo of Julia Ideson at her desk.

Mason Building on Main Street. One reason for the move was because the previous location—in the Market House at the corner of Travis and Congress—was considered "not a suitable place for a lady to venture unescorted." In 1898 the city of Houston appropriated $2,400 a year toward the establishment of a central library. The Woman's Club asked Andrew Carnegie for his help, and with his donation of $50,000 and the city's appropriation, the Carnegie Library was constructed, opening to the public in 1904. Built in the Italian Renaissance style, the two-story building had columns fronting an elaborate entrance. Julia Ideson, a member of the first library science class offered at the University of Texas, was chosen as librarian. She held that position for forty-two years, during which she was responsible in large part for the expansion of the library.

🐿 🐿
From a Central Library to a Complex

By 1922 the city had outgrown the Carnegie Library. Residents approved a $200,000 bond issue and planned a new library building. They commissioned Architect Ralph Adams Cram of the Boston firm of Cram and Ferguson. William Ward Watkin and Louis Glover of Houston were appointed associate architects. Cram, who had just returned from a trip to Spain, had fallen in love with Spanish Renaissance architecture, and when the contract for the new library was offered, he proposed a building in that style. Moreover, the city leaders recognized a connection between that style and the colonial past of Texas. Julia Ideson worked closely with the architects, helping to plan an interior that would be not only equal in beauty to the exterior but also be functional. She envisioned three floors with a fluid, open plan that would allow for rearrangements as the library grew and changed.

In 1926 the three-story library was completed. Constructed of concrete and buff-colored brick, with marble columns and arched windows, its L shape reflected the Spanish influence. The top of the main building had wrought iron gratings and red tiles. All

The Julia Ideson Building was designated a City of Houston Historic Landmark in 2004.

rooms had ample natural light and proper air circulation. The floor plan included a central lobby, the Children's Room and Story Hour Room, the Lecture Room with seating for three hundred, the Reading Room, the Club Room designed for meetings of up to 125 people, the Periodical Room, Reference Room, and a central hall in the rotunda on the second floor where patrons checked out books or looked up materials in the card catalog. The basement provided storage, whereas the second floor was given over entirely to books. The third floor held administrative offices, and a mezzanine between the two floors held the librarian's offices. Marble columns, oak rafters and paneling, and Spanish blue tiles gave the building a feeling of elegance. Floors were finished in red quarry tile or cork tile, terraza, or wood. Clerestory windows bathed the rotunda in light. Oak reading tables were made to look like refectory tables. Renaissance carvings crowned open bookcases. The new library reflected Julia Ideson's vision: "It is not enough to be functional; a library must offer delight to the eye."

In 1951 the building that Ideson helped establish was named after her. The Julia Ideson Building served as Houston's public library for fifty years. As the city continued to grow, the library's collection grew with it, and eventually a new library, one more architecturally modern, was needed. In 1976 the Jesse H. Jones Building was built across the courtyard from the Julia Ideson Building. Thirty years later that building, too, is scheduled for remodeling, an undertaking that will add 34,000 square feet of space to the library, update it technologically, and reorganize the collection for easier accessibility.

In 1977 the building was entered in the National Register of Historic Places of the U.S. Department of Interior. That same year, a restoration effort was undertaken. When the building reopened in 1979, it became the location for the Texas Room, a collection of local and Texas history, including photographs, archival material, and cultural history items, and the Houston Metropolitan Research Center, where Houston's history is documented and made available to researchers. The Julia Ideson Building was designated as a City of Houston Historic Landmark in 2004.

Today the Houston Public Library circulates almost six million items a year from its central library and branches.

Interior of the library.

Round Rock Public Library

◆

Round Rock, Texas

Address: 216 East Main Street
                        Round Rock, TX 78664
Date Founded: 1960s
Date Built: 1980; 1999 (expansion)
Architect: Ray Gill; John Moman
Director: Dale Ricklefs
Special Collections: Local History and Genealogy

"How do you eat an elephant?"

That's the riddle that an employee posed to Sarah Samson, reference services manager of the Round Rock Public Library, when Samson told the employee that she wanted to help the library of Gretna, Louisiana, rebuild and reopen after it was destroyed by Hurricane Katrina.

Front view of the library.

"I told her I wanted to help, but I just wasn't sure how one librarian in Round Rock, Texas, could help make a difference," Samson recalled. "The task seemed overwhelming.

However, the employee supplied the answer to the riddle.

Question: "How do you eat an elephant?"

Answer: "One bite at a time."

"When you use the elephant analogy," Samson said, "anything is possible."

A friend asked Samson recently, "Why are you raising money to help their library? Why don't you raise money for the Round Rock Library?"

Samson answered, "Round Rock has a library, it has books, librarians, many computers, CDs, movies, a roof, and two stories. We have a library. The people in Gretna have no library."

The Round Rock library's goal was to raise $5,000. To help raise the money, the library raffled off two quilts made by the staff and volunteers. The money will be used to help pay for a $22 million library to replace the Gretna library and the library in neighboring Terrytown.

※ ※

Expanding Population =
Library Expansion

The Round Rock library began in the early 1960s when a group of private residents created the city's first public library board. The board bought the old Ford dealer's building on East Main Street, where the present library stands. The old showroom provided space but needed to be remodeled. The project took twenty months, the work performed by students of a building and trades class from Round Rock High School and local craftsmen.

That building was replaced in 1980, and explosive population growth—going from 2,700 residents in 1970 to a current 85,000—fueled the need for library expansion. (Located fifteen miles north of Austin, Round Rock is home to Dell Inc.,

The volunteer fire department bell by the front door.

among other leading companies.) In 1996 voters passed a $3.5 million bond issue to expand the library from 11,000 to 43,000 square feet. The new building opened in 1999. It has four public meeting rooms, four private study rooms, twenty-three Internet computers for adults, and ten Internet computers with filters for children. Oh, and one python. Rocksssanne No Feet, the library's pet, is seven years old and four feet long.

As a child I was a very shy little blonde kid that didn't speak at all to anybody . . . And what was wonderful about the library was that you didn't have to say a word. So it was my oasis. And you didn't have to ask for things in full sentences. You could just point to a shelf and say, "18th century dolls," and the librarians would lead you there. It was amazing. I felt like a queen.

—Adrienne Yorinks

One of the handmade quilts created for the raffle to benefit the Gretna Public Library Katrina effort.

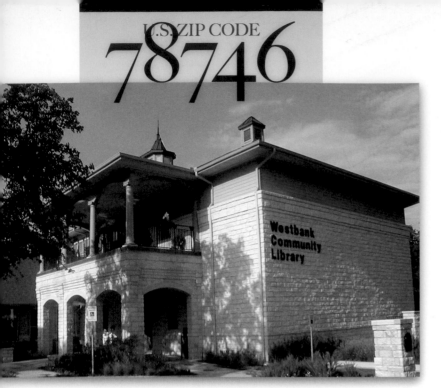

Westbank Community Library

Austin, Texas

Address:	1309 Westbank Drive
	Austin, TX 78746
Date Founded:	1983
Date Built:	1989
Architect:	G. Tim Aynesworth
Director:	Beth Wheeler Fox

In 1983 Texas had no library districts. It was with Texas grit that Doris Walcutt, Eleanor Drake, and sixty-five Austin residents created a library for the Westbank area. Relying on donations and volunteers to stay open, the Westbank Community Library was first located in Texas Commerce Bank in southwest Austin. With the advice, support, and active encouragement of library leaders and local legislators, the Westbank Community Library led the charge in 1998 to pass legislation to create their own library district (and, to date, a dozen others) in Texas. Stable funding was at last guaranteed; the current library was built and dedicated in 1989.

> Libraries are community treasure chests, loaded with a wealth of information available to everyone equally, and the key to that treasure chest is the library card.
>
> —Laura Bush

Potluck and Chocolate

Westbank Community Library has more than a half-million items in circulation. More than 250,000 people use the 15,640-square-foot facility each year. It offers twenty-five computer terminals for public use, more than four thousand video and audio tapes, and 150 magazine and newspaper subscriptions. The library also has one of the most successful volunteer programs in the area: More than one hundred volunteers a week process books, keep the shelves organized, and operate the circulation desk. The library makes sure that the volunteers know how much they are appreciated with yearly potluck dinners, training luncheons, and a steady supply of chocolate. Many volunteers are teens who serve after school, on weekends, and during their summer vacations. They earn credit hours toward their school's community service requirements as they learn how important the library is to their community and how important they are to it.

Westbank Community Library's goal has always been to serve every sector of the community. It offers a summer reading program that begins with the Kick-Off Party, which more than a thousand people attend on a Saturday to enjoy live musical performances, crafts, face painting, and organized games. During June and July there are weekly story times for the younger set,

craft and science activities, special performances, and a kids' book group, all culminating in an end-of-program celebration that includes a walk down a red carpet, a certificate, and a prize. For teens there are special book groups, Game Day, and Library Lock-In featuring pizza and a scavenger hunt. Even adults have their own Raffle Readers program, in which each book they read becomes an entry in a prize drawing. As a result of these efforts, there is increased interest in reading as well as in the library.

Partnering with the Community

In addition to entertainment, the library is keen on education. It has established a working relationship with area schools, sponsoring a brunch in the autumn for teachers, another in the spring for local school librarians, and a special event for booster club presidents. The library's collection is designed in part to enrich the schools' curriculum and to be a source of homework help. Research databases and help from a library technician in how to use them are available. After-hours database training sessions are held for home educators and other groups.

The library also serves as a community center. Young children

Mark Twain sculpture by Scott Sustek, presented by the Friends of the Library as a twentieth anniversary gift in 2004.

and mothers meet for morning story hour. Teens meet to study after school. Adults use the upstairs meeting rooms for daytime group meetings; tutors and their students use them in the evening. The Teen Advisory Committee meets at least four times a year to suggest programs, recommend purchases, and give input on other library matters. The committee has helped to sponsor Teen Read Week, which includes guest speakers, informal meetings with teens who like to write, and a creative group activity. The library holds an annual craft sale, and there's even a space where people learning to speak English can meet and converse. Twice a year the library hosts library districts meetings, at which training and networking opportunities are made available to fledgling districts in the state.

Thousands of books are donated to the library each year—many are redistributed to library branches, non-profit organizations, and schools. Each week a box of books is donated to the Rotary Literacy Reach Out and Read Program, which delivers books to clinics serving low-income families. Each child receives a book and a "prescription for reading." The library also participates in the American Library Association's Adopt a Library Program to help rebuild a Gulf Coast public library after Hurricane Katrina.

❧ ❧

Just Rewards

Westbank Community Library was named a Great American Public Library by the Hennen American

Public Library ratings in 1999. The Texas Municipal Director's Association has honored the library with a statewide Achievement of Excellence Award, and Library Director Beth Wheeler was honored by the Texas Library Association as the 2006 Librarian of the Year.

The library's dream of better serving the growing western portion of their district has become a reality with the one-million-dollar donation of ten acres of land. The design phase for a branch library began in 2006.

Teens show off their favorite reads at the Teen Lock-In.

I had always imagined paradise as a kind of library.

Jorge Luis Borges

Denver Public Library

Central Library
Denver, Colorado

Address:	10 W. 14th Avenue Parkway Denver, CO 80204
Date Founded:	1889
Date Built:	1910; 1956; 1995
Architect:	Fisher & Fisher/Burnham Hoyt (1956); Michael Graves and Klipp Colussy Jenks DuBois (1995)
Director:	Shirley Amore
Special Collections:	Western History Collection

The development of the Denver Public Library has been as dramatic as that of the West itself: from a "center of public happiness" in a wing of the Denver High School in 1889, to a building designed like a Greek temple and funded by industrialist and philanthropist Andrew Carnegie, to a second structure expected to house the library for no more than a decade, to the current 540,000-square-foot building (the largest library between Los Angeles and Chicago).

Keeping Up with the Times

City Librarian John Cotton Dana is credited with opening the city's first library in a wing of the Denver High School in 1889. In 1910 the city, using funding provided by Carnegie, built an elegant building in downtown's Civic Center. There Dana created the first children's library by cutting down the legs of adult-sized tables and chairs to tot height. Although popular fiction was a controversial issue in those days, the library provided such reading material at the request of its patrons.

The "Old Main" library served downtown for forty-five years, but the building had insufficient space for the library's growing collection. The firm of Fisher & Fisher/Burnham Hoyt was hired to design a second structure, and in 1956 the new library building was opened. However, even though the space was double that of the Carnegie building, it was not enough to serve the burgeoning population. The city experienced great growth during the 1950s and 1970s. By the late 1980s the library and several of its branches had outgrown their spaces. Three-quarters of the Central Library's books and materials languished in basements and warehouses. Nor were any of the buildings adaptable to the rapidly expanding technology of the Information Age. In 1990 Denver voters approved a $91.6 million bond issue to build a new central library as well as to expand current branch library buildings or construct new ones. Architect Michael Graves and the Denver firm of Klipp Colussy Jenks DuBois were hired, and in 1995 the new Central Library opened.

Past and Present

Denver, the capital of Colorado, is located on the high plains at the eastern foot of the Rocky Mountains. Established in 1858 by a party of gold prospectors, it was named after James W. Denver, then governor of Kansas territory, of which eastern Colorado was then a part. The Colorado Territory was established in 1861, and

Schlessman Hall.

The Central Library opened in 1995 to better serve Denver's burgeoning population.

> A great library contains the
> diary of the human race.
> —George Mercer Dawson

Denver, with its breweries, bakeries, and meat-processing plants, emerged as a hub for agricultural products and as a manufacturing hub for ranch equipment, barbed wire, seed, and feed. By 1890 it had a population of 106,713—plenty of folks to require the services of a good library.

Today the city considers the library to be one of its notable institutions, along with the Denver Museum of Nature & Science, the Colorado History Museum, the Denver Art Museum, the Denver Center for the Performing Arts, and the U.S. Mint. The library, a recipient of the 2001 Award of Excellence for Library Architecture, houses a world-renowned western history collection, a federal deposit library, and has a circulation of nine million items a year. The library has entered the technological age with more than one hundred computers, its own website, and support for online transactions. It houses two art galleries visited by people from not only the metropolitan area, but also the state and the rest of the country. One gallery holds a collection of western art; the other holds special exhibits, including those of both national and local artists. Known for its model Children's Library, celebrated for its collection of American West memorabilia as well as historic books and photographs, the library also contains papers and photographs of the 10th Mountain Division, which trained in the Colorado Rockies as preparation for fighting in the Alps during World War II.

The library also offers more than 100,000 photographs online, including rare pictures of Native Americans and early pioneers. The Library of Congress in Washington, D.C., includes many of these photos in its American Memory Project.

Heart of the Community

Service to its public has always been the library's main mission. To this end it has established a number of electronic services, including remote access to a number of subscription databases, e-books, and audio e-books. An entire section of the library, El Centro, is devoted to the non-English-speaking population. It contains popular Spanish-language materials as well as services for recent immigrants. The Central Library also supports branch libraries with staff and materials for non-English-speaking patrons.

In 2005 the library conducted a community poll to help it better understand the needs of Denver's residents. The poll resulted in improved services for patrons seeking information and researchers requiring primary sources and provided as well improved access to current bestsellers and children's literature. In-depth reference hotlines and deliverable collections are also available to any branch library. In addition to its collection of materials, the Central Library is a center for cultural programming, hosting a series of thematically interrelated programs for adults known as "Fresh City Life."

More than a million people use the Central Library annually. More than 72 percent of Denver's residents hold library cards and check out more than nine million items a year.

Boulder
Public Library

◆

Boulder, Colorado

Address:	1000 Canyon Boulevard
	Boulder, CO 80302
Date Founded:	1895
Date Built:	1906; 1961; 1974; 1992
Architect:	Midyette/Seieroe/Hartronft (1992)
Director:	Liz Abbott
Special Collections:	Local History

First there was "gold in them there hills," and then there was a world of words in them there books: People could read romance and adventure and mystery and learn history and geography and, yes, proper grammar.

In 1895, a scant thirty-seven years after the first gold prospector appeared on Arapaho lands at the foothills of the Rockies, the women's groups of Boulder consolidated into a corporation, issued shares of stock at ten dollars each, established a $600 yearly budget for books and supplies, and opened a small reading room stocked with two hundred books. Today the Boulder Public Library serves a diverse population of more than one hundred thousand with a main library, three branches, free cultural programs, wireless Internet access, and multicultural outreach programs.

Past

Boulder was incorporated as Boulder City in 1873, and Colorado achieved statehood in 1876, the same year the University of Colorado was established. By 1898 the library women were seeking money from the city council to help them increase the reading room's collection. When a patron complained about having to pay to use the room, the council promised ongoing support and declared the reading room to be the new Boulder Public Library, accessible to all city residents. In 1906 the city applied for and received a Carnegie grant and purchased land downtown for a freestanding library building. The Carnegie Library served the city until 1961, when the building that is now the north wing of the main library was constructed. Today the Carnegie building houses historic documents and photos of Boulder.

Present

The new library on Canyon Boulevard had 38,000 square feet of space. In 1992 renovations increased that space to more than 92,000 square feet, making possible a 208-seat auditorium for films, concerts, and plays. A partial atrium and stepped clerestory windows allow maximum daylight to illuminate the reading and stack areas of both the first and second floors. Energy-efficient lighting and an evaporative cooling system keep maintenance costs down. To meet patrons' technological needs, the library has wireless Internet access, electronic reference resources, Internet partnerships with other libraries, and other digitized resources.

The library also sponsors free cultural programming, hold-

Night shot of the library exterior. Courtesy of Andrew Kramer.

The Central Library opened in 1995 to better serve Denver's burgeoning population.

> ### A great library contains the diary of the human race.
>
> —George Mercer Dawson

Denver, with its breweries, bakeries, and meat-processing plants, emerged as a hub for agricultural products and as a manufacturing hub for ranch equipment, barbed wire, seed, and feed. By 1890 it had a population of 106,713—plenty of folks to require the services of a good library.

Today the city considers the library to be one of its notable institutions, along with the Denver Museum of Nature & Science, the Colorado History Museum, the Denver Art Museum, the Denver Center for the Performing Arts, and the U.S. Mint. The library, a recipient of the 2001 Award of Excellence for Library Architecture, houses a world-renowned western history collection, a federal deposit library, and has a circulation of nine million items a year. The library has entered the technological age with more than one hundred computers, its own website, and support for online transactions. It houses two art galleries visited by people from not only the metropolitan area, but also the state and the rest of the country. One gallery holds a collection of western art; the other holds special exhibits, including those of both national and local artists. Known for its model Children's Library, celebrated for its collection of American West memorabilia as well as historic books and photographs, the library also contains papers and photographs of the 10th Mountain Division, which trained in the Colorado Rockies as preparation for fighting in the Alps during World War II.

The library also offers more than 100,000 photographs online, including rare pictures of Native Americans and early pioneers. The Library of Congress in Washington, D.C., includes many of these photos in its American Memory Project.

Heart of the Community

Service to its public has always been the library's main mission. To this end it has established a number of electronic services, including remote access to a number of subscription databases, e-books, and audio e-books. An entire section of the library, El Centro, is devoted to the non-English-speaking population. It contains popular Spanish-language materials as well as services for recent immigrants. The Central Library also supports branch libraries with staff and materials for non-English-speaking patrons.

In 2005 the library conducted a community poll to help it better understand the needs of Denver's residents. The poll resulted in improved services for patrons seeking information and researchers requiring primary sources and provided as well improved access to current bestsellers and children's literature. In-depth reference hotlines and deliverable collections are also available to any branch library. In addition to its collection of materials, the Central Library is a center for cultural programming, hosting a series of thematically interrelated programs for adults known as "Fresh City Life."

More than a million people use the Central Library annually. More than 72 percent of Denver's residents hold library cards and check out more than nine million items a year.

Boulder
Public Library

◆

Boulder, Colorado

Address:	1000 Canyon Boulevard
	Boulder, CO 80302
Date Founded:	1895
Date Built:	1906; 1961; 1974; 1992
Architect:	Midyette/Seieroe/Hartronft (1992)
Director:	Liz Abbott
Special Collections:	Local History

First there was "gold in them there hills," and then there was a world of words in them there books: People could read romance and adventure and mystery and learn history and geography and, yes, proper grammar.

In 1895, a scant thirty-seven years after the first gold prospector appeared on Arapaho lands at the foothills of the Rockies, the women's groups of Boulder consolidated into a corporation, issued shares of stock at ten dollars each, established a $600 yearly budget for books and supplies, and opened a small reading room stocked with two hundred books. Today the Boulder Public Library serves a diverse population of more than one hundred thousand with a main library, three branches, free cultural programs, wireless Internet access, and multicultural outreach programs.

🐿 🐿
Past

Boulder was incorporated as Boulder City in 1873, and Colorado achieved statehood in 1876, the same year the University of Colorado was established. By 1898 the library women were seeking money from the city council to help them increase the reading room's collection. When a patron complained about having to pay to use the room, the council promised ongoing support and declared the reading room to be the new Boulder Public Library, accessible to all city residents. In 1906 the city applied for and received a Carnegie grant and purchased land downtown for a freestanding library building. The Carnegie Library served the city until 1961, when the building that is now the north wing of the main library was constructed. Today the Carnegie building houses historic documents and photos of Boulder.

🐿 🐿
Present

The new library on Canyon Boulevard had 38,000 square feet of space. In 1992 renovations increased that space to more than 92,000 square feet, making possible a 208-seat auditorium for films, concerts, and plays. A partial atrium and stepped clerestory windows allow maximum daylight to illuminate the reading and stack areas of both the first and second floors. Energy-efficient lighting and an evaporative cooling system keep maintenance costs down. To meet patrons' technological needs, the library has wireless Internet access, electronic reference resources, Internet partnerships with other libraries, and other digitized resources.

The library also sponsors free cultural programming, hold-

Night shot of the library exterior. Courtesy of Andrew Kramer.

Second floor, looking through to Boulder Creek. Courtesy of Andrew Kramer

ing forty concerts a year, showing films on the big screen in the Canyon Theater, and hosting rotating art exhibits in the Canyon Gallery. The events are paid for by grants from the Boulder Public Library Foundation, making admission almost always free. Support services include the Grillo Health Information Center. Staff and trained volunteers answer health questions or direct patrons to reference materials, and the center hosts talks by medical experts. All Boulder Public Library cardholders have access through a unified catalog called "Prospector" to materials in academic, public, and special libraries located in Colorado and Wyoming. The Boulder Arts Resource Online lets patrons access information and grant forms from the Boulder Arts Commission.

To promote reading and discussion, groups meet at the library to discuss everything from Arabic literature to women of the West, from physics and metaphysics and cosmology to the United Nations and international affairs. In the Conversations in English group people learning English can hone their language skills, and in another group people learning Spanish can practice with a Spanish-speaking volunteer. The Marcelee Gralapp Children's Library draws youngsters in past two murals painted by artist Mario Miguel Echevarria, and Teen Space features programs for young people.

Bhutanese monks create a sand mandala in the Canyon Gallery.

The Braille Computer Center offers help to the sight-impaired with technologies such as a magnification reader, and a TTY telephone typewriter provides help for the hearing impaired. The library operates a homebound delivery program, offers ESL and citizenship classes, and holds workshops in computer use.

To pursue its mission to assist in the personal development of its patrons, the Boulder Public Library also offers BoulderReads!, a free one-on-one tutoring program for adults. With a goal of helping people discover the power and the joy of reading, the program teaches adult learners to master basic life skills such as preparing for their driver's license test, passing their citizenship test, assisting their children with homework, or improving their employability.

Future

To meet the needs of Boulder's highly educated and an increasingly diverse population, the library continues to develop ways to provide all members of the community with access to electronic information resources, and with training in how to use these tools. The library is also committed to presenting Boulder's arts-conscious community with first-rate programming in culture and the arts.

Orem Public Library
Orem, Utah

Address: 58 N. State Street
Orem, UT 84057
Date Founded: 1939
Date Built: 1970; 1995 (addition)
Architect: Dell Ashworth; Ken Pollard
Director: Louise Wallace
Special Collections: Storytelling; Folktales; Jazz; Film

Once upon a time the Orem Public Library occupied a basement, where volunteers on the home front wrapped bandages during World War II. Today the library is located above ground, in the light, with a children's wing where stories are told in which characters live happily ever after.

WPA Project

Orem was founded in 1919 as a small community of about 150 farming families. When the Orem Public Library was established in 1939, it immediately became a hub for the community. Built by the federal Work Projects Administration (WPA), the library opened with books that were donated by local families or discarded from other libraries. The library was located in the basement of the old Stratton Home, the site of the city's first town hall. Funds to hire a librarian for the first few months were donated anonymously by an Orem citizen, and civic clubs raised money to purchase books.

The library was used during World War II as a rationing office and a place where volunteers could help the war effort by rolling bandages. In 1948 the City Council levied for library services. In 1970 the library moved to its current home in a new city center located at the site of the original town hall. The 16,000 square feet of space on the main floor and mezzanine housed the entire collection. The basement was used during the next few years as collection size and circulation grew.

Stories as Windows to the Imagination

By the early 1990s more space was desperately needed. In 1990, to raise funds for a children's wing, the Friends of the Orem Library began the Timpanogos Storytelling Festival in the backyard of chairperson Karen Ashton. The children's wing addition would move the children's collection out of the basement and into an open space where the imagination has no limits. The success of the festival, named for nearby Mount Timpanogos, allowed for a 1993 groundbreaking in which hundreds of children participated with their shovels, spoons, spades, and Tonka trucks. The festival, meanwhile, has blossomed into an annual community event that celebrates the art of storytelling with Orem families as well as visitors from across the nation. The Timpanogos Storytelling Festival is now the third largest storytelling festival in the nation, with more than twenty-three thousand people attending events held at its new permanent home, the forty-four acre Mount Timpanogos Park. The Friends of the Library continue to raise funds through the Festival in support of the library's collections.

Two years after the groundbreaking the doors opened, providing a 35,000-square-foot wing devoted to the library's expansive children's and non-print media collections. An exterior spiral staircase, a secret garden, thirty-foot ceilings, and tree motifs are

The library's architecture is meant to represent trees, and allows for a sense of grand space. Courtesy of Ken Pollard.

The "Windows to the Imagination" stained-glass window. Courtesy of James Westwater.

a few of the architectural features. A stained glass "Windows to the Imagination" spans 36 feet of the west end of the children's main floor. The 8-foot-high panels contain more than five thousand pieces of glass and were created by local artists Tom Holdman and Ralph C. Barksdale.

✿ ✿
Doorway to a Lifetime of Learning

Whether it's an evening of tales told by the Timp Tellers, a performance by the Skyline Barbershop Chorus, or a "What Have We Here?" presentation spotlighting hidden treasures of the collection, patrons find a retreat from the stresses of everyday life. Nearly twenty-five thousand patrons attend more than seven hundred library programs featuring readings by authors and poets, musical performances, puppeteers, storytellers, dancers, and book discussion groups for children, teens, and adults. The 2,100 patrons who enter the library daily check out more than 1.3 million items each year and receive help finding answers to their 250,000 questions. They use Internet workstations for everything from researching school assignments to keeping in touch with family through e-mail to researching employment opportunities.

✿ ✿
Local Wordsmiths

At the Orem Public Library all patrons are treasured, but two treasured patrons of note are Alex Caldiero and Leslie Norris.

Performance poet Alex Caldiero has been a library patron for twenty years. Born in the ancient town of Licodia Eubia, Sicily, Alex immigrated to the United States at age nine and was raised and educated in New York. Alex is best known for his performance works that integrate poetry with music, dance, and art. He has performed at numerous venues, including *Day to Day,* a feature of National Public Radio. His work has been reviewed in *Village Voice* and the *New York Times.* Caldiero says of the library:

> Whenever I talk to my buddies from New York and San Francisco about the arts, the Orem Library invariably comes up. They are incredulous when I tell them about the library's extensive foreign film and documentary collections; and the incredible jazz, classical, and experimental music collections. "In Orem?" they ask. I always get a big kick when I boldly respond, "Yes, in Orem."

Acclaimed Welsh poet Leslie Norris is has also been a regular patron and friend of the library. Norris read his work at the groundbreaking ceremony for the new children's wing, and has since given readings at several library programs. He was awarded the Cholmondeley Poetry Prize, the David Higham Memorial Prize, the Katherine Mansfield Memorial Award, and the Welsh Arts Council Senior Fiction Award. He is has been a fellow of the Royal Society of Literature and of the Welsh Academy, holds two honorary doctorates, and has been a poet-in-residence at Brigham Young University. He has also written poetry and prose for children. His Christmas story, *Albert and the Angels,* was published by Farrar, Straus & Giroux. He is the subject of the documentary *Crossing Borders: The Life and Works of Leslie Norris* and the portrait *Welsh Poet with a Dog* by Utah artist Brian Kershisnik, which is owned by the Utah Arts Council.

The City Library

Salt Lake City Public Library System

Salt Lake City, Utah

Address:	210 E. 400 South
	Salt Lake City, UT 84111
Date Founded:	1898
Date Built:	2003
Architect:	Moshe Safdie
Director:	Nancy Tessman
Special Collections:	Salt Lake Valley History

It provides common ground in an uncommon setting. As one visitor to The City Library wrote, "Congratulations to the people of the Salt Lake region for valuing libraries and reading enough to fund such a splendid building—one of the most spectacular libraries in the world. Truly an example of enlightenment."

Salt Lake City has embraced The City Library since it opened on 8 February 2003. In fact, the library attracts three million visitors a year (making it the second-most popular attraction in Utah). Many visitors are drawn to the building's architecture. The American Institute of Architects (AIA) recognized the building in 2004 with its AIA Honor Award, the profession's highest recognition of works that exemplify excellence in architecture, interiors, and urban design. The library was designed by architect Moshe Safdie, whose works also include Vancouver's Library Square and Los Angeles' Skirball Cultural Center. *The Architectural Record* stated that Safdie's library projects "break down the distinction between commerce and culture, entertainment and enlightenment."

Beginnings

The Church of Jesus Christ of Latter-day Saints brought the first books into Utah in 1851, forming the Utah Territorial Library. In 1872 the Ladies Library Association was organized and maintained a 400-volume public reading room until 1876. The Masonic Public Library was established in 1877, but due to a lack of public and fi-

Getting my library card was like citizenship; it was like American citizenship.

—Oprah Winfrey

nancial support, the 10,000-volume collection was donated to the newly founded Pioneer Library Association in 1891. Within a year of Utah's admission to the Union in 1896, legislation provided for the establishment of free public libraries. Under this law, the Free Public Library of Salt Lake City opened in 1898 with a collection of 11,910 books from the Pioneer Library Association.

A Soaring Wall of Glass

Fast forward to a century later, when visitors enter the Main Library's sunlight-filled interior through the five-story Urban Room, and their eyes are drawn upward to the glass roof. A soaring wall of glass referred to as the "lens" fills the library with mountain vistas. A view of the city draws patrons to the rooftop garden. In addition, the building has a five-story walkable wall with shops and cafes at the ground level and reading galleries above. Public meeting rooms and a three hundred-seat auditorium encourage community discussions. Fireplaces on every level invite conversation and reading. A coffee shop in the Browsing Library lets readers enjoy a cup-of-the-day, bestseller, or newspaper. Patrons read whimsical and thought-provoking quotes placed throughout the building. Children have their own library, which sits at the base of the lens and includes fanciful nooks and crannies such as Grandma's Attic and the Crystal Cave. Teens gather in the "Canteena" to find timely materials, watch the large plasma screen, study in café-style booths, and interact with librarians wearing "No Shhh!" buttons. A quiet place? Not even.

Library Square

More important than the architecture, however, are the library's resources, collections, and public programs. One patron's comment echoes the sentiments of the community: "There is no

Heart of the Community: **The Libraries We Love**

Night life at the City Library. Courtesy of Sohm Photografx, © Dana Sohm.

question in my mind that our library is the best thing that has happened to Salt Lake City in decades."

In November 1998, 68 percent of Salt Lake City voters approved an $84 million bond issue to expand two branch libraries and to construct a larger main library for downtown. Building community and creating a rich environment at the Main Library were a high priority. The idea of designing a community of compatible organizations and small shops grew. Soon the term "Library Square" was being used to describe this block in the heart of the city. Now Library Square is home to KCPW public radio station, the Salt Lake City Film Center, the Community Writing Center, an artists' co-op, and a downtown information center, as well as a coffee shop, deli, comic book shop, florist, and gift shop operated by the Friends of the Library. Each works in harmony with the library to enhance visitors' experience.

More than one thousand groups—from the League of Women Voters to the Utah Quilters, from Wasatch Coalition for Peace and Justice to the Utah Storytelling Guild, from Women in Recovery to the Utah Science Center, from the Authors Club to the Leukemia and Lymphoma Society—use the library to meet, discuss, debate, and enjoy. "The new Main Library embodies the idea that a library is more than a repository of books and computers—it reflects and engages the city's imagination and aspirations," says library director Nancy Tessman. "Our library represents common ground and encourages civic dialogue, cultural exploration, and community celebrations."

When the library opened, the Dewey Lecture Series debuted. Monthly lectures by some of the best minds in the nation addressed the wide range of topics that makes up the Dewey Decimal Classification System. The goals were to challenge the community; to host speakers who offer fresh perspectives; and to broaden patrons' view of the world. The program was so well received that it became an annual series. Speakers have included William Safire, Terry Waite, Kay Redfield Jamison, Sherman Alexie, Oliver Sacks, M. D., David Halberstam, and Will Shortz. The scope of the program reaches beyond the walls of the library when local National Public Radio affiliate KCPW broadcasts the lectures live.

The Dewey Lecture Series is just one of the programs that has established the Main Library as the community's gathering place. The public enjoys story times, book discussions, author readings, and art exhibits. Working dogs from Intermountain Therapy Animals visit the library monthly and listen attentively as children read in a relaxed, nonthreatening environment. In partnership with the SLC Film Center patrons see documentary films and often meet the director or producer. Cultural events occur throughout the year. The Diwali festival reaches the Indian population. The Chinese New Year celebration draws hundreds from the growing Chinese community. The Hispanic Festival at Library Square attracts enthusiastic crowds. The Utah Arts Festival has made Library Square its permanent home, as has the Great Salt Lake Book Festival. Working in conjunction with organizations such as the Utah Symphony and Opera, the Utah Museum of Natural History, and the Utah Science Center expands the range of information and events the library offers to the public.

When the Main Library opened, architect Safdie stated, "Libraries are cultural storehouses and a community of readers where people interact with the material and with each other. The architecture must celebrate that and in so doing, not only make a wonderful library, but go beyond that to create a placemaker." The library world agrees: Salt Lake City Public Library was named Thomson Gale/Library Journal's 2006 Library of the Year.

U.S. ZIP CODE

85331

Desert Broom Branch

◆

Phoenix Public Library

Cave Creek, Arizona

Address:	29710 N. Cave Creek Road
	Cave Creek, AZ 85331
Date Opened:	2005
Date Built:	2005
Architect:	Richärd + Bauer Architecture, LLC
Director:	Theresa Shaw, Branch Manager

Borrowing from the symbiotic relationship between a young Saguaro and a nurse tree, the Desert Broom Library creates a shaded microclimate for growth, providing day light, shelter and a nurturing environment for intellectual growth. The Desert Broom Library opened in February 2005. The library serves the residents of Phoenix and the community of Cave Creek, and outlying county properties.

The library is distinguished by the beauty and innovation of its design. Outdoor reading spaces are enclosed and shaded by a series of coiled metal screens, following the natural form of the adjacent arroyo, and are cooled by building relief air. The roof is penetrated by a series of openings, allowing filtered light into the interior and exterior spaces. Each of the openings is treated with a fritted or colored glass creating an ever-changing series of colors and patterns throughout the space. Stone-filled gabion walls anchor the base of the building and provide a natural contrast to the steel structure. Designed to fit into the desert site with a minimum of disturbance, the library has already won six major architectural awards for excellence in design and sustainable commercial development.

❧ ❧

Programming to Fit Community Needs

Through countywide reciprocal borrowing agreements, residents of almost all county towns and cities can borrow freely from area libraries; so the Desert Broom Library, as part of the Phoenix Public Library system, serves a wide clientele. In its service area, there is a population of about 79,000 people, 27 percent of whom are under the age of 18 years.

Library services include a materials collection of 94,000 items, as well as access to the library's catalog, subscription databases, and the Internet through forty public computers and wireless access. Responding to the large number of commuters in the area, Desert Broom offers a large collection of audio books, in addition to DVDs and music CDs.

A primary programming focus is children and their caregivers. Desert Broom offers programs for babies, toddlers, preschoolers, and school-age children. Attendance at these programs averages about 250 participants each week. In keeping with the Phoenix Public Library's commitment to youth, teens have their own space, and are active participants in the planning of collections and services especially for them. A teen advisory group meets

Outside reading area. Courtesy of Bill Timmerman.

Library interior looking into the sunset. Courtesy of Bill Timmerman.

monthly to plan programs and fundraising activities. The group also selects music for the teen area's listening center and offers suggestions for book, movie, and music purchases. The Phoenix Public Library also supports a summer reading program and a winter reading program, with much needed help provided by teen volunteers.

Adult programming includes computer classes, author programs, and parenting workshops. The library's meeting room provides space for a wide variety of community organizations, from homeowners associations to support groups. Desert Broom enjoys the support of a large and active Friends group with a charter membership of 250.

Children's area. Courtesy of Bill Timmerman.

Poised for Change

As the area grows, develops and changes, the library is ready to do likewise. The 15,000-square-foot facility is configured to expand to 25,000 square feet and 150,000 items. The 3-acre site is located within a larger 45-acre parcel that is being developed as a regional park by the city. Several natural washes cross the site, with the library located on one side of a wash and parking accessed by an elevated pedestrian walk. This natural arroyo is augmented with additional planting and reinforced with trails leading down into the park.

With a design focused on natural light and energy conservation, and a respect for nature and the environment—along with a commitment to providing access to the latest forms of technology—the Desert Broom Library effectively reflects the heart and life of its community.

Ernie Pyle Library

Albuquerque-Bernalillo County Library System
Albuquerque, New Mexico

Address:	900 Girard S.E.
	Albuquerque, NM 87106
Date Founded:	1948
Date Built:	1940
Architect:	Arthur McCollum and Earl Mount
	(Contractors)
Director:	Eileen Longsworth; Joani D.
	Murphy, Branch Manager
Special Collections:	Ernie Pyle Memorabilia

If these walls could talk, they would talk of war and peace: the war that Ernie Pyle experienced first hand and wrote about so prophetically and the peace that he found in this little white house with the picket fence in Albuquerque.

Journalist Ernest Taylor Pyle (1900–1945) was not a desk reporter. He and his wife, Jerry, built the little clapboard house in 1940 as a place to call home while they wandered the country for Ernie's job as a roving human-interest writer for Scripps-Howard newspapers. After his death in 1945, and Jerry's seven months later, the Pyle estate offered the property to the City Of Albuquerque, and in 1948 the house became the first branch of the city's public library system.

A Perfect Fit Overall

Pyle's travel assignments kept him moving about the country during the 1930s, writing columns in a down-to-earth, folksy way that earned him a wide following. The columns from those times are collected in *Home Country* and *Ernie Pyle's Southwest*. By 1940 Ernie was famous. However, after crossing the country thirty-five times, he and Jerry began to feel as though they were, in Ernie's words, "swinging forever through space without ever coming down." They decided to build a house in Albuquerque where they could spend a month out of every year just relaxing. In an article entitled "Why Albuquerque?" Ernie listed all the reasons why he and Jerry had chosen the town: they had a country mailbox instead of a slot in the door; people were friendly yet allowed the Pyles their privacy; Ernie could wear overalls every day, even to the cantina in the old Alvarado Hotel, and nobody raised an eyebrow; the days were warm, the nights were cool, and the air was unsullied by smoke and soot; meadowlarks sang in the morning, rabbits nibbled the lawn at night, and the quail didn't fly away when the Pyles came out onto the porch. Ernie thought the sunsets so violently beautiful they almost frightened him; there were no streetcars; men wore cowboy boots instead of street shoes; and the tempo of life was slow. Besides, he said, half the horizon was his just for the looking.

At the outbreak of World War II, Ernie became a war correspondent during the blitz in England. He went with the U.S. Army to North Africa and from there to the invasion of Italy. He witnessed the landings at Normandy and the liberation of France. By 1944 *Time* magazine was calling him "America's most widely read war correspondent." Instead of the mass media reports about what the armies or the commanding generals were doing, Pyle wrote from the perspective of the common soldier, an approach that furthered his popularity. His wartime writings are preserved in the books *Brave Men, Here is Your War,* and *Ernie Pyle in England.* He came home when he could to Jerry and the little white house. He won the Pulitzer Prize for journalism in 1944. In 1945 Ernie accompanied U.S. troops to the South Pacific, and on April 18 he was killed by a Japanese sniper on the island of Ie Shima.

The library houses Pyle memorabilia as well as books.

THE DEATH OF CAPT. HENRY T. WASKOW

Another man came. I think he was an officer. It was hard to tell officers from men in the dim light, for everybody was bearded and grimy. The man looked down into the dead captain's face and then spoke directly to him, as though he were alive. "I'm sorry, old man."

Then a soldier came and stood beside the officer and bent over, and he too spoke to his dead captain, not in a whisper but awfully tenderly, and he said, "I sure am sorry, sir."

Then the first man squatted down, and he reached down and took the captain's hand and he sat there for a full five minutes holding the dead hand in his own and looking intently into the dead face. And he never uttered a sound all the time he sat there.

Finally he put the hand down. He reached over and gently straightened the points of the captain's shirt collar, and then he sort of rearranged the tattered edges of the uniform around the wound, and then he got up and walked away down the road in the moonlight, all alone.

FROM BRAVE MEN BY ERNIE PYLE

Memorial for Captain Waskow, the subject of one of Ernie Pyle's most famous columns.

⚘ ⚘
A Lasting Memorial

When the Pyles' house was converted to a library, every attempt was made to keep the character of the place intact. The room configuration remains the same, and the picket fence that Ernie built is kept white with fresh paint. The grave of their favorite dog, Cheetah, is there as is the memorial for Captain Waskow, the hero of one of Ernie's most famous columns. The place has the flavor of the old days in Albuquerque, before the war changed everything. Inside the library, a collection of memorabilia honors the war correspondent. His hat and his sun goggles are on display along with numerous photographs, scrapbooks of articles by and about Ernie Pyle, and the newspaper announcing his death in front-page headlines.

Since the Ernie Pyle Library is a full-service library in the Albuquerque-Bernalillo County Library System, visitors can read children's books in the kitchen, check out bestsellers at the living room, read fiction in Ernie's bedroom, or look in the bathroom mirror where Ernie himself must have looked while he shaved in the morning. The bathroom is stocked with periodicals.

In 2004 the Ernie Pyle Library underwent a makeover. Mayor Martin Chavez, who remembered riding his bike to the library as a boy, saw to it that the buildings were refurbished. The library has recently been listed as the only historic landmark in Albuquerque. Visitors from all over the world come to see the little house that Ernie built and pay their respects to his memory. Patrons come to read quietly, enjoy the summer reading club events, or take part in the storytime picnics underneath the old sycamore tree.

The grave of Ernie's beloved dog, Cheetah.

Only one hour in the normal day is more pleasurable than the hour spent in bed with a book before going to sleep, and that is the hour spent in bed with a book after being called in the morning.

—Rose Macaulay

Aztec Public Library

❖

Aztec, New Mexico

Address:	201 W. Chaco
	Aztec, NM 87410
Date Founded:	1911
Date Built:	1964, 2005
Architect:	DLR Group (2005)
Director:	Leanne Hathcock
Special Collections:	Local History, UFO History;
	Southwest ArchaeoAstronomy
	Research

When a little library has a big funding problem, where does it look for help? This town's library turned to the skies (and its own area history) for inspiration. Ten years later, thanks to outer space, the Aztec Public Library has much more inner space: It's five times larger and is the sponsor of an annual event that draws crowds—and dollars—to support even more innovative and technological improvements.

🦎 🦎

Better UFOs than IOUs

In 1911 a woman's group known as the Altrurian Club vowed to "establish some kind of library" in the city of Aztec. Housed first in several downtown locations, the library was eventually

granted space in the Aztec City Complex, where it remained for just over forty years. When a larger facility was needed, the Aztec Public Library met with the Friends of the Library to talk about raising the money necessary for expansion. Library Director Leanne Hathcock proposed turning a far-out bit of Aztec's history into a not-so-far-out idea that eventually allowed the library to quintuple its useable space. In 1998 the first Aztec UFO Symposium was launched. Now in its ninth year, the weekend symposium draws international attention and has helped fund a $2 million, 9,400-square-foot multi-use library building. The Friends of the Aztec Library, a nonprofit organization, sponsors the weekend's activities commemorating the alleged March 1948 crash of a UFO twelve miles northwest of the town. According to author Timothy Good in his book, *Above Top Secret,* that particular UFO incident is one of history's all-time best-kept secrets regarding alien landings. All proceeds from the weekend directly benefit the library.

🦎 🦎

Four Corners and Ten Years

Located about fourteen miles northeast of Farmington and not far from the famous Four Corners (where the borders of Arizona, Colorado, New Mexico, and Utah meet), Aztec is named after the nearby ruins of a twelfth-century Aztec village. The town was laid out in 1890 and became the San Juan county seat in 1897. Unlike most northern New Mexican towns, Aztec has hilly, tree-lined streets and a mix of midwestern and Victorian architecture. Produce farming and tourism fuel the economy. The library is part of the Aztec Family Center Complex, a ten-year, phased community development project sharing space and cost with the City of Aztec, the Aztec Boys and Girls Club, San Juan Col-

David Achubeque's winning entry in the library's 2001 Space Art Contest.

Aztec Public Library, part of the Aztec Family Center Complex. Courtesy of Leanne Hathcock.

lege East, and the Aztec School District. The single facility is designed to provide after-school and educational programs, library services, and fitness and recreation opportunities. The building itself is modern in aspect—long, lean, and ground-hugging. The library houses a collection of twenty thousand books and serial volumes as well as audio and video materials, offers a variety of children's programs, and hosts its own online Web catalog.

🜨 🜨

Extraterrestrial Excitement

Besides a stunning, high-desert landscape set in the foothills of the Rocky Mountains, what puts the Aztec Public Library in the spotlight are the annual UFO Symposium and related events that take place in late March. The symposium draws authors and lecturers, investigative journalists, and, most recently, filmmakers, from around the world. Perhaps because the event is closely connected to the library, the whole affair has taken on scholarly overtones. Library Director Hathcock has been interviewed for radio programs from Johannesburg, South Africa, to CBS Radio in New York. Among the many notable speakers at the symposium are Jim Marrs who wrote *Alien Agenda: Investigating the Extraterrestrial Presence among Us;* Andrew Kissner, a former state representative of Las Cruces who works in the satellite communication industry; Anthony Dellaflora and James Lujan, producer/writers of the prize-winning film, *High Strange New Mexico,* and authors of the first articles that appeared regarding the UFO Symposium; Dr. Ron Craig (now deceased) who was the last surviving member of Project Blue Book (U.S. Air Force studies on UFOs) and author of *UFOs: An Insider's View*

of the Official Quest for Evidence; Stanton Friedman, nuclear physicist and author of *Top Secret/Majic;* and researcher Scott D. Ramsey, whose eighteen-year investigation of the Aztec UFO landing is documented in a film entitled *Aztec 1948.* Speaker fees are donated to the library, as are proceeds from the Alien Run Mountain Bike Competition. There's also a tour to the crash site and the Space Art Contest as well as staged plays and the nighttime Stargaze conducted by Suman Krishniswami, a local astrophysicist.

🜨 🜨

Future Stargazing

The Aztec Public Library will play a vital role in the newest town project: A coalition of federal, state, and local partners plans to turn the Aztec Courthouse into a cultural and educational center for the study of archeoastronomy (the study of sky myths and astronomical practices of the ancients) and ethnoastronomy (traditional astronomy as understood by contemporary native peoples). Tentatively called Four Corners Center for Universe Studies, the plans call for a partnership with the University of New Mexico's Lodestar Astronomy Center, which will work with the town to create a planetarium able to re-create the skies the ancient Native Americans observed. In addition, the Four Corners Center hopes to garner the support of area national parks, including the Aztec Ruins National Monument, Chaco Canyon National Historical Park, Mesa Verde National Park, and Salmon Ruins. A key component of the plan is to have the Aztec Public Library provide local citizens and visitors with access to the technology and information generated by the center.

Northwest Reno Library

◆

Washoe County Library System
Reno, Nevada

Address:	2325 Robb Drive
	Reno, NV 89523
Date Founded:	1999
Date Built:	1988; 1999 (renovation)
Architect:	Robert A. Fielden, Inc. (1999)
Director:	Nancy Cummings; Dianne Varnon,
	Branch Manager
Special Collections:	Shia Szrut Holocaust Studies
	Memorial Collection

The Northwest Reno Library is one place where seldom is heard a discouraging word, especially the word *shush*.

Instead, children are encouraged to play with puzzles and to cuddle up with parents in oversize chairs or rockers to be read to while enjoying the views from the windows. All year, toddlers, preschoolers, and older children come and go to programs and reading clubs. The Young People's Area includes a Story Cottage for story times, which has a mini-puppet theater for children to use. The cottage has its own hobbit-like door in a tree trunk. Through the Sierra Arts Foundation, teen landscapers developed a circular maze defined by rocks and Nevada plants in the island in the street. And children's activities, including safe trick-or-treat, are presented in cooperation with local businesses such as Microflex and Western Village.

The Northwest Reno Library was the first of fourteen branches of the Washoe County Library System (WCLS) to become a commons—a gathering place for the community. The library exemplifies one of the system's service roles: to address the need of people to interact with others and to participate in public discourse.

The library opened in June 1999 to serve a fast-growing residential area of northern Nevada. A citizens' library committee had met for several years, and its recommendations were followed in designing and locating the library. It was funded by a county tax override approved in 1994. Community focus groups and the West Reno Branch Library Planning Committee, which was comprised of a cross-section of the community, participated in planning. A mission statement identified the branch as

The Young People's Library. Courtesy of William Carlin.

"a primary information and community activity center providing broad resources to all generations." Subsequent planning and development proceeded from this statement.

❧ ❧

Creative Partnerships

Development and construction were done by a public-private partnership among Washoe County and Trainor and Associates, developer; Robert A. Fielden, Inc., architect; and Q&D Construction. Library staff worked with Fielden on the physical design of the building and, more importantly, on the vision of the library as place.

Money and time were saved by remodeling an existing 30,000-square-foot building, located high above the valley floor. The architecture was designed to reflect the surrounding environment. The façade has a mountain motif using the colors of the high desert mountains. Interiors reflect the outside views of nature by using a tree-and-leaf pattern and multiple shades of wood.

The atmosphere of the library is intentionally similar to a bookstore, and the interior and exterior design draw on a visual theme that emphasizes the view. Designers added extra windows and a pair of skylights to maximize the available natural light. Inside the building, which once housed a pharmaceutical manufacturer, is a maze of pillars. Interior designer Jane Fielden disguised these structural supports by painting the pillars

Deborah Curtis reads a story to youngsters inside the Story Cottage. Courtesy of William Carlin.

green to create stylized trees, whose branches appear to support a solid canopy of leaves.

Library visitors enjoy views of Peavine Mountain to the north and can look out over the city of Reno and across the high-desert valley to the Virginia Range. Windows were installed in the south side of the building to capture views of the beautiful Sierra Nevada.

Building for Community Needs

Tables and chairs are scattered throughout the building for individuals or groups to choose for comfort and to take advantage of the views as they read or study. Internet stations also are located in several areas. The library offers a community meeting room and two study rooms. The Friends of the Library operate Second-hand Prose, a used-book store and gift boutique. An art gallery provides exhibits, including paintings, photography, sculpture, pottery, and even jewelry, all selected annually by a community committee. Patrons can use a drive-up window to pick up reserved items and return library materials.

In designing the library, the architect, Robert Fielden, envisioned a building that "beyond a full palette of programs and services, would serve as the neighborhood's Center of Place." At the Northwest Reno Library, "neighbors come together both formally and informally to meet one another, for getting to know each other better, and for discussing common issues," Fielden noted. "A neighborhood library provides countless contributions to the quality-of-life for the citizenry it serves. Even for those neighbors who may not be frequent users of programs and services, the public library represents a significant added-value for real property appraisal and imagery that elevates the status of surrounding development." And, he added, "Transferring information while enriching the sense of community go hand-in-hand in today's life."

Collaboration across the Community

The library collaborates to offer a range of programs. For example, Lifescapes, a joint project of the University of Nevada, Reno, WCLS and Nevada Humanities, sponsors book readings, discussions, and "life writing" for seniors. This program has received national recognition. "Children of Children," a still/audio exhibit by photographer Michael Nye, was presented in 2000. Another Nye exhibit, "The Fine Line," depicting mental health issues, was on display during 2006, in cooperation with the University of Nevada School of medicine. The library also houses the Shia Szrut Holocaust Studies Memorial Collection, which is used by the public and teachers. In support of the Holocaust Collection, the library provides space for teacher training and presents programs related to themes of tolerance and understanding.

Community members have a say in what the library offers and recommend selections for Spanish and Chinese materials as well as donate materials in other languages. People can view movies at one of four viewing stations. Newspaper and magazine reading areas are located near the Vending Café, which offers snacks and beverages. Snacks and beverages, like food for thought, are welcome throughout the library.

East Los Angeles Library

◆

County of Los Angeles Public Library

Los Angeles, CA

Address:	4837 East 3rd Street
	Los Angeles, CA 90022
Date Founded:	1923
Date Built:	1967; 2004
Architect:	Stephen Finney, with artist Jose
	Antonio Aguirre (2004)
Director:	Alice Medina
Special Collections:	Chicano History

At the East Los Angeles Public Library one detail of the mural on the wall says it all: the book of knowledge, intended to reflect human origins and traditions. East Los Angeles, with its multicultural past and present, remains mindful of its origins and traditions.

> A great public library, in its catalogue and its physical disposition of its books on shelves, is the monument of literary genres.
>
> —Robert Melancon

Humble Beginnings

The library began in June of 1923 with a small number of books housed in the corner of a local store. In August of that year a small building was constructed to hold the collection, and a year later a second building was erected. In 1932 the library moved from Whittier Boulevard to Fetterly Avenue, where it remained for thirty-five years. It moved again to the corner of Third and Fetterly in 1967. In 2004, thanks to funding from Gloria Molina, a member of the Los Angeles County Board of Supervisors who initiated the East Los Angeles Civic Center Renovation Project, a new library was erected on East 3rd Street with 26,000 square feet of space. Included was a separate room for the Chicano Resource Center established in 1976, where scholars from around the world have come to study the multimedia collection of Mexican-American history and culture.

The new building, with its east and west entrances and lobby planned by architect Stephen Finney of CWA AIA, Inc., was designed in conjunction with public mural artist Jose Antonio Aguirre. Community input was vital during planning of the library. In response to the request that Mayan themes be represented, the building incorporates images of the sun and the moon in the pavement at the entrances and in the lobby. Jose Aguirre's mosaic mural, *Our Legacy: Forever Presente*, covers more than 2,176 square feet of wall space. He calls it a mural cycle in four movements, the first of which—"The Gift of Humanity"—is featured on the east wall. In addition to the book of knowledge appear the rays of the sun, symbolizing the directions of the universe, while the generic human portrait is the face of humanity. The second

part of the mural, "Arrival," on the interior wall of the east tower, portrays mythical themes from ancient Mexico. "Heart of the People" on the exterior wall of the west tower merges the ancient with modern and symbolizes the individual as a vital member of his or her community. "Departure" on the interior of the west tower depicts significant public leaders who have opened the way for future generations. The mural is a tribute to East Los Angeles's cultural heritage and sociopolitical struggles.

East Los Angeles has a long history of diverse populations. In the area where the library now stands, the original settlers were Tongva Indians, and into the 1980s the population remained sparse. In the beginning of the twentieth century, the population began to expand. Armenians established a community there. A dissenting sect of the Russian Orthodox Church immigrated, followed by an influx of Japanese Americans after the San Francisco earthquake of 1906. The years between 1910 and 1920 brought the large-scale immigration of Mexicans driven from their homeland by the Mexican Revolution. By the mid-1920s overcrowding in eastern and midwestern cities led to an influx of additional ethnic groups. Jewish settlers, as well as Italians, Poles, African-Americans, and Serbians, arrived. In the 1930s and 1940s the Great Depression caused a wave of Mexican-American deportations. One-third of the local population of East Los Angeles was encouraged or forced to return to Mexico. As a result, in 1939 the first Latino Civil Rights Assembly was held in the city, drawing more than a thousand delegates from all over the United States.

Heart of the Community: **The Libraries We Love**

The library from across the lake in adjacent Belvedere Park. Courtesy of Alex Huang, County of Los Angeles Public Library.

Finally, when Pearl Harbor was bombed, Japanese Americans were relocated to internment camps for the duration of the war. Only a few returned to their former homes. Through the years the Latinos who remained held many more demonstrations in their pursuit for equal rights and currently make up 96 percent of the East Los Angeles population.

From Symbolism to Service

A number of projects have been undertaken to remind East Los Angeles residents of their multicultural past. The construction of the library, with its bilingual staff and one of the largest Spanish collections in the County Library, is one of them. The library serves 65,415 residents, more than 75 percent of whom are Spanish-speaking and who take pride in their cultural traditions.

Other exterior features of the library include a patio and walkways that afford views of adjacent Belvedere Park and its lake. Inside the library houses adult and children's collections totaling 139,542 volumes, 5,990 audio cassettes and CDs, nearly 9,000 videocassettes, 123 periodical subscriptions, a meeting room for 175 people, a computer room, and the Friends of the Library bookstore. There is also a homework center and a variety of children's programs, including a story hour. Fully automated, the library provides public access to computers, online library catalogs and electronic databases, and a microform reader-printer. "Your Librarian/Live Reference" is an experimental project that lets patrons ask questions and get answers in real time via the Internet from reference staff throughout Los Angeles and Orange Counties. East Los Angeles has traditionally been characterized by high population density, low literacy level, high crime and school dropout rates, and low-income residents. However, the library's mission—to provide its diverse communities with access to the information and knowledge needed to nurture their cultural exploration and lifelong learning—has led to an increase of 100,000 patrons since 2004.

East wall mural, "Arrival." Courtesy of Martin Zamora.

Los Angeles Public Library

◆

Richard J. Riordan Central Library

Los Angeles, California

Address:	630 W. Fifth Street
	Los Angeles, CA 90071
Date Founded:	1872
Date Built:	1926; 1993 (expansion)
Architect:	Bertram Grosvenor Goodhue;
	Hardy Holzman Pfeiffer Associates
Director:	Fontayne Holmes
Special Collections:	Maps; Genealogy

Lights! Camera! Reading glasses! Actors are just some of the famous faces you might see with a nose in a novel at the Richard J. Riordan Central Library (known simply as the "Central Library" to patrons) in downtown Los Angeles. An average of seven thousand people a day use the collection of more than 2.6 million items and 300 public-access computers, including Prince Charles, who chose the library as the location for his Business Leaders Forum during a trip to the United States. You can hobnob with the stars, including Sharon Stone, Kevin Spacey, and Morgan Freemen at the Gregory Peck Reading Series (the library is located in the entertainment capital of the world), enjoy the work of authors and performers at the Aloud Cultural Program Series, peruse one of the largest collections of maps in the United States, view major art exhibitions in the gallery, dine at the café, or stroll in the 1.5-acre garden.

The library also features an area for teens, a library-within-a-library that is the first of its kind in the nation and that serves as a model for others around the world. Teen'scape features a "cyber space" with Internet computers; a "living room" with sofa, magazines, and a 50-inch plasma TV; and a study lounge with resources and homework help material just for teens.

❦ ❦

Building for History

Incorporated in 1850, Los Angeles sprawls across nearly 463 square miles and is the second-largest city in the United States. Often called the "City of Angels," it is comprised of the most diverse population of

The Central Library. Courtesy of Foaad Farah of Hardy Holzman Pfeiffer Associates.

any city in the world. Set along the coastline, the Los Angeles area incorporates beaches, dunes, wetlands, hills, mountains, and rivers and is home to a variety of native plant species. Though the rainy season lasts from November through February (perfect indoor library weather), the air is mostly balmy, and the area claims 325 days of sunshine a year. The economy is driven by international trade, entertainment, aerospace, agriculture, petroleum, manufacturing, and tourism, all of which make Los Angeles a culturally rich, cosmopolitan city.

Noted architect Bertram Grosvenor Goodhue designed the original building (one of his last major works) in 1926, and for nearly fifty years the library served its patrons. The structure combined influences from Egyptian, Roman, Byzantine, and Islamic styles as well as Spanish Colonial and Revival. A colored tile

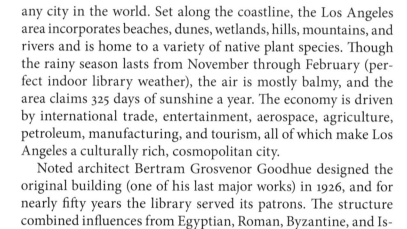

pyramid featuring a sunburst and a torch meant to symbolize the light of learning topped the four-story rotunda. Limestone sculptures of literary and historical figures decorated the building's exterior, and the interior contained large reading rooms, with murals depicting California's history.

❦ ❦

Rising from the Ashes

By the 1970s, however, the aging, overcrowded building had begun to deteriorate, and there was talk of demolition. Before that could happen, a fire set by an arsonist in 1986 nearly destroyed the library, incinerating almost 400,000 books,

Interior of the library. Courtesy of Foaad Farah of Hardy Holzman Pfeiffer Associates.

melting metal shelves, and injuring forty-six firefighters. Water damaged about 700,000 more volumes. A second fire on 3 September of the same year destroyed the contents of the Music Department Reading Room. The near disaster roused the residents of Los Angeles, who came to the library's aid by launching a recovery campaign called "Save the Books." Its goal: to raise $10 million to replace materials lost to the fire. The outpouring of support from southern California and across the nation accelerated the expansion and renovation of the library. Designed by the Hardy Holzman Pfeiffer Associates, a new wing was added and the original building was restored, doubling the size of the library to 540,000 square feet. The doors reopened on 3 October 1993 to a cheering throng of eighty thousand.

☙ ❧

Into the Future

Renamed for former Mayor Richard Reardon in 2001, the Central Library serves as the headquarters for the Los Angeles Public Library system and is the largest public library facility in the western United States. It is a designated cultural heritage monument and is listed on the National Register of Historic Places. The Tom Bradley Wing, named for another former mayor, has an eight-story atrium. There is gallery space for major exhibitions, one of which was "American Originals: Treasures from the National Archives," featuring the original Emancipation Proclamation. There is a two hundred-seat auditorium and a gift shop. The library holds a collection of 3 million historic photographs of Los Angeles, is a depository for U.S. trademark and copyright information, and has more than ten thousand periodical subscrip-

tions. In addition, it is one of the western United States' major public genealogy resources. Thousands of public programs are held at the Central Library annually. The building also serves as a classroom and resource center for local students enrolled in the Electronic Information Magnet High School. The Los Angeles Public Library's Central Library and seventy-one branches offer subscription databases, an online catalog, downloadable e-book and e-music collections, an electronic reference section that is available twenty-four hours a day, seven days a week, and automated cardholder services—all available from the library's website.

The Library Foundation of Los Angeles, created to raise funds to enhance the Central Library and branches, continues its support. Since 1992 individuals, companies, and foundations have donated more than $60 million to the foundation. In the words of City Librarian Fontayne Holmes, "Befitting its location in the entertainment capital of the world, the Central Library is perhaps the library world's greatest star."

Ornamental mosaic roof design. Courtesy of Foaad Farah of Hardy Holzman and Pfeiffer Associates.

Brand Library and Art Center

◆

Glendale Public Library

Address:	1601 W. Mountain Street
	Glendale, CA 91201
Date Founded:	1956
Date Built:	1904; 1969 (addition)
Architect:	Nathaniel Dryden (1904)
Director:	Alyssa Resnick
Special Collections:	Art and Music

Some come to look, some come to listen, and some come just to toast the ghost of the former host. With a beautiful building located in a family-friendly park, Brand Library and Art Center is the art and music branch of Glendale Public Library of Glendale, California. Situated in the foothills of the Verdugo Mountains, the library is the century-old former residence of Leslie C. Brand, a Glendale founder and a key figure in Southern California history. Through the years the library has become a unique asset for Glendale and surrounding Southern California communities.

Glendale is a suburb of Los Angeles and the third-largest city in Los Angeles County with a population of more than 207,000. Glendale also has the third-highest (54 percent) foreign-born population for a city of its size in the nation, including many Armenian, Arab, Filipino, Latino, and Asian residents. For its diverse population, the Brand Library and Art Center offers a unique compilation of art and music materials, including more than 110,000 works on art and music history, theory, criticism, and techniques as well as specialized encyclopedias, dictionaries, indexes, and other guides. Formats include books, exhibition catalogs, compact discs, phonograph records, librettos, sheet music, 35-mm colored slides, videos, DVDs, and framed art prints.

🎌 🎌
El Miradero

Leslie Coombs Brand (1859–1925), a businessman and banker, was a major figure in Southern California's early settlement and economic growth. Brand purchased 650 acres in the Verdugo foothills and in 1904 built a 5,000-square-foot family residence. Brand named his estate "El Miradero," meaning a "high place overlooking a wide view." Because of its distinctive style and location, Glendale residents soon began referring to it as the "Brand Castle."

Brand made his fortune in utilities, transportation, and Southern California real estate. He and Henry E. Huntington, who built

his own mansion in Pasadena (now the Huntington Library, Art Collections, and Botanical Gardens), were leaders in developing land, establishing local mass transportation, and connecting points north and south. Brand and Huntington collaborated to bring the Los Angeles and Glendale Electric Railroad, known as the beloved "Red Cars," to the area. Brand built a private airstrip in 1919 and established his own fleet of airplanes. In 1921 he hosted what the international press dubbed the world's first fly-in luncheon. All one hundred guests were required to arrive by airplane.

At the time of his death, Leslie C. Brand was one of Southern California's wealthiest and most influential residents. As part of his legacy, Brand bequeathed his estate to Glendale to be converted to a public library and park. This conversion was realized in 1956 when Brand Library was officially opened.

Interior of El Miradero Library, c. 1906–1910.

"Opulent Splendor" exhibition, 2005, at the Brand Galleries. Courtesy of John E. Baer, photographer.

Saracenic Architecture

An architectural marvel of its day, the exterior of the Brand Castle was modeled after the East Indian Pavilion that Brand admired at the 1893 Columbian World Exposition in Chicago. The architecture is considered "Saracenic," incorporating bulbous domes, minarets, and crenellated arches, combining characteristics of Spanish, Moorish, and Indian styles. The interior reflected the Victorian period in which it was built. Its design was invigorated by a unique central solarium, outfitted with palms, ferns, and flowering plants, and leading to almost all first-floor interior rooms.

Designed by Nathaniel Dryden, Brand's brother-in-law, the mansion is sited at the elevated end of a palm-lined driveway and is surrounded by lawns and trees. The stark white of the building creates a striking image against the green hillsides. The facility is listed in the Glendale Register of Historic Resources and is qualified for listing in the California and National Registers.

The Brand

Because of its prominence in the history of the city, its setting in Brand Park, its unique collection of art and music materials, and its responsive staff and services, Brand Library and Art Center—now affectionately referred to as "the Brand"—is a popular destination for people from all over Southern California. As the *Los Angeles Times* (30 December 2004) put it:

Today bookshelves and desks crowd the former estate's interior. But, devoted to art and music, the Library's contents have the power to transport you. Traffic, time clocks, and dirty dishes fade away while you leaf through Chopin sheet music or "The Letters of Michelangelo." Grazing from counterpoint to criticism to calligraphy, only the finer things matter . . . the world comes to a dead halt in a record room—record as in vinyl—complete with turntables and headphones. Just try not to sing along out loud . . .

Through the years Brand Library and Art Center has expanded to include an art studio (operated by Glendale Parks, Recreation and Community Services Department), two art galleries, and a recital hall with two concert pianos. The 448-acre park surrounding the library hosts picnics, weddings, soccer matches, and baseball games and has a playground and hiking trails.

A Mysterious Presence

The Brand Family cemetery is tucked into the hills above the park, its presence marked by a pyramid where the family members are buried along with their dogs at Brand's request. Through the years library staff and visitors have reported hearing sounds or seeing moving objects or simply "having a feeling" that the ghost of Leslie C. Brand still inhabits the old family estate. If this is the case, no one is complaining. In fact, the idea that there is a haunting only contributes to the popularity of the Brand Library and Art Center.

Ojai Library

◆

Ventura County Library
Ojai, California

Address:	111 E. Ojai Avenue
	Ojai, CA 93023
Date Founded:	1893
Date Built:	1928; 1980
Architect:	Carleton Monroe Winslow; Fisher and Wilde
Director:	Jackie Griffin; Kit Willis, Branch Manager
Special Collections:	"Ojai Valley News," 1891 to present

Some libraries operate in the red, others operate in the black. The Ojai Library operates—at least for a moment each day—in the pink.

Because the valley that the town of Ojai (pronounced "o-high") is located in has an east-west orientation, for an instant at sunset the sun paints Topa Topa Mountain at the east end of the valley a pastel pink. Ojai residents call that time the "Pink Moment."

As early as 1889 Ojai residents dreamed of having their own circulating library, a place "where young men and others can go and get whatever reading matter they may select." Starting with a modest reading corner in the local Congregational church, a core group of residents held a variety of fund-raising events, ranging from a candy sale netting $10.65 to an ice cream social under the oaks at the Theodore Woolsey ranch that brought in another $80. When a local educator, Sherman Thacher, chipped in $500 in memory of his brother, George, library supporters agreed to his two stipulations: that there be proper housing for the books and that the library be known as the "George Thacher Memorial Library." A library supporter donated a downtown lot, a local builder put up a simple wooden building, and Sherman Thacher traveled to New York to select and purchase books for the new library.

A kerosene stove provided heat, and two kerosene lanterns lighted the first library building, but as time went by Ojai townspeople introduced many improvements: first a wood-burning stove, then a gas radiator, gasoline lamps, and, in 1913, electric lights. The building was moved to a larger lot and expanded in 1908, and in 1916 the Ojai Library became the first branch of the Ventura County Free Library and thus eligible for public funding.

The George Thacher Memorial Library, which opened in 1893.

❦ ❦
Westward Ho

Ojai, located 75 miles north of Los Angeles, has a temperate climate and a physical beauty that attracted an increasing number of well-educated easterners who built winter homes and became supporters of expanding library service. One of those easterners was Edward Drummond Libbey of the Libbey Glass Company in Toledo, Ohio. Libbey was one of the most influential benefactors of the valley's library, envisioning a larger building in a style more in harmony with the Spanish flavor of the town and directing that it be situated on a lot that his heirs later donated.

With the donation of the lot, Ojai townspeople formed a committee that in one month raised $20,000 for a new library building. The committee hired architect Carleton Monroe Winslow, who also designed the Los Angeles Public Library, Santa Barbara Public Library, and many churches, residences, and public buildings throughout California. The building he designed was basically a symmetrical composition recalling the haciendas of the Mexican period but substituting for their heaviness a lightness and grace while preserving their effect of timelessness and peace. *The Ojai* newspaper reported, "For what excellent design, artistic judgment and a nice sense of value can do, has been done."

By 1979 the library needed more space. J. K. "Ken" MacDonald, county supervisor from Ojai, spent the next few years working to add a wing. He persuaded the Ventura County Board of Supervisors to finance a portion of the project, and the newly formed Ojai Valley Friends of the Library raised the

The interior of the library, showing the magazine area. Courtesy of Fred Rothenberg.

additional $50,000 needed to complete the project. The architectural firm of Fisher and Wilde designed an addition that melds seamlessly with the Winslow building, forming an ell and doubling the size of the library to 5,200 square feet.

Crisis Averted

A funding crisis in the mid-1990s led to a grass-roots effort to pass a parcel tax that brings in an additional $140,000 a year for the library's operating budget and enables the library to be open seven days a week—remarkable for a library of its size.

One of the busiest libraries in Ventura County, the Ojai Library circulates 126,000 items a year and averages five hundred visits per day. In a city of eight thousand people, Ojai Library has seventeen thousand cardholders, indicating use by residents of the surrounding valley as well.

In a typical month the Ojai Library hosts eight preschool story times, two Shakespeare Reading Salons with refreshments, an adult book discussion group, a writers group, one to four bilingual story times for children and their families, sixteen K–12 homework center

The interior of the current library in 1928.

sessions, class visits and one-on-one tutoring sessions for adults learning to read or improve their English, and one or more Friday night lectures or book signings. The library's collection of fifty thousand books and eight public Internet computers are in constant use.

Home Away from Home

A hub of activity, the Ojai Library is the heart of the community or, as one staffer put it, "There's home, and then there's the Ojai Library." The downside of the library's success is that again it has outgrown its quarters. Thus, the Grow Your Library committee recently formed and raised $400,000 to purchase adjacent property for an expansion. Two local architects have donated their services to create a design that preserves the library's great "bones" while adding a children's wing, teen area, meeting room, outdoor reading areas, Friends of the Library bookstore, and more space for books, computers, and people. The fund-raising effort for the $5 million project is just getting under way, and Ojai townspeople are again rallying to keep their library in the pink.

Dr. Martin Luther King, Jr. Library

◆

San José, California

Address:	150 E. San Fernando Street
	San José, CA 95112
Year Founded:	1857; 1880
Year Built:	2003
Architect:	Carrier Johnson; Gunnar Birkerts;
	Anderson Brulé
Director:	Jane Light, San José Public Library;
	Ruth Kifer, Dean, San José State
	University Library
Special Collections:	California History, Cultural
	Heritage Center; Beethoven Studies,
	Steinbeck Studies

"Pass the catsup and the cooperation, please": The Dr. Martin Luther King, Jr. Library—the first co-managed city-university library in the nation—is the result of collaboration between a university president and a city mayor that began at a breakfast meeting.

✿ ✿

A Marriage of Convenience

Despite challenges, the partnership between the City of San José and San José State University has yielded a valuable resource for the community. San José Public Library and the San José State University Library have been recognized for the "path breaking collaboration" that culminated in the joint-use King Library through receipt of the 2004 Library of the Year Award from Thomson Gale/*Library Journal,* the 2004 Helen Putnam Award of Excellence for Intergovernmental Relations & Regional Cooperation from the League of California Cities, and the 2005 James C. Howland Award for Municipal Enrichment Among Cities with Populations Over 500,000 from the National League of Cities.

✿ ✿

Rooted in Tradition

The people of San José have supported library services for more than one hundred years and San José State University has served its students for 150 years. Groundbreaking for the current King Library took place in 2000. The event honored city and university history as it took place 130 years after the groundbreaking of the first building in San José for the California Normal School, the forerunner of San José State University. The Normal School was established in San Francisco in 1857, and in 1871, the Normal School moved to San José on the Washington Square site, which was donated by the City of San José. The Normal School's library collection survived fire in 1880 and the 1906 earthquake, and numbered 12,000 volumes when the third Normal School

building was completed in 1910. Growth and relocation of the collection continued through the period that witnessed the Normal School's transformation to a Teachers College (1921), a State College (1935) and finally, a State University (1972). Prior to the opening of the current King Library, the university's collection of more than a million items was housed in two facilities: the Clark Library and Wahlquist North.

The King Library is located on the site of the City's Carnegie Library, which was built on land transferred from the Normal School to the City. In 1901, the trustees of the Normal School agreed that the northwest corner of its Washington Square site would be transferred to the City of San José so that a public library could be built to hold a collection housed in temporary locations since 1880. In 1903 the San José Carnegie Library opened at the corner of 4th and San Fernando Streets, but the collection soon outgrew it. In 1936 the city council agreed to sell the Carnegie Library to what was then known as "San José State College."

✿ ✿

Silicon Valley

San José was the first town in the Spanish colony of Nueva California, founded in 1777, just one year after the founding of the United States. It was a farming community that provided food for nearby military installations, and it remained an agricultural community for nearly two hundred years. Prunes, grapes, and apricots were some of the major crops, even after IBM established its West Coast headquarters there in 1943.

The San José area underwent extraordinary and sometimes disconcerting changes that buffeted Silicon Valley in the 1970s, 1980s, and 1990s. Now the tenth-largest city in the nation, San José blends the spirit of its small-town beginnings with the spirit of innovation that has made the area a world center of technology innovation.

Following "temporary" housing in the old Post Office (now a wing of the San José Art Museum) the collection was trans-

Dr. Martin Luther King, Jr. Library.

ferred to San José's original main library, which opened in 1970 and was later renamed in honor of Dr. Martin Luther King, Jr. in 1990. This gesture expressed a commitment by the City and the Library Department to serve all residents. The current King Library continues to embody the spirit of the city and the dreams that hard work, respect for diversity, and unique vision brought to life in Silicon Valley.

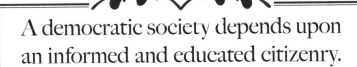

A democratic society depends upon an informed and educated citizenry.
—Thomas Jefferson

international language collections housed under one roof further contribute to making the King Library a cultural hub for the entire community.

Well-Organized Joy

The Dr. Martin Luther King, Jr. Library opened in 2003 as the largest new library built at one time west of the Mississippi River. Rather than appear daunting, as a big city library can, the eight-story, 475,000-square-foot building maintains a welcoming atmosphere. This atmosphere is a result of the city-university collaboration, the architectural design that infuses the building with natural light, and the warmth that staff members convey to patrons. As the *San Francisco Chronicle* noted in 2003, "At once academic and active, humming with well-organized joy, the new Dr. Martin Luther King, Jr. Library makes a convincing case that traditional libraries can hold their own in the computer age." Each day, during the course of the academic year, more than twelve thousand people visit the library, located in the heart of downtown. The rare blend of university and community-sponsored adult programming enables those who are interested to take part in discussions with well-known authors, scholars and policy makers. Unique special collections such as the Ira F. Brilliant Center for Beethoven Studies and the Martha Heasley Cox Center for Steinbeck Studies, as well as one of the largest

Harvestings

As part of the City's commitment to the arts, the San José Public Art Program commissioned artist Mel Chin to create thirty-three works of art integrated into the King library. The works are sited throughout the library and pay homage to the collections, provoking interest and curiosity, and encouraging circulation throughout the building. Entitled *Recolecciones (Harvestings)*, the artworks manifest as both functional installations such as chairs, tables, and shelves; wall paneling, sculptural ceilings and unique light projections; as well as more traditional, formal sculptures.

Consistent with the commitment to the community and a shared desire by all to reflect the diversity of the library's users, the artist's methodology involved public forums in which he facilitated discussions on personal and civic issues that inspired the design of *Recolecciones*. The resulting collection of artworks represents the highest level of artistic expression through an engaged and engaging collaboration between the artist, community and library.

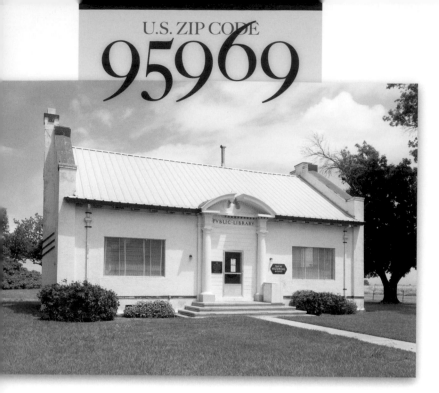

U.S. ZIP CODE

95969

Bayliss Library

◆

Willows Public Library

Glenn, California

Address:	7830 County Road 39
	Glenn, CA 95969
Date Founded:	1917
Date Built:	1917
Architect:	W. H. Weeks
Director:	Linda Peelle-Haddeman, Branch Supervisor

Sometimes a hand-me-down can be a perfect fit: In the heart of northern California in a farming area with an unusually stable population, grandparents bring their grandchildren to little Bayliss Library and explain that it is the library they came to when they were children. Bayliss Library is the only Carnegie library in the United States built in a truly rural area rather than in a city or town. It is also the smallest Carnegie library. However, it has been the object of a great deal of love by the residents since it was built in 1917.

❦ ❦

Resistance to Rural Libraries

In 1915, when people of the region applied to the Carnegie Foundation for a library construction grant, they were turned down. The foundation was skeptical that a library could survive in a

> Books, books, books. It was not that I read so much. I read and re-read the same ones. But all of them were necessary to me. Their presence, their smell, the letters of their titles, and the texture of their leather bindings.
>
> —Colette

farming area that was unincorporated and without a government. However, the people of Bayliss were determined to have a library of their own to save them the day-long trip to the library in Willows. So they convinced the Sacramento Valley Irrigation Company to donate the land, gathered hundreds of signatures on a petition of support, and received a promise from the county government that it would fund the library after it was built. With this new evidence, the foundation granted the library $4,000—$3,500 for the building and $500 for furniture. That furniture—twenty-four chairs, a desk, and five oak tables—is still in use eighty-five years later.

❦ ❦

Determined to Keep It Alive and Well

The story of Bayliss Library is one of its users doing whatever it takes to keep the library open. In 1987 library budgets were being slashed across California. By then Bayliss Library had been added as a branch to

The library's checkout desk. Courtesy of Pat and Bernie Skehan.

Interior view with portrait of Andrew Carnegie. Courtesy of Pat and Bernie Skehan.

the Willows Public Library, located in a small town about thirteen miles from Bayliss. Because of dwindling financial support from city, county, and state government, Bayliss Library was cut out of the budget entirely and scheduled to be closed. However, Bayliss residents refused to let their library close. Mildred Tucker and Virginia Chappell offered to volunteer as long as necessary to keep the library open. They staffed the library for three years, providing basic library services to the area in trying circumstances. They worked without even a telephone in the library.

In 1990 Susan Rawlins, the new director at the Willows Library, convinced the city and county governing boards that the Bayliss Library represented a value far greater than the relatively small amount of funding necessary to operate it with a professional staff person. A branch supervisor was hired, a telephone was installed, and the volunteers were able to resume their own lives with the satisfaction that their work had kept the library from being closed. A few years later open hours at the library were increased from four to eight hours a week. And in 1997 the first computer was installed, connecting the rural library to the whole world through the In-

Children's section of the library.
Courtesy of Pat and Bernie Skehan.

ternet. Ms. Rawlins also initiated the effort to have the library designated a California Point of Historical Interest, which was granted in 2001.

However, the library was not yet safe. In 2002 the city and county library budgets were slashed again, and the threat of closing arose again as well. Again the people of Bayliss rallied to save their library. One heroic resident, Betty Ainger, stepped forward to provide leadership to form a nonprofit organization to provide funding for the library if the governmental bodies could not come up with it. Many other Bayliss residents, willing to spend time and effort to save the library, joined to sponsor bake sales, Unique Treasure sales (a classy name for a yard sale), and other fund-raising activities. A Carnegie library calendar (2004) with Bayliss Library on the front cover and on the January page was donated to the Bayliss nonprofit by the people at Carnegie Libraries of California. A fund-raiser sold 150 of these calendars.

The residents of Bayliss and the other communities in Glenn County are now cooperating on long-range plans for library funding so that the continual budget crises will be eliminated.

Heart of the Community: **The Libraries We Love**

Multnomah County Central Library

◆

Portland, Oregon

Address:	801 S.W. 10th
	Portland, OR 97205
Date Founded:	1864
Date Built:	1913
Architect:	Albert E. Doyle
Director:	Molly Raphael
Special Collections:	Historic First Editions;
	Native American Collection

It's all here, from birds (a complete folio of Audubon's *Birds of America*) to words (a first edition of Johnson's 1755 *Dictionary of the English Language*).

In fact, the Multnomah County Central Library has more than 875 tons of books and other materials stored on 17 miles of bookshelves—and it all grew from the Library Association of Portland's collection of two thousand books and periodicals, housed in a rented room in a frontier settlement of frame buildings and muddy streets.

> In the nonstop tsunami of global information, librarians provide us with floaties and teach us how to swim.
>
> —Linton Weeks

Librarian's Library

In 1902 the association became a tax-supported free public library, and a year later its services extended to all Multnomah County. Construction of the Central Library began in 1911. The architect, Albert E. Doyle, worked with library director Mary Frances Isom to design what he called in the dedication speech a "librarian's library." Its Georgian Revival look was inspired by the University of Virginia, its arched windows were reminiscent of the Boston Public Library. Inside the building was a series of open rooms surrounding a central tower of bookcases. The design made it not only easy to manage many people at once, but also allowed for easy interaction between the librarian and the patrons. Completed in 1913, it has remained the heart of a system of branch libraries throughout Multnomah County. It is known as "Portland's Crown Jewel."

In 1990 the Library Association of Portland transferred ownership of the library buildings and their contents to the people of Multnomah County, who govern its holdings through the Multnomah County Board of Commissioners.

Prior to the latest renovation, begun in 1994 and completed three years later, the American Library Association reported that the Central Library was the most used public library in the nation. Each day about three thousand people check out books, CDs, and audio-visual materials, use its periodical and reference materials, or view the ever-changing exhibits and programs.

Paradise Found

Engraved in gold leaf in the library's entrance are Argentine writer Jorge Luis Borges's words, "I have always imagined that paradise will be a kind of library." The library's three stories feature engraved granite staircases, a bronze sculptured tree that stretches to the ceiling of the Children's Library, a ceiling sculpture of gilded leaves in the foyer, faux-marble-painted columns and roses underfoot in the custom carpets.

The first floor contains the Children's Library, named for children's author Beverly Cleary, who lived in Portland and interned at the Central Library. Throughout the year hundreds of programs introduce children to the world of words. Also on the first floor are the Popular Library, containing a collection

"Pelican" by James Audubon, from *Birds of America*.

Central Library, second floor stairs. Courtesy of Fletcher Farre Ayotte.

of fiction and young adult titles; the Clark Story Theater; the Friends' Library Store; and the U.S. Bank public meeting room. The second floor houses the microfilm area, the periodical section of 1,500 titles, and the Sterling Room for Writers, where authors and scholars may reserve time to write. Author Jean Auel researched her bestseller *The Clan of the Cave Bear* at the Central Library, and author Ursula Le Guin was a member of the Library Advisory Board. When the library was renovated in 1997, Le Guin wrote a poem in its honor.

The Meyer Memorial Trust Science and Business Library, with its collection of business directories and books on medicine and health, cooking, and gardening, is located here, as are the John Wilson Special Collections, containing 10,000 books, photographs, maps and manuscripts. Its treasures include the 1943 *Nuremberg Chronicle,* the complete double-elephant folio of John Audubon's *Birds of America,* and a first edition of Samuel Johnson's *Dictionary of the English Language* (1755). There are also fine-press titles by regional artists, writers, and publishers and rare and valuable materials donated by patrons. The third floor contains the Collins Gallery, where educational and artistic exhibits are regularly hosted; the Henry Failing Art and Music Library (Failing was one of the founders of the library and his commitment to the library continues with an annual gift to the art collection from his estate); and the Helen Kroll Literature and History Rooms, which include genealogy records, history, literature in multiple languages and maps. (The library treasures all its gifts, but Helen Kroll's bequest stands as the most unexpected. Ms. Kroll was a legal secretary who lived modestly and visited the library regularly over her lifetime. When she passed away in the late 1990s, she gave her entire estate—$2 million—to the library.)

The renovation in the mid-1990s also brought technology to the Central Library: It offers 117 public-access computers situated on made-to-order tables that hide unsightly cables, an automated book checkout system, and a high-tech gravity chute for returned books.

Multnomah County Central Library.

Heart of the Community: **The Libraries We Love**

U.S. ZIP CODE
98107

Ballard Branch
◆
Seattle Public Library
Seattle, Washington

Address:	5614 22nd Avenue N.W.
	Seattle, WA 98107
Date Founded:	1904
Date Built:	2005
Architect:	Bohlin Cywinski Jackson; Swift &
	Co. (landscape architect)
Director:	Sibyl de Haan, Branch Manager
Special Collections:	Maritime and Fishing Collection;
	Native American History

Andrew Carnegie may have planted the seed, but the residents of Ballard provided everything else necessary to grow a public library from the ground up: land, labor, and, of course, books. Now Seattle's Ballard Branch is an architectural highlight of the twenty-two-branch public library system and an example of environmentally sustainable architecture in U.S. public buildings. The branch, built in 2005, has an updated collection and the capacity to hold 66,700 books and materials. One of the highlights include materials related to the local maritime and fishing industry.

❧ ❧
A Series of Libraries for a Community of Readers

Established in 1889, Ballard was a separate city before it was annexed by the burgeoning city of Seattle in 1907. It was the center of the region's lumber and shingle mills, boat-building yards, and fishing fleet, attracting a population of predominantly Scandinavian heritage, which gave the neighborhood its identity for the next hundred years.

The first library in Ballard was a "freeholders' reading room" formed by settlers in the 1860s. Forty years later, at the turn of the twentieth century, Ballard had grown into a city in its own right (not yet a Seattle neighborhood), and its residents determined they needed a library of their own.

In 1903 the Ballard City Council sought funding from Andrew Carnegie to build a free public library. Carnegie gave $15,000 for a new building with the proviso that Ballard furnish the land and operating funds. The library opened on 24 June 1904; its first librarian was George C. Hitchcock, publisher of the *Ballard Register,* who was paid $50 a month. Beyond the stacks of the main room, the library initially served as a gathering place for the community with both a men's smoking room and a ladies' conversation room, and upstairs an auditorium with five hundred opera-style seats. Carnegie's name was carved into the frieze. This classic brick structure, which has survived three earthquakes and still stands a block away from the new library building, is now a restaurant called Carnegie's.

Because Carnegie's gift did not provide for books, *The Ballard News* made an appeal to its readers, "It is hoped each visitor will bring a book to start the collection." They did.

Space quickly became an issue in the building, which was only 64 feet by 57 feet. The men's smoking room was turned into a reading room, and the ladies' conversation room made way for a children's reading room. After two thousand more books arrived in 1914, the reading room fireplaces had to be used for book storage, and more efficient shelving replaced the radiating stacks. The auditorium (sans its seats) had to be transformed into the clubroom.

The residents of Ballard had to wait nearly fifty years to get their new branch, however. In 1963 a branch opened at 5711 24th Avenue N.W., offering patrons not only more room for books and reading, but also specially commissioned works of art. By the 1990s the Ballard Branch offered two significant special collections: one concentrating on maritime and fishing coverage, the other focusing on Native American history. The maritime collection expanded over the decades to include commercial and sport fishing and recreational boating. The location of Daybreak Star Cultural Center (which focuses on Native American culture) in nearby Discovery Park spurred the development of the library's Native American collection.

Books are the plane, and the train, and the road. They are the destination, and the journey. They are home.

—Anna Quindlen

The west elevation of the Ballard Branch and the Neighborhood Service Center. Courtesy of Nic Lehoux.

Wooly Yarrow, Sea Pink, and Creeping Phlox

The new Ballard Library was built with environmental sustainability in mind. It has many "green" features, the most dramatic being the green roof—a long, sweeping arc reminiscent of a ski jump, which is covered with planting material and planted with over 18,000 low-water-use species of grasses, sedums, and other native plants.

The plantings provide natural insulation and reduce rainwater runoff significantly, an important benefit in the soggy Northwest climate. The contractor used a big nozzle to blow the dirt onto the roof, and work crews moved it around in wheelbarrows. A biodegradable coconut fiber mat on top of the four-inch-thick dirt helped the plants get established; these plants include wooly yarrow, sea pink, creeping phlox, and thyme. Other green features include lots of natural light; solar panels on the roof; recycled carpet, glass, ceramic, and ceiling tiles; and waterless urinals.

The architects were proud of their innovation and wanted to be able to show it off to the public, so they built a stairway up to a small observation room for a 360-degree view of the roof garden and an eyeful of the surrounding city and mountains. They also designed a periscope from which to view the roof indirectly from the ground floor.

A Place to Be

The Ballard Library never faltered in its popularity even as the pundits spun convincing variations of the "it's all on the Web" argument. It has consistently placed first or second as the most used branch in the Seattle Public Library system. Since the new building opened in May of 2005, circulation has increased by 11 percent, and door count has risen by about 40 percent. Across the street from the library, construction is underway for a new park, which will enrich the experience of Ballard as a small town within a big city and reaffirm the enthusiasm for the library as a shared community asset and a place to be.

The garden roof, looking south. Courtesy of Nic Lehoux.

Bainbridge Public Library and Gardens

Bainbridge Island, Washington

Address: 270 Madison Avenue N.
              Bainbridge Island, WA 98110
Date Founded: 1962
Date Built: 1962
Architect: John Rudolph
Director: Cynthia Harrison, Branch Manager
Special Collections: Pacific Northwest Artists

Some come to read; some come to write. Others come to honor the island's Japanese-American heritage. Still others come to enjoy the fern garden. Or the art exhibits. Or the speakers. The Bainbridge Public Library is an island within an island: located on Bainbridge Island in Washington State's Puget Sound just six miles and a half-hour by ferry from downtown Seattle.

Opened in 1962 by a determined group of volunteers, the centrally located building (near two churches, a high school, an elementary school, and senior housing) was built entirely from donated funds. The founders were determined never to tax the residents of Bainbridge Island for the maintenance of their public library building. As this community grew, from about 5,000 residents in 1962 to 22,000 today, the library has been enlarged twice—both times through citizens' donations only. It is still operated and maintained through donations. No taxes have ever been levied to support the facility. Over 75 percent of the residents carry library cards, and the library logs nearly 400,000 visits from patrons per year.

A Writer's Community

The Bainbridge Public Library has been home to many gifted writers. Perhaps the most popular in recent history is David Guterson, whose book *Snow Falling on Cedars,* a fictionalized story based on Japanese-American experiences during World War II, has been a worldwide bestseller.

Others associated with the Bainbridge library include poet Linda Bierds; Rebecca Wells of *Ya-Ya Sisterhood* fame; the late Jack Olsen, true crime storyteller; Aaron Elkins, mystery writer/forensic anthropologist; children's book author, George Shannon; and novelists Kristin Hannah and Susan Wiggs.

These writers, led by David Guterson (a former teacher) and others dedicated to the craft of writing, have organized a writers' community affiliated with the library. Called Field's End, it has become a center for the literary arts in the Puget Sound area. Its meetings and public forums in the library draw people from all over western Washington.

The Haiku Garden

Bainbridge Island was the site of the first evacuation of Japanese-American citizens from their homes to relocation camps during World War II, and most of those Bainbridge Islanders returned to their island homes after the war. A unique feature of the Bainbridge Public Library is its Haiku Garden created to honor the Issei, first generation Japanese immigrants, for their sacrifices and struggles. Designed by local nursery owner Junkoh Harui with funding from the Bainbridge Island Japanese-American Community, the Haiku Garden is a tranquil space that celebrates the Issei commitment to learning.

Front entrance to the library.

In Harmony with Nature

Designed in 1962 by John Rudolph, a young Pacific Northwest architect influenced by Frank Lloyd Wright and others dedicated to the integration of buildings with their natural surroundings, the cedar building nestled in a stand of tall cedars and firs was fresh and contemporary when first built. It has remained so through two expansions. Soaring ceilings let in the light, and the building and its remarkable gardens merge into one continuous whole. (Just one example: A large rock, at home on the site for centuries and too large

Bainbridge's own Japanese Haiku garden, created to honor first-generation Japanese immigrants.

to move, was incorporated into the design of the main reading room during the most recent expansion in 1997.)

The gardens draw almost as many visitors as the library building itself. The Japanese-American memorial Haiku Garden is on the west side. On the east side the Hardy Fern Foundation has created a unique fern garden, featuring hundreds of varieties of ferns hardy in the temperate zones. On the south side of the building a perennial garden was created and is maintained, like the building itself, by volunteers—no tax money here, either—under the direction of best-selling garden writer (and library board president) Ann Lovejoy.

The green parking lot, adjacent to the perennial garden, has an ecologically friendly, permeable surface (covered with hardy grasses) that puts Pacific Northwest rainwater to good use.

🎴 🎴

A Community Cultural Center

Bainbridge Island is a community noted for its dedication to the arts: literary, visual, musical. No other institution in this city plays a more central role in the lives of its residents—from toddlers to great-grandparents. More than 200 volunteers contribute their time and skills to the library.

The children's and young people's library serves families not only with a great selection of books, computers, audio-visuals and other materials, but also with events including children's story hours, puppet shows, and a summer reading program that attracts more than one thousand youngsters every year. Teenagers have their own retreat, with comfy cushions, games, magazines and books.

Visually impaired persons are welcomed to a group that meets monthly to share the latest information on improvements to help those with low vision—and to socialize.

The Library Speakers Forum, now in its eighth year and always a sellout, brings distinguished speakers and artists to the area six or seven times a year. Recent speakers have included Egil Krogh, sharing Watergate memories, and Dee Boersma, the "Penguin Lady" of the University of Washington.

Instead of a standard "newsletter," the library publishes a quarterly community newspaper (mailed to all households on the island), which prints features on staff, volunteers, and library patrons as well as information about upcoming events and reading or listening recommendations.

An art collection—including works by Dale Chihuly, Kenneth Callahan, and other Pacific Northwest artists—enhances the architecture within, and rotating exhibits feature local artists.

The library checkout area.

*Heart of the Community: **The Libraries We Love***

Everett
Public Library
◈
Everett, Washington

Address: 2702 Hoyt Avenue
Everett, WA 98201
Date Founded: 1894
Date Built: 1903; 1934, 1991
Architect: Carl F. Gould (1933); Cardwell/
Thomas & Associates and Dykeman
Architects (1991)
Director: Mark Nesse
Special Collections: Pacific Northwest History

In the fifteenth century Gutenberg revolutionized the distribution of the printed word in Europe with movable type. In the twentieth century the Everett Public Library revolutionized the distribution of the printed word in Washington with the state's first bookmobile.

That rolling revolution had stationary—and simple—beginnings. In 1894 a group of women who wanted to start a library in the newly incorporated town of Everett met to form the Woman's Book Club. Although the nation had just been plunged into a depression, the women solicited and received books from other women's book clubs around the country. A temporary library service was set up in the home of one of the club members, and shortly thereafter the collection was moved to City Hall, where three rooms were made available.

✾ ✾
Ups and Downs

In 1903 that small library was awarded a $25,000 Carnegie grant. (Andrew Carnegie spent $55 million of his own wealth in the late nineteenth and early twentieth centuries to establish 2,509 libraries throughout the English-speaking world; 1,679 of them were built in the United States.) Constructed in the Italianate style, the library served Everett for more than a quarter of a century. By 1924, however, after a surge in population, Everett had outgrown its little library. No funds were available to build a bigger one, but tight budgets make for innovation, and Everett became the first town in Washington state to offer bookmobile services in addition to its housed collection.

The Great Depression hit at the end of the 1920s, when Everett's lumber and shingle mills were operating at their peak. A $75,000 bequest from the estate of industrialist Leonard Howarth made it possible to build a new library precisely as the city, and the world, entered a decade of severe depression. In 1933 the Library Board decided to construct a larger facility. The board chose architect Carl F. Gould, designer of the University of Washington's Indus-

trial Gothic edifice. Gould drew plans for what was then considered a modern building; covering nineteen thousand square feet, it was made with brick and terra cotta detailing. From the rear of the library one could see the waterfront with the Olympic Mountains looming behind. The entrance faced a downtown that was surviving in the 1930s but wasn't really thriving. During hard times public libraries are especially important to financially stressed communities. This helped to make the library a cultural center. The new Everett Public Library was opened in 1934. Built into a hillside, the structure featured a children's room entrance at the basement level, a main floor and a mezzanine level, and works of art by local artists—painter Guy Anderson, sculptor Dudley Pratt, and muralist J. T. Jacobson. The interior was also hung with works of art purchased through the Public Works of

Everett Public Library, showing barrel vaulted reading room with bowstring trusses. Courtesy of Perspective Image.

The lobby of the library. Courtesy of Carol Ellison.

Art Program. The original Carnegie building was sold and for many years was used as a funeral parlor.

Growth of the collection and burgeoning use resulted in an expansion and remodel in 1962 and finally, in 1991 an award-winning renovation and addition. Carl Gould's son provided Dykeman Architects and Cardwell/Thomas & Associates (now Cardwell Architects) access to his father's original architectural files, enabling a faithful restoration and an addition in keeping with the library's Art Moderne character. The addition nearly doubled the building's capacity and added some dramatic focal points such as a two-story rotunda and a barrel-vaulted main reading room. Dykeman and Cardwell/Thomas's renovation of the library has received awards from the American Institute of Architects and the Washington Trust for Historic Preservation.

❧ ❧
Heart of a Community

The Everett Public Library serves 101,100 residents with a collection of 345,000 items located in a main library and one branch. One million items are circulated annually. The library's Children's Department provides story times and programs for children of all ages. The Northwest Room contains maps, oral histories, photographs, and pamphlets relating to the history of Everett and Snohomish County, and presents approximately fifty public programs a year. The Outreach Department provides library services to child-care centers, preschools, nursing homes, senior apartments, and home-bound individuals. At the Career Center patrons can get advice from a career and education advisor and search for employment, education, and training opportunities. The library maintains a

website, and provides public-access computers. The original 1920s bookmobile, known as Pegasus, has recently been purchased and is being restored. The Everett Woman's Book Club, the organization that founded the library more than a century ago, is now over four-hundred members strong, and still meets at the Main Library. And finally there's the coffee shop, Espresso Americano, where one can relax in a quiet atmosphere and enjoy a drink, listen to local musicians, or see periodic exhibits of Everett's art community.

A close-up view of one of the library's stained-glass windows. Courtesy of Carol Ellison.

Z. J. Loussac Public Library

Anchorage, Alaska

Address: 3600 Denali Street
Anchorage, AK 99503
Date Founded: 1917
Date Built: 1986
Architect: Environmental Concern
Director: Karen Keller, Acting Municipal Librarian
Special Collections: Alaska Collection; Genealogy; Social Justice and Nonviolence

Books were surprisingly important to early settlers who followed the gold rush north to the ragtag tent town of Anchorage. While the long days of summer allowed plenty of light for the exhausting work of mining, the dark frigid months of winter made reading a favorite pastime. A lending library was demanded almost immediately.

The first library, established in 1917, was run by the Women's Club. During the World War II population boom, the library grew, too, thanks to book donations from residents and the military.

In 1950 Z. J. Loussac, a Russian immigrant and local pharmacist, established the Loussac Foundation, which pledged to pay off bonds for a new library. The Z. J. Loussac Library opened in 1955. Loussac continued to support the library throughout his life.

As Anchorage grew, the library system attempted to keep pace with the demand for books. Bookmobile service, started in 1965, was discontinued six years later—the vehicle's size limited its capacity for distributing books and, more important, it could be driven only in summer. Branch libraries numbered eight by the late 1970s. Flush with the boom times generated by construction of the Trans-Alaska Pipeline System, Anchorage voters approved municipal projects for the expanding metropolis: a visitors and convention building, a performing arts center, a sports arena, and a headquarters for the public library system.

Biggest in the Biggest State

Two years after groundbreaking ceremonies, the $42 million library opened in 1986. The Seattle architectural firm Environmental Concern created a design that incorporates function, style, and space. Set on 17 acres in midtown Anchorage, Alaska's largest city, Z. J. Loussac Public Library, at 140,000 square feet, is the largest public library in Alaska.

The building is anchored by three round towers. On the first level of the main part of the building are the Assembly Cham-

> If this nation is to be wise as well as strong, if we are to achieve our destiny, then we need more new ideas for more wise men reading more good books in more public libraries.
>
> —John F. Kennedy

bers, home of the municipality's legislative branch, in one tower and the Wilda Marston Theatre, a 220-seat performance space, in the other tower. In between is a lobby with features echoing the building's curved elements and a public conference room that seats fifty.

The library's main entrance is on the second level. Patrons climb stairs to the outside patio or enter at the first level and take the inside elevator or stairs. The patio overlooks the lawn and the Kay Linton Memorial Fountain, the city's only fountain, which transforms into an ice sculpture during the winter. In summer hundreds of people gather on the patio and lawn to listen to live music performed by local musicians. The two-story glass atrium on the front wall slants up and over the balcony on the third level, bringing natural light to both areas.

The View from the Bridge

One of the most important parts of the library is the Alaska Collection, which includes books by Alaskans and about the

The Kay Linton Memorial Fountain, with the Loussac Library in the background.

state, as well as all the state's media publications. Housed in the third tower, the Alaska Wing is accessed through a bridge on the third level. The bridge incorporates two special elements of the library. The Galleria features floor-to-ceiling windows facing the Chugach Mountains on one side and the Z. J. Loussac art collection by Alaskan artists on the other. Paralleling the Galleria is the Ann Stevens Room. A memorial to Alaska Senator Ted Stevens's first wife, who died in a plane crash, the room has the quality of a drawing room, with cherry woodwork, leather furnishings, marble buffet area, and windows overseeing the patio and fountain.

The Alaska Wing has architectural features reminiscent of the rotunda in the nation's Capitol. The circular room at the third level entrance continues the glass-dominated face of the bridge and overlooks a circular area for study. The majority of the collection of Alaskana is housed on the first level.

Among the most arresting features of the building are its works of art, some donated and some designed for the space, purchased with funds from a state program that mandates that 1 percent of a public building's total cost be dedicated to art for the public.

The second level of the library houses the Youth Services Department, the fiction collection, and the circulation desk. Children hide out in the reading alcove and attend programs in the Story Theater. Public computers, reference services, the nonfiction collection and magazines are found on level three.

As Anchorage continues to grow so does the demand on Loussac resources. Whether it is designing intriguing programs, adding wireless capability, or building foreign language collections for the city's one hundred cultural minorities—whatever it takes—Loussac Library will remain the heart of this community for generations to come.

The Ann Stevens room overlooks the patio and fountain.

Heart of the Community: **The Libraries We Love**

Wolfville
Memorial Library

Wolfville, Nova Scotia, Canada

Address: 21 Elm Avenue, Wolfville,
Nova Scotia, Canada B4P 2A1
Date Founded: 1949
Date Built: 1912; 1993 (redeveloped)
Architect: Herbert E. Gates; Ron Peck
Director: Lisa Rice, Library Manager

It's the little library that could.

The Wolfville Memorial Library is housed in a building that once was a train station, built by the Dominion Atlantic Railway in 1912. The architect was Herbert E. Gates of Halifax. The east end of the building was used for baggage, and the west end was a waiting room. When Via Rail discontinued passenger service through the Annapolis Valley in 1989, the red brick and stone station sat abandoned and vandalized.

The idea of converting the station into a library was conceived in 1988 by the local branch of the Canadian Federation of University Women, who said, "We think we can, we think we can, we think we can." Townsfolk agreed and quickly got on board the project because the town's one-room library (located in the town's public works building) was cramped and because the sta-

tion held so many memories from the days of passenger travel. In two years a twenty-member board purchased and transformed the building.

Heritage architects and librarians volunteered their services, and a capital campaign met with great success. More than 480 individuals, foundations, businesses, and the province of Nova Scotia contributed.

The Sites and Monuments Board of Canada designated the building as a national heritage railway property during the process. The adaptive reuse project was completed in September of 1993 at one-third the cost of building a new structure. The local newspaper termed the project "a genuine exhibition of civic pride."

Elected representative Robbie Harrison, who had been a volunteer canvasser, called the new library a legacy. "I don't know of a more precious gift to leave behind."

The main floor is divided into a youth wing and an adult wing, with the staff counter in between. A vintage model train is parked in the youth wing, along with plenty of cozy nooks to sit and read. In the summer especially it is full of youthful energy. Upstairs, where the station agent used to live, is a meeting room and CAP (Community Access Project) computer lab. Authors give frequent readings.

The library collection consists of both print and nonprint material, including audio books, videos/DVDs, large-print material, reference material, magazines and newspapers, and computers with public Internet access. In many ways the library is a community center. Senior citizens stop in on a daily basis to read national and community newspapers. People meet friends, and no one shushes those who stop briefly to chat. The staff members become friends to many through repeated visits.

Residents and tourists are able to obtain a free library card and borrow materials by presenting identification.

WOLFVILLE LIBRARY FOUNDATION

You are invited to attend the official opening of the Wolfville Memorial Library

(Wolfville Branch, Annapolis Valley Regional Library)

This ribbon cutting ceremony will be at the newly renovated train station

(former DAR /VIA rail station), Elm Avenue, Wolfville, Nova Scotia

Saturday, September 11, 1993

2 o'clock pm

Entertainment and refreshments will be offered

An invitation to the library's ribbon-cutting ceremony.

A vintage model train parked in the Wolfville Library children's room.

Programs include story time, after-school programs, and special events. Recently the CAP site manager challenged staff members to raise funds to donate books to Nunavut, the northernmost territory of Canada. He became a "Book Hero" and had his head shaved outside the library while friends and patrons looked on admiringly.

The library is a branch of the Annapolis Valley Regional Library System, which is one of nine regional library systems in Nova Scotia. The regional library system was established in 1949. The library serves the wider community of Wolfville and beyond. Its circulation annually is more than eighty thousand items, which makes it the most-used branch in the system. As far back as five years ago a visitor observed that the library was bursting. Discussions are ongoing, and expansion might be down the track.

Postcard of the original train station.

The library connects us with the insight and knowledge, painfully extracted from Nature, of the greatest minds that ever were, with the best teachers, drawn from the entire planet and from all our history, to instruct us without tiring, and to inspire us to make our own contribution to the collective knowledge of the human species. I think the health of our civilization, the depth of our awareness about the underpinnings of our culture and our concern for the future can all be tested by how well we support our libraries.

—Carl Sagan

Heart of the Community: **The Libraries We Love**

H3Z 1G1

Westmount Public Library

◆

Westmount, Quebec, Canada

Address: 4574 Sherbrooke Street W.
Westmount, Quebec,
Canada H3Z 1G1
Date Founded: 1897
Date Built: 1899; 1995
Architect: Robert Findlay; Peter Rose
Director: Ann Moffat
Special Collections: Foreign Novels in Translation

The tribute—in both its occasion and its location—was royal.

In 1897 the town of Westmount was looking for a way to celebrate Queen Victoria's Diamond Jubilee marking sixty years of her reign. What better testament to their love of reading and education than a library? Money for the library's construction came from a default payment by a local gas company, making Westmount Public Library the first library in Quebec entirely funded by a municipality. Westmount resident and architect Robert Findlay (who designed many homes and public buildings in Canada) was hired to create a structure that would reflect the civic pride of residents. There weren't many examples of library architecture in Canada at that time, so Findlay turned to the designs of U.S. architect Henry H. Richardson for inspiration. The resulting building, with its arched entrance, gabled roof, and peaked tower, reflects Richardson's influence, Findlay's own neoclassical background, and some suggestions from librarian Charles Gould of McGill University's Redpath Library.

🕮 🕮

Westmount

Located in southwestern Quebec, Westmount is an enclave (a separate municipality) of Montreal. More than twenty thousand people of multiple ethnic and linguistic backgrounds call it home, although originally the population was predominantly English and Scottish. The city lies on the western slope

Library turret.

of Mount Royal, and although it is within walking distance of downtown Montreal, Westmount retains its residential, small-town air. The birthplace of actress Norma Shearer and poet and songwriter Leonard Cohen, Westmount is proud of its thirteen tree-filled parks, community center, and its library.

The Westmount Public Library opened in 1899 with a collection of nearly two thousand books. Records show there were 694 borrowers that year. In 1911 an extension, again designed by Robert Findlay, included a children's department as well as a workroom and a receiving room in the basement. Morning story hour was introduced, and a separate reference desk service was put in place.

In 1925 a second addition designed by Findlay and his son, Frank, made room for more stacks, a librarian's office, and an additional reading room along with space for a music collection, an art section, and shelves for reference books. Windows bearing the names of Canadian authors were installed. The library also began its first cooperative effort with local schools. The library was remodeled again in 1936, this time to include a new workroom, new concrete floors, air-conditioning, and new counters for borrowers. In 1940 the library became a receiving station for books and magazines for members of the armed forces, and in 1943 it was appointed curator of all material collected by the newly formed Westmount Historical Association.

The 1950s brought more modernization and an extension of library

Looking in from the outside of the Runnymede Branch.

With collections in English, French, Lithuanian, Polish, Russian, and Ukrainian, Runnymede is responsive to the diverse community it serves. Since reopening, the library has become even busier, becoming one of Toronto Public Library's top five neighborhood branches.

The entrance to the library.

I read because life isn't enough, and in the pages of a book I can be anybody; I read because the words that build the story become mine, to build my life: I read not for happy endings but for new beginnings: I'm just beginning myself, and I wouldn't mind a map; I read because I have friends who don't, and young though they are, they're beginning to run out of material; I read because every journey begins at the library, and it's time for me to start packing; I read because one of these days I'm going to get out of this town, and I'm going to go everywhere and meet everybody, I want to be ready.

—Richard Peck

Heart of the Community: **The Libraries We Love**

POSTAL CODE
S4P 3Z5
PICTURE BOOKS

Regina Public Library
◆

Regina, Saskatchewan, Canada

Address: 2311 12th Avenue
Regina, Canada S4P 3Z5
Date Founded: 1908
Date Built: 1912; 1962
Architect: Storey and Van Egmond; Izumi, Arnott, and Suglyama
Director: Jeff Barber
Special Collections: Original Canadian Artwork; Prairie History

Hundreds of public libraries in North America are indebted to Andrew Carnegie for their start. Regina's library is indebted to Carnegie for its start *and* its restart.

Regina was established in 1882 as the headquarters of the North-West Territories and incorporated as a city in 1903. In 1907 a number of residents petitioned the city council to establish a free public library. The city council responded by passing a bylaw in 1908, and in 1909 the library was given three rooms on the second floor of the new City Hall. A year later Andrew Carnegie was approached for a grant and donated $50,000. However, six weeks after the new library building opened in 1912, a tornado swept through Regina, damaging a number of buildings, including the library. Carnegie donated more money for reconstruction. Before long, however, Regina recognized the need for extended library services. Branch after branch was added until, by 1959, five branches and three book trailers were serving the growing city.

❧ ❧
Building on the Past

In 1960 a measure to demolish the original Carnegie building and construct a new Central Library was passed. The stone bearing the words "Regina Public Library" from the original building was saved and inserted in the lobby of the new library, and a medallion bearing the library's crest of a torch and an open book declared, "He who reads, rules." The new library opened in 1962, complete with a children's department, an art gallery, and a theater. In 1973 a mezzanine was constructed to house the Prairie History Room and Learning Centre.

❧ ❧
More Than You Imagine

Today the Regina Public Library consists of nine locations; the Central Library is located in the heart of downtown Regina, and eight branches serve other areas of the city. Total circulation is more than two million articles a year. The library seeks to enhance the quality of life in Regina by providing an environment in which anyone can access information for work, study, or recreation. "More Than You Imagine," proclaims its website. The Central Library has a number of special departments, including the RPL Film Theatre, where domestic and foreign films are shown Thursday through Sunday. Created as a community film society in the mid-1960s, the RPL Film Theatre is the only cinema in the city that consistently presents Canadian, foreign, and independent films and the only repertory film theater in southern Saskatchewan.

The library has exhibited art since 1949. First presented in the periodicals reading room, exhibits later found a home in the multipurpose Dunlop Art Gallery, built as part of the new Central Library. Named in 1972 after Ms. Marjorie Dunlop, former chief librarian, the gallery hosts a variety of exhibits and programs. With facilities at both the Central Library and the Sherwood Vil-

The original stone medallion crest from the original Central Library, reinstalled in present-day Central Library. The text says, "He who reads, rules."

Marjorie Dunlop, chief librarian from 1948 to 1971, and Kiyoshi Izumi, one of the architects of the present Central Library, examine a time capsule retrieved in 1961. Courtesy of Regina Archives.

lage Branch, the Dunlop Art Gallery presents a range of visual culture with a focus on the contemporary. Using programs that pose questions, the gallery staff then presents lectures, screenings, and publications to answer those questions. Exhibitions and programs are conducted from the gallery offices at the Central Library. The gallery also offers an art rental service, which allows patrons to borrow original Canadian artwork to display in their home or office for a modest fee. Over time, the Dunlop Art Gallery has grown to be a nationally recognized art gallery. Children's programming includes annual summer reading programs and puppet shows, homework help, and a toy library where small children can check out toys just as they do books. Several of the branches offer infant and toddler resources and programs and separate story times for babies, toddlers, and preschool children. Teens have their own section of the library with an up-to-date suggested reading list and hundreds of current titles, online help lines for teen-related social issues, and resources on health and fitness. Computer lessons are offered, and educational computer games are available. A poetry project and writing guidance encourage students to explore their creative side, and music Web pages and links are posted on the website. Teen advisory committees give teens a voice in the activities of their library. Senior citizens can get information on continuing education, finance, health, and life transitions, much of it through links on the website. The library provides a list of support services available in town, as well as travel and volunteer opportunities, and hosts programs designed for seniors who are looking for advice on managing their money or making their lives more meaningful. Regina Public

Library also has an award-winning literacy program that has a long history of providing high-quality literacy services to Regina citizens. The program offers tutor training, one-on-one tutoring for adult learners, a computer lab with literacy software, and an extensive literacy collection.

Regina Public Library recently held a contest inviting patrons to tell their own library love story. Stories were to include how Regina Public Library has played a positive role in their lives, and what they loved best about their Library. Library Director Jeff Barber submitted his personal story where he wrote about his career in library service. He summed up the value of libraries in this way: "It's what libraries are that keeps my love light burning. It's the assumption of intellectual freedom and free speech. It's access for anyone. It's benefit for all."

The Regina Central Library.

Heart of the Community: **The Libraries We Love**

Additional Photo Credits

Unless otherwise noted in the photo captions, images were provided by the individual library. The design of the book, however, did not allow for the inclusion of credits for the opening photo of each library. Below are credits for opening photos that were provided by an individual or organization other than the library itself.

162

Libraries of Distinction

Although scores of wonderful libraries nominated for inclusion in the book did not make the final selection, we honor all the nominees on the following pages as "Libraries of Distinction."

We invited all the nominated libraries to submit a photo of their buildings, and many responded. We were bowled over by the diversity of the architecture through the centuries. And libraries that don't have a "building" per se are also proudly represented. Photos include the Four County Cybermobile that brings Internet access to unserved residents of four counties in central upstate New York and King County, Washington's high-tech Library Connection @ Crossroads that brings electronic access to the resources of its forty-two libraries (along with loads of books to peruse) in a shopping center storefront location.

We know there are many other libraries that somehow didn't hear about the project or weren't able to put together a nomination package in time. They, as well as all our nominated libraries, share the distinction of being much-loved by their communities. This book is designed not only to celebrate certain stellar libraries but also to show the breadth of what libraries—and librarians—do for our towns, our students, our communities, and our country.

01075   01880   02346   02459

02660   02719   03801   06371

07075   10940   11520   11733

Libraries of

Zip Code	Library	Zip Code	Library
01007	Clapp Memorial Library	03442	Peterborough Town Library
01027	Emily Williston Memorial Library	03801	Portsmouth Public Library
01060	Forbes Library	04005	McArthur Public Library
01075	Gaylord Memorial Library	06103	Hartford Public Library
01262	Stockbridge Library Association	06371	Old Lyme Phoebe Griffin Noyes Library
01262	Lenox Library Association	07044	Verona Library
01274	Gleason Library	07075	Woodridge Memorial Library
01608	Worcester Public Library	07643	Little Ferry Library
01742	Concord Free Public Library	08852	South Brunswick Public Library
01852	Pollard Memorial Library	10541	Mahopac Public Library
01880	Lucius Beebe Memorial Library	10927	Haverstraw Kings Daughters Public Library
01890	Winchester Public Library	10940	Middletown Thrall Library
01960	Peabody Institute Library	11520	Freeport Memorial Library
02169	Thomas Crane Library	11576	Bryant Library
02332	Duxbury Free Library	11733	Emma S. Clark Memorial Library
02346	Middleborough Public Library	11756	Levittown Public Library
02459	Newton Free Library	12037	Chatham Public Library
02719	The Millicent Library	12061	East Greenbush Community Library
02740	New Bedford Free Public Library	12078	Gloversville Public LIbrary

Libraries of Distinction

Although scores of wonderful libraries nominated for inclusion in the book did not make the final selection, we honor all the nominees on the following pages as "Libraries of Distinction."

We invited all the nominated libraries to submit a photo of their buildings, and many responded. We were bowled over by the diversity of the architecture through the centuries. And libraries that don't have a "building" per se are also proudly represented. Photos include the Four County Cybermobile that brings Internet access to unserved residents of four counties in central upstate New York and King County, Washington's high-tech Library Connection @ Crossroads that brings electronic access to the resources of its forty-two libraries (along with loads of books to peruse) in a shopping center storefront location.

We know there are many other libraries that somehow didn't hear about the project or weren't able to put together a nomination package in time. They, as well as all our nominated libraries, share the distinction of being much-loved by their communities. This book is designed not only to celebrate certain stellar libraries but also to show the breadth of what libraries—and librarians—do for our towns, our students, our communities, and our country.

| 01075 | 01880 | 02346 | 02459 |

| 02660 | 02719 | 03801 | 06371 |

| 07075 | 10940 | 11520 | 11733 |

Libraries of

Zip Code	Library	Zip Code	Library
01007	Clapp Memorial Library	03442	Peterborough Town Library
01027	Emily Williston Memorial Library	03801	Portsmouth Public Library
01060	Forbes Library	04005	McArthur Public Library
01075	Gaylord Memorial Library	06103	Hartford Public Library
01262	Stockbridge Library Association	06371	Old Lyme Phoebe Griffin Noyes Library
01262	Lenox Library Association	07044	Verona Library
01274	Gleason Library	07075	Woodridge Memorial Library
01608	Worcester Public Library	07643	Little Ferry Library
01742	Concord Free Public Library	08852	South Brunswick Public Library
01852	Pollard Memorial Library	10541	Mahopac Public Library
01880	Lucius Beebe Memorial Library	10927	Haverstraw Kings Daughters Public Library
01890	Winchester Public Library	10940	Middletown Thrall Library
01960	Peabody Institute Library	11520	Freeport Memorial Library
02169	Thomas Crane Library	11576	Bryant Library
02332	Duxbury Free Library	11733	Emma S. Clark Memorial Library
02346	Middleborough Public Library	11756	Levittown Public Library
02459	Newton Free Library	12037	Chatham Public Library
02719	The Millicent Library	12061	East Greenbush Community Library
02740	New Bedford Free Public Library	12078	Gloversville Public LIbrary

13053　　　13066　　　13850　　　15017

17257　　　19312　　　19380　　　27546

32541　　　33161　　　36732　　　36908

Distinction

Zip Code	Library
12106	Kinderhook Memorial Library
12147	Rensselaerville Library
12414	Catskill Public Library
12464	Phoenicia Public Library
12561	Elting Memorial Library
12946	Lake Placid Public Library
13053	Southworth Library
13066	Fayetteville Free Library
13667	Hepburn Library of Norfolk
13815	Guernsey Memorial Library
13850	Four County Library Cybermobile
15017	Bridgeville Public Library
15202	Avalon Public Library
16036	Foxburg Free Library
16117	Ellwood City Area Public Library
17214	Blue Ridge Summit Free Library
17257	Shippensburg Public Library
17543	Lititz Public Library
18077	Riegelsville Public Library

Zip Code	Library
18701	Osterhout Free Library
18938	Free Library of New Hope and Solebury
19040	Union Library of Hatborough
19312	Easttown Library and Information Center
19380	West Chester Public Library
19507	Bethel-Tulpehocken Public Library
22801	Massanutten Regional Library
24954	Pocahontas County Free Libraries
26554	Marion County Public Library
27402	Greensboro Public Library
27546	Harnett Central Library
31635	W. L. Miller Library
32541	Destin Library
33161	North Miami Public Library
34243	Jane Bancroft Cook Library
35209	Homewood Public Library
36010	Tupper Lightfoot Memorial Library
36732	Demopolis Public Library
36908	Choctaw County Public Library

38261   45662   46601   47710

49046   49412   59711   60016

60045   60046   60153   60523

Libraries of

Zip Code	Library	Zip Code	Library
37086	LaVergne Public Library	48605	Hoyt Public Library
37804	Blount County Public Library	49046	Delton District Library
38225	Ned R. McWherter Weakley County Library	49412	Freemont Area District Library
38261	Obion County Public Library	49740	Harbor Springs Library
42003	McCracken County Public Library	52317	North Liberty Community Library
43211	The Ohio Historical Society Archives/Library	55102	Saint Paul Central Library
44048	Kingsville Public Library	56345	Little Falls Carnegie Library
44112	East Cleveland Public Library	59711	Hearst Free Library
44123	Euclid Public Library	59715	Bozeman Public Library
45014	Lane Library	60016	Des Plaines Public Library
45662	Portsmouth Public Library	60045	Lake Forest Library
46077	Hussey-Mayfield Memorial Public Library	60046	Lake Villa District Library
46208	Indianapolis-Marion County Public Library	60153	Maywood Public Library District
46601	Saint Joseph County Public Library	60523	Oak Brook Public Library
47408	Monroe County Public Library	60605	Chicago Public Library
47710	Willard Library	60957	Paxton Carnegie Library
48185	William P. Faust Public Library	63103	St. Louis Public Library
48236	Grosse Pointe Public Library	64105	Kansas City Public Library

60605   63103   75941   77954

78613   80104   93721   93921

94115   97217   98027   98353

Distinction

Zip Code	Library
66604	Topeka and Shawnee County Public Library
68506	Charles H. Gere Library
75757	Bullard Community Library
75941	T. L. L. Temple Memorial Library
77954	Cuero Public Library
78610	Buda Public Library
78613	Cedar Park Public Library
78954	Round Top Family Library
79015	Canyon Area Library
79601	Abilene Public Library
79761	Ector County Library
79830	Alpine Public Library
80104	Philip S. Miller Library
83843	Moscow Community Library
84720	Cedar City Library
87024	Los Alamos County Public Library System
87102	Albuquerque-Bernalillo Country–Special Collections
87544	Mesa Public Library

Zip Code	Library
88021	Valley Community Library
90018	Los Angeles Public Library–Jefferson Branch
90026	Beverly Hills Public Library
90274	Malaga Cove Library
90703	Cerritos Library
92373	Smiley Library
92410	Norman F. Feldheym Central Library
93721	Fresno County–Leo Politi Branch
93921	Harrison Memorial Library
94104	Mechanics Institute Library
94115	San Francisco Public Library–Presidio Branch
97217	North Portland Public Library
98027	King County–Library Connection @ Crossroads
98250	San Juan Island Library
98353	Kitsap Regional Library
99111	Whitman County Library

Index

A

Abbey, Edwin Austin, 5
Adams, John, 5
Aguirre, Jose Antonio, 132
Audubon, John James, 144
Aztec UFO Symposium, 128–129

B

Barksdale, Ralph C., 121
Barrett, John, III, 3
Barry, Robert, 22
Bartram, John, 38
Bates, Joshua, 5
Battle of Antietam, 44
Battle of Oriskany, 32–33
Best, Ken, 2
Blackinton, Sanford, 2
Bowman, Judy, 98–99
Bradford, Emma Staples, 10
Brand, Leslie Coombs, 136
Brigham, Charles, 12
Brockway, George A., 50
Butts, William Davis, 43

C

Caldiero, Alex, 121
Carnegie, Andrew, 28, 34, 64, 76, 78,
    80, 86, 92–93, 94, 96, 104, 108, 116,
    118, 142, 146, 150, 160
Changing Lives Through Literature
    (CLTL), 101
Chin, Mel, 141
Civil rights, 42–43, 55, 58–59
Cleary, Beverly, 144
Clinton and Kalamazoo Canal, 70
Collinson, Peter, 38

Cooke, James "Slim," 31
Cossitt, Frederick W., 58
Cramer, Ambrose C., 15
Cuesta, Angel, 52

D

Dana, John Cotton, 116
Denkmann, Frederick, 94
Dewey, Melvil, 6
Doner, Michele Oka, 25
Dunlop Art Gallery, 160–161

E

Eldridge, Isabella, 18
Eliot, Charles W., 36
Estes, Dana, 57

F

Failing, Henry, 145
Falter, John, 91
Family Place Libraries, 30
Field's End, 148
Finney, Stephen, 132
Freeman, Christopher, 25

G

Gale, Ellen, 95
Gale, Napoleon Bonaparte, 12
Goodhue, Bertram Grosvenor, 134
Gould, Carl F., 150
"Green" building, 2, 62–63, 66–67,
    68–69, 124–125, 147

H

Haiku Garden, 148
Hanlon, Brian, 25
Hardy Holzman Pfeiffer Associates,
    30–31, 134
Holder, Reggie, 53
Holdman, Tom, 121
Hooks, Benjamin L., 58–59
Houghton, A. C., 2
Hovey, Ida Fuller, 92
Howard, Robert E., 108–109
Hudson River School, 27
Hugh B. Wheeler Reading Room, 25
Hughes, Thomas, 56
Hurricane Katrina, 102–103, 112, 115

I

Ideson, Julia, 110
Immigrants, services for, 28–29, 49,
    60–61, 72
International Resource Center, 29
Inventory of Heritage Properties, 158

J

Jackson, Arthur C., 32
Jean S. Picker Memorial Garden, 15
Johnson, Philip, 4
Jones, Allan D., Jr., 43
Jones, David H., 98

K

Kaltenborn, H. V., 81
Kang, Ik-Joong, 22
Kay Linton Memorial Fountain, 153
Keillor, Garrison, 82

Kerens, R. C., 104
Kittredge Maritime Collection, 8
Kroll, Helen, 145

L

Latter family, 102
Leadership in Environment and
    Energy Design (LEED), 2, 67
Lectores, 52
Libbey, Edward Drummond, 138
Lothrop Genealogy Collection, 8
Lothrop, Reverend John, 8
Loussac, Z. J., 152
Lyle, John M., 158

M

Malpass, Michael Allen, 24
McKim, Mead, and White, 4, 20–21,
    64
McKinley, William, 62
Millay, Edna St. Vincent, 14
Miller Business Resource Center,
    30–31
Molina, Gloria, 132
Morgan, J. P., Mrs., 26
Myers, Eliah J., 76

N

Newport, Christopher, Captain, 43
Newton family, 90
Norris, Leslie, 121

O

Orlowski, Dennis, 70
Osler/Milling Architects, 76

P

Pacheo, Ferdie, Dr., 53
Pickens, T. Boone, 106
Pickens, Grace, 106
Prescott, Martha, 12
Prescott, Wilbur L., 12
Price, Gary, 70
Proctor, Frederick T., 32
Proctor, Thomas R., 32
Puvis de Chavannes, Pierre, 5
Pyle, Ernest Taylor, 126–127
Pyle, Jerry, 126

R

Read to Rover Program, 48–49
Reeve, Christopher, 23
Register of Historic Places, 2, 8, 34,
    43, 52, 55, 82, 96, 104, 109, 134, 137
Robeson, Paul, 23
Roundwood construction, 88
Rugby Colony, 56
Rylant, Cynthia, 46

S

Safdie, Moshe, 122–123
Saint James, Synthia, 53
Salemme, Antonio, 23
Samson, Sarah, 112
San Cherico, Joanie, 24
San José State University, 140
Santa Fe Trail, 100
Sargent, John Singer, 5
Scott, Thomas Blythe, 80
Smith, Abel I., 18
Spencer, Clara Nell, 109
Stout, Frank B., 78
Struthers, Thomas, 36
Sturgis, R. Clipston 6
Sturgis, William, 8
Swift, Jane, 3

T

Taylor, Mary, 22
Thacher, George, 138
Thacher, Sherman, 138
Thompson, W. Hale, 42
Tilton, Edward L., 64
Timpanogos Storytelling Festival,
    120–121
Tully, Christopher, 85
Twain, Mark (Samuel Clemens),
    18–19, 90–91, 115

V

Vattemare, Alexandre, 4
Vender family, 86
Vonnegut, Kurt, 9

W

Warren, Frank L., 106
Watson, Samuel, Reverend, 10
Wetmore, Charles Delevan, 36
Weyerhaeuser, Frederick, 94
Whittemore, John Howard, 20
Wilda Marston Theatre, 153
Williams, Edward, Dr., 16
Williams, Norman, 16
Windmills, 90

Y

Yohn, Frederick, 32

Z

Zimbalist, Mary Curtis Bok, 14–15

The Look

In these pages, the tangible beauty of libraries—their architectural grandeur and regional distinctiveness—and their intangible qualities of warmth, inclusiveness, and excitement about ideas and knowledge are evident. We wanted a look full of delicate touches but also plenty of movement and energy. To achieve this, we used the whimsical and elegant Humana Serif as the font for the main headings and Bodoni Ornaments to echo the heart motif as well as the shape of a book. Minion Pro, used for the book's text and subheads, is inspired by classical, old-style typefaces of the late Renaissance, a period of elegant, beautiful, and highly readable type designs. Because the nomination process finished on Valentine's Day, the image of a chocolate box became an inspiration for the book's color scheme, and we like to think that readers will find the entire collection as delectable as we do.

Day lily in the garden at the library that first inspired this book, Stoneridge Public Library in upstate New York.

About the Editors

Karen Christensen and David Levinson founded Berkshire Publishing Group in 1998. Levinson, a cultural anthropologist, had been the vice president of a major think-tank at Yale University, the Human Relations Area Files, and served as editor-in-chief of the 10-volume *Encyclopedia of World Cultures.* Christensen had returned to the United States after a decade in London, where she worked in scientific publishing and with Valerie Eliot editing the first volume of the T. S. Eliot letters. They founded Berkshire with a vision of promoting a greater knowledge of other nations and peoples. Berkshire's library reference and other publications are the result of dynamic collaborations by an worldwide network of scholars, thinkers, editors, and authors.

What's Next

Heart of the Community: The Libraries We Love is a grand celebration of public libraries and their role in America's history, America's communities, and America's heart. This celebration continues at the book's website, **www.librarieswelove.org**, where more material, photographs, and comments will be available all the time. In addition, beginning in 2008, Berkshire will be publishing an annual calendar celebrating libraries. Berkshire's *Good Library Guide* will also follow. This compact reference will include not only public libraries but also academic, private, corporate, and even some school libraries, with separate U.S. and U.K. editions.